D0330501

Traveler's Language Guides: Japanese

Fumiko Kimura-Hoffmeister
Gerhard Hoffmeister

All inquiries should be addressed to:
Barron's Educational Series, Inc.
250 Wireless Boulevard
Hauppauge, NY 11788
http://www.barronseduc.com

ISBN-13: 978-0-7641-3208-7
ISBN-10: 0-7641-3208-3
Library of Congress Control Number 2005921548

Photo Sources

Bundesverband Selbsthilfe Körperbehinderter, Krautheim: 81;
Cycleurope, Bergisch-Gladbach: 64; Fordwerke AG: 60; Japanische
Fremdenverkehrszentrale (JNTO), Frankfurt: 77, 87, 99, 147, 169;
Killroy media, Asperg: 11, 15, 19, 31, 51, 119, 129, 141, 183;
Wolpert Fotodesign, Stuttgart: 110-114, 153
Graphics on page 43: Business Sprachführer Japanisch, Ernst Klett
Sprachen GmbH
Cover: Corbis

Printed in China
9 8 7 6 5 4 3 2 1

Along with the Chinese writing system, from which it is derived, the Japanese system of writing is the most complicated of all the *Kultursprachen,* or "culture-bearing languages." It consists of two phonetically identical syllabic scripts, *hiragana* and *katakana,* and Chinese characters, or *kanji,* and with considerable work it can be learned by foreigners up to a certain level of proficiency.

The Japanese Writing System

In the fifth century, Buddhist monks came from Korea to Japan, bringing the Chinese writing system along with the teachings of Buddhism. At that time Japan did not yet have its own system of writing, so this system was adopted along with the Buddhist doctrine.

The Chinese characters are not phonetic symbols like our alphabet letters. Instead, a character is the equivalent of a word. Thus there were two options: Either a Japanese word could be rendered with the Chinese character that had the same meaning, or the corresponding Chinese word could also be adopted as a loan word along with the Chinese character. As a result, the language was greatly enriched, but it also became more difficult to learn.

A Chinese character, or *kanji,* can be read in different ways: either in a Chinese reading or in a Japanese reading. In compound words, the Chinese reading predominates, in isolated words, the Japanese. This mean that the very same *kanji,* depending on the context, can have sounds as different as *gai* (Chinese reading) and *soto* (Japanese reading). Incidentally, we're not the only ones who find this difficult. During all their school years and until they enter university, the Japanese continue to learn new characters. An additional difficulty is presented by the fact that the Japanese language is completely different from Chinese. Japanese is an agglutinating language; that is, there are grammatical endings, prefixes, and particles that can be combined with a word. That is not true of Chinese, where different meaning = different character. That probably accounts for the fact that there exist two syllabaries, or syllabic alphabets, both developed in the Middle Ages, in Japanese, in addition to the *kanji.* These syllabic alphabets, whose characters were developed from the kanji by simplifying them, made it possible to take the linguistic features of Japanese into consideration. The more rounded syllabic alphabet is *hiragana.* Many hundreds of years ago, it was used chiefly by women. The more angular syllabic alphabet, *katakana,* came into being at the same time. It was used predominantly by monks, in order to take notes quickly. Today *katakana* is used to write words of foreign origin.

Both these syllabic alphabets are purely phonetic writing systems; that is, they can be read like our system. The official number of syllables in each is 46. They are written from top to bottom and from right to left. With the help of these syllabaries, Japanese words and entire texts as well can be rendered. For both syllabic alphabets, there are two government-approved systems, called *romaji*, for transcribing them into our Roman alphabet. The romanization system used in this book is the Hepburn System, named for a missionary and philologist who compiled a Japanese-English dictionary in the late nineteenth century.

Thus one could ask: Why don't the Japanese just use our Roman alphabet to write their language?
And again we are confronted with both the richness and the difficulty introduced into the Japanese language through the Chinese language. The Chinese inventory of sounds differs from that of Japanese. Thus, because of the inadequate phonetic capabilities of Japanese there is, for example, only one Japanese word for Chinese words with different pronunciations.
Consequently there are an incredible number of words that sound alike but have very different meanings. Only the Chinese characters make it possible for the Japanese to express themselves unambiguously and make it clear which word is intended. Often Japanese can be seen talking to each other while tracing the kanji in the air or on their palms. They do this to communicate without ambiguity.
Without the Chinese characters, Japanese probably would be quite imprecise. The beauty of these characters and the fluidity with which the Japanese write these complicated characters are part and parcel of Japanese culture.
The syllabic alphabets, which can be learned relatively quickly, allow foreigners to make themselves understood in Japan. Learning the *kanji* well enough to be able to read simple texts requires a great deal of hard work and persistence.

Here we show only the two syllabaries and their standard romanization (*romaji*), for which we use the Hepburn system (*hebonshiki*).

Syllabary
With few exceptions, Japanese consists of open syllables. In the simplest case, these syllables are a combination of a hard consonant with the vowels *a, i, u, e, o,* which also occur independently as syllables. In addition, the consonant *n* functions as a syllabic nasal. That is exactly how it is rendered in the syllabic scripts *hiragana* and *katakana.*

This also results in a simple classification system for the syllabic alphabet and *romaji* (rendered in *hebonshiki*).

(In each column, the first character is *hiragana*, the second, *katakana*. The syllabic characters are to be read as a combination of the consonant appearing in the left consonant and the vowel at the top. Note the divergent pronunciation in the case of the syllables *chi, tsu,* and *fu,* which are also written this way in the Hepburn System.)

—	あ ア	い イ	う ウ	え エ	お オ
k	か カ	き キ	く ク	け ケ	こ コ
s	さ サ	し シ	す ス	せ セ	そ ソ
t	た タ	ち チ chi	つ ツ tsu	て テ	と ト
n	な ナ	に ニ	ぬ ヌ	ね ネ	の ノ
h	は ハ	ひ ヒ	ふ フ fu	へ ヘ	ほ ホ
m	ま マ	み ミ	む ム	め メ	も モ
y	や ヤ	—	ゆ ユ	—	よ ヨ
r	ら ラ	り リ	る ル	れ レ	ろ ロ
w	わ ワ	—	—	—	を ヲ
syllabic nasal	—	—	—	—	ん ン n

Next, this simple system is adapted to the realities of the language by the use of diacritical marks. With the semi-voiced (half-turbid) sign (*handakuten* modifier) and the voiced (turbid) sign (*dakuten* modifier), the originally unvoiced consonants *k, s, t, h* can easily be turned into voiced ones:

$$k \rightarrow g \ (k + handakuten)$$
$$\text{unvoiced } s \rightarrow \text{voiced } s \ (s + handakuten)$$
$$t \rightarrow d \ (t + handakuten)$$
$$h \rightarrow b \ (h + handakuten), \ h \rightarrow p \ (h + dakuten)$$

Examples of modifiers:

か カ ka	さ サ sa	し シ shi ち チ chi	た タ ta	は ハ ha	*kana character*
が ガ ga	ざ ザ za	じ ジ ji ぢ ヂ ji	だ ダ da	ば バ ba	*+ handakuten*
—	—	—	—	ぱ パ pa	*+ dakuten*

(The same procedure is followed with the other syllables.)

Note that the handakuten changes the /s/ sound or /t/ sound + *i* into the syllable *ji.*

Other sounds can be represented by adding syllabic characters written small: In the katakana syllabary, used for foreign words, *fu* + *a* vowel written small represents the sounds *fa, fi, fe, fo*:
ファ、フィ、フェ、フォ.

By adding *ya, yu,* and *yo,* written small や、ゆ、よ /ヤ、ユ、ヨ to the characters in table column "i," we obtain the palatalized equivalents (roughly a consonant + *j* + the corresponding vowel) of the syllables shown there: for example, *hya, hyu, hyo* ひ ゃ、ヒ ュ、ひ ょ (correspondingly in *katakana*), or, with a *dakuten, ja, ju, jo* じ ゃ、じ ゅ、じ ょ、ち ゃ、ち ゅ、ち ょ (correspondingly in *katakana*).

Notes on Pronunciation

The pronunciation of Japanese words, which, as previously mentioned, consist largely of open syllables, is quite easy. You are not likely to have any problems in this regard. The vowels in the syllables are pronounced as follows:

a	as in	mat, rat
i	as in	tip, active
u	as in	pull, book
e	as in	bed, peck
o	as in	saw, caught

Since the Hepburn System is based on English, the pronunciation of consonants closely follows that of our language.

Then there are just three more important things to keep in mind:

1) In pronunciation, a strict distinction must be made between a short vowel—in *hebonshiki,* a normal vowel letter without a diacritical mark—and a long vowel (vowel letter with a macron, or long mark, above it: $\bar{a}, \bar{i}, \bar{e}, \bar{u}, \bar{o}$). If you ignore this distinction, you will not be properly understood. A long *i* is usually written as *ii*, while ī appears in words of foreign origin. A long *e* usually is written as *ei*, or as ē in words of foreign origin. This results from the different spelling conventions of *hiragana* and *katakana*.

2) The doubling of the syllabic consonants (noted in the syllabary with a preceding *tsu* つ written small) is written in *hebonshiki,* as in English, as a double consonant and is also pronounced that way: い っ て *it t e.*

3) In addition, a peculiarity in the pronunciation of *i* and *u* must be taken into account. In certain cases, these sounds are pronounced as voiceless or even almost entirely swallowed. In Roman script, that can be noted by raising the vowel in question; however, that disrupts the typeface and possibly would only confuse a Japanese, if he had to read a sentence written in

Roman script in order to communicate. Most Japanese, in any event, are not used to Japanese written in romaji.

Therefore we will dispense with the use of the elevated *i* and *u*, and instead give the exact rules for vowel loss.

The vowels *i* and *u* are pronounced as unvoiced or swallowed:
1. after *s*, *sh*, and *ts* at the end of a word.
2. between two voiceless consonants, unless both are /*s*/ sounds.

Examples:
(Here the apostrophe represents a voiceless or swallowed *i* or *u*)

desu	→	*des'* (Rule 1)
toshi	→	*tosh'* (Rule 1)
hitotsu	→	*h'tots'* (Rule 2, Rule 1)

yakusoku	→	*yak'soku* (Rule 2)
tsutaeru	→	*ts'taeru* (Rule 2)

but:	*shiso* →	*shiso* (exception, since both are *s* sounds)
	sushi →	*sushi* (exception, since both are *s* sounds)

Otherwise the apostrophe designates a syllable-final *n*; see dictionary section.

Abbreviations Used in This Book

adj.	adjective
adv.	adverb
f.	feminine
m.	masculine
n.	neuter
v.	verb
con.	conjunction

Different Countries, Different Customs

Intercultural Tips

Forms of Address

To address someone formally, use the family name, to which the word –san is appended. In Japanese, no distinction is made between men and women. If your last name is Roberts, for example, you are addressed as **Roberts-san**, whether you are Mr. or Mrs. Roberts.

Never add –san to your own name or to that of someone who is accompanying you, however, since this sign of respect is shown only to the person being addressed.

With Japanese names—on business cards, for example—keep in mind that the order of the names is reversed: the family name appears first, and then the given name, etc.

If you speak to someone out in public—for example, to ask for directions—preface your question with Sumimasen, ga ... (Excuse me, ...) and say thank you: Arigatōgozaimasu.

Greetings—Aisatsu

In Japan, people greet each other by bowing. The deeper the bow, the greater the respect being shown to the other person.

The Western custom of shaking hands is not common practice in Japan. Hugging or kissing in public would be totally improper. Such things are restricted to the private sphere.

In the morning, until about 10 o'clock, people greet each other with Ohayōgozaimasu—Good morning!—and after that time, until about 5 P.M., they say Kon'nichi wa—Good day!

Later in the day, until about 9 P.M., they say Konban wa—Good evening! Oyasumi nasai is the equivalent of Good night!

Home Visit Program

The Home Visit Program offers an opportunity to spend a few hours visiting in a private home and talking with the family members.

The Japanese welcome contact with foreigners. It is a way to cultivate international contacts, and you will have a chance to immerse yourself in an authentically Japanese setting for a few hours.

Both the placement services and the invitation are on a voluntary basis.

This Home Visit Program is offered in the following cities: Narita, Yokohama, Nagoya, Kyōto, Ōsaka, Ōtsu, Kōbe, Kurashiki, Okayama, Hiroshima, Fukuoka, Kumamoto, and Miyazaki.

The respective addresses can be obtained either from the TIC in Tōkyō or from the information centers in each city. In some cities, you need to sign up in person at the office counter at least one day before the home visit. Further requirements should be verified in advance.

Visiting a Private Home

When you enter a house or an apartment—this also applies to the *ryokan,* the traditional Japanese inn—you absolutely must remove your shoes at the door. Then, wearing the slippers that are placed there for your use, you can enter the hall. The room with a tatami straw mat floor must be entered only in your stocking feet, with even the slippers left outside! Special slippers are provided for wearing in the toilet room. Never forget to remove them again afterwards and put on the regular indoor slippers once more!

Japanese Bathrooms

The setup of the bathroom in Japanese homes and in the *ryokan* is different from that common in Europe. It consists of a room with a drain on the floor. Also in this room is an *o-furo,* which looks like a bathtub and is filled with very warm, almost hot water. But a tourist simply must not confuse this with a European bathroom and make the mistake of soaping down or washing in the *o-furo*: If there is no shower in the room, you should take the bucket that is provided there and fill it with water. While standing or sitting on the stool provided, wash yourself. Then you can get into the warm *o-furo* to relax. Thus the o-furo is *not* a bathtub, but a kind of pool. After using the *o-furo,* never pull the plug and let out the water, because the *o-furo* is meant to be available just as it is for the next bather to enjoy. To keep the water at the proper temperature, the *o-furo* is covered with an insulating cover.

The same rules apply for the Japanese *onsen,* a bath fed by a natural hot spring.

Saying Good-bye

In general, people say good-bye by using the word *sayōnara,* while bowing slightly. In a family setting, people say *itte kimasu* (I'm leaving and coming back), and the response is *itte'rasshai* (Please come back). When you come back, you say *tadaima* in greeting, meaning "I'm back (home)." The family member or members who stayed at home answer by saying *o-kaeri nasai* (Welcome home).

In a Restaurant

Eating out and shopping are two of the favorite activities of the Japanese. Consequently there are a great many places to eat. Some serve only Western foods (*yōshoku*), while others offer Japanese (*washoku*) and Chinese cuisine (*chūka-ryōri*).

In Japanese restaurants, realistic wax representations of the foods on the menu are displayed in the front window. Guests can simply point to the food they want.

In addition, there are many specialty restaurants that serve only one or two dishes. Typical of these are the sushi restaurant, *sushiya*, and various noodle restaurants such as *sobaya* and *ramenya*.

To order, you say *Kore o kudasai!* and give the number of the dish as shown on the menu, on a sign outside, or in the window display. Chopsticks are used, and you will be provided with a warm cloth to wipe your hands with and a glass of cold water. Western flatware is usual only with Western food (*yōshoku*).

Before the meal, the Japanese say *itadakimasu,* and after eating they say *gochisō-sama deshita.*

Business Travel

If you are in Japan on a business trip at the invitation of a Japanese company, you can assume that everything will be extremely well organized.

For American businesspersons, it is important to have plenty of time. From the Japanese point of view, an overall good atmosphere is a precondition for good business. You will be invited to dinner, and you may issue an invitation as well. As the evening wears on, the Japanese also like to sing. They know and love American songs. Don't be embarrassed to join in the singing.

It would be unimaginable to deliberately steer the conversation toward the subjects of the business dealings. Once you enter into the negotiations, it is important to keep the following in mind: Japanese will not interrupt someone who is talking, since from their standpoint this is considered very impolite. Refusal and agreement are not expressed either verbally or through a facial expression. You will never hear a direct *iie*—"no"—from a Japanese. Instead, a negative attitude will be perceptible from the overall atmosphere and will be hinted at with expressions such as "that is difficult …" or "that is somewhat inconvenient …" A clear *hai*—"yes"—entails an absolute obligation for a Japanese, which he absolutely must fulfill to keep from losing face.

In addition to plenty of time, you also need a bilingual business card with the exact name of your company and your title. Do not wear casual clothing. Even in high temperatures, a suit, light-colored shirt, and tie are compulsory. Bring brochures and documents in Japanese or English with you.

Travel Preparations

When you're going on a trip ...
The best source of useful information is the internet. It will tell you all you need to know about your travel destination. In addition to information for travelers, look for these online:
- on a daily basis, news of interest to travelers and interesting reports
- on a regular basis, theme-related specials and contests
- mini-guides to print and use

Some Useful Internet Addresses

http://japanvisitor.com/

http://www.jnto.go.jp/

http://gojapan.about.com/

http://www.japantravelinfo.com/tips/travel_tips.html

http://www.jal.co.jp/japantravelinfo/main.html

http://www.jinjapan.org/

Reserving a Hotel Room by E-Mail

Dear Sir or Madam,
I would like to book a single/double/twin-bedded room for 2 nights on the 24th and 25th June.
Please let me know if you have any vacancies and the cost per night plus breakfast.
Yours faithfully,

Reserving a Car by E-Mail

Dear Sir/Madam,
I would like to hire a small/mid-range/luxury saloon car/minibus from July 20 – 25 from XXX Airport. I depart from YYY Airport so wish to leave the car there. Please inform me of your rates and what documents I shall require.
Yours faithfully,

I'm planning to spend my vacation in … Can you please give me information about accommodations in the area?
… de kyūka o sugosu tsumori desu, Sono atari no yadoya no jūsho arimasu ka?

What kind of accommodations do you have in mind?
Dono yō na yado o gokibō desu ka?

a hotel.
hoteru
a pension.
penshon
a room in a private home.
kyakushitsu
a vacation apartment.
kyūka yō apāto

Questions About Accommodations

Hotel – Pension – Bed-and-Breakfast

I would like a hotel that's not too expensive—something in the mid-price range.
Hoteru o sagashite imasu, amari takakunaku tegoro na tokoro o.

I'm looking for a hotel with an indoor swimming pool/golf course/tennis court.
Okunai pūru/gorufujō/tenisukōto no aru hoteru o sagashite imasu.

Can you recommend a nice room in a private home with breakfast?
Kirei na chōshoku tsuki kyakushitsu arimasu ka?

How many people should it be for?
Nan'nin desu ka?

Are dogs allowed?
Inu wa yoi desu ka?

Is it possible to set up an additional bed in one of the rooms?
Betto o mō hitotsu irete kuremasen ka?

How much does it cost per week?
Isshūkan ikura desu ka?

General

Yes.
Hai.

No.
Iie.

Japanese view *iie* (no) as very abrupt, and it is rarely used. If you want to refuse or decline something, say *chotto muzukashii desu*, "It is inconvenient."

Please.
Dōzo.

Thank you.
Arigatō!

Thank you very much.
Dōmo arigatō gozaimasu!

You're welcome.
Dō itashimashite!

Not at all.
Dō itashimashite!

What is it?/What did you say?
Nan desu ka?/Ē, nan to osshaimashita ka?

Of course.
Mochiron!

I understand.
Wakarimashita!

Okay.
Okē!

I got it.
Wakarimashita!

Excuse me./I'm sorry.
Sumimasen!/Gomen nasai!

Just a moment, please.
Chotto matte kudasai!

It's enough, thank you.
Mō ii desu!

Help!
Tasukete!

Who?
Dare?

What?
Nani?

Who?/Which?
Dore?/Dono ...?

To whom?
Dare ni?

Whom?
Dare o?

Where?
Doko?

Where is ...?
... wa doko desu ka?

Why?/Why?/What for?
Dōshite?/Naze?/Nan' no tame ni?

How?
Dono yō ni?

How much?
Ikura?

How long?
Dono kurai nagaku?

When?
Itsu?

At what time?
Nan'ji ni?

Give me ..., please.
... o kudasai.

Do you have ...?
... ga arimasu ka?

Numbers—Measures—Weights

0	zero, rē
1	ichi
2	ni
3	san
4	shi, yon
5	go
6	roku
7	shichi, nana
8	hachi
9	kyū
10	jū
11	jū-ichi
12	jū-ni
13	jū-san
14	jū-shi, jū-yon
15	jū-go
16	jū-roku
17	jū-shichi, jū-nana
18	jū-hachi
19	jū-kyū
20	ni-jū
21	nijū-ichi
22	nijū-ni
23	nijū-san
24	nijū-shi, nijū-yon
25	nijū-go
26	nijū-roku
27	nijū-shichi, nijū-nana
28	nijū-hachi
29	nijū-kyū
30	san-jū
31	sanjū-ichi
32	sanjū-ni
40	yon-jū
50	go-jū
60	roku-jū
70	nana-jū
80	hachi-jū
90	kyū-jū

100	hyaku
101	hyaku-ichi
200	ni-hyaku
300	sanbyaku
1000	sen
2 000	nisen
10 000	ichiman
100 000	jūman
1 000 000	hyakuman
1.	ichiban(me)
2.	niban(me)
3.	sanban(me)
4.	yonban(me)
5.	goban(me)
6.	rokuban(me)
7.	nanaban(me)
8.	hachiban(me)
9.	kyūban(me)
10.	jūban(me)
1/2	nibun no ichi
1/3	sanbun no ichi
1/4	yonbun no ichi
3/4	yonbun no san
3.5 %	san ten go pāsento
27 °C	nijū nana do
–5 °C	mainasu go do
1999	sen kyūhyaku kyūjū kyū nen
2005	nisen go nen
millimeter	miri/mirimētoru
centimeter	senchi/senchimētoru
meter	mētoru
kilometer	kiro/kiromētoru
square meter	heihō-mētoru
liter	rittoru
gram	guramu
pound	pondo
kilogram	kiro

Telling the Time

What time is it?
Nan'ji desu ka?

Exactly ... o'clock./About ... o'clock.
... -ji chōdo/daitai ... desu.
  3 o'clock
  San-ji desu.
  5 after 3
  San-ji go-fun (sugi) desu.
  10 after 3
  San-ji juppun.
  3:15
  San-ji jūgo-fun.
  3:30
  San-ji han.
  a quarter to 4
  Yo-ji jūgo-fun mae.
  5 to 4
  Yo-ji go-fun mae.
  12 noon/12 midnight
  Shōgo jūni-ji/Mayōnaka jūni-ji.

At what time?/When?
Nan'ji ni?/itsu?

At 1 o'clock.
Ichi-ji ni.

At 2 o'clock.
Ni-ji ni.

Around 4 o'clock.
Yo-ji goro.

After 1 hour.
Ichi jikan go ni.

After 2 hours.
Ni jikan go ni.

Not before 9 in the morning.
Asa ku-ji mae de wa naku.

After 8 in the evening.
Yoru, hachi-ji sugi ni.

Between 3 and 4.
San-ji kara yo-ji no aida.

How long?
Dono kurai nagaku?

For 2 hours.
Ni jikan.

From 10 to 11.
Jū-ji kara jūichi-ji made.

Till 5 o'clock.
Go-ji made.

From what time?
Itsu kara?

From 8 in the morning.
Asa no hachi-ji kara.

From 30 minutes ago.
San juppun mae kara.

Since the 8th./Since 8 days ago.
Yōka irai/mae kara.

Since a week ago.
Isshūkan mae kara.

after 2 weeks	nishūkan go ni
after a week	isshūkan go ni
around noon	hiru goro
at noon	hiru ni
before	izen wa
during the morning	gozenchū ni
during the weekend	shūmatsu ni
early tomorrow morning/ . .	ashita no asa hayaku/ashita no ban
tomorrow night	
every hour	ichijikan-goto ni
everyday	mainichi
immediately/soon	sugu ni, mamonaku
in the afternoon	gogo ni
in the daytime	hiruma ni
in the morning	asa ni, gozen ni

late	osoku
later	ato de
Monday of last week	senshū no getsuyōbi
next year	rainen
night	yoru
now	ima
occasionally	tokidoki
on Sunday	nichiyōbi ni
quickly	hayaku
recently/the other day	saikin/senjitsu
sometimes	tokidoki
the day after tomorrow	assatte
the day before yesterday	ototoi
these days	konogoro
this morning/tonight	kesa/konban
this week	konshū
today	kyō
tomorrow	ashita
within a week	isshūkan inai ni
yesterday	kinō
10 minutes ago	jippun mae ni

The Days of the Week

Monday	getsuyōbi
Tuesday	kayōbi
Wednesday	suiyōbi
Thursday	mokuyōbi
Friday	kinyōbi
Saturday	doyōbi
Sunday	nichiyōbi

The Months

January	ichigatsu
February	nigatsu
March	sangatsu
April	shigatsu
May	gogatsu
June	rokugatsu
July	shichigatsu
August	hachigatsu
September	kugatsu
October	jūgatsu
November	jūichigatsu
December	jūnigatsu

The Seasons

spring . . . . haru
summer . . . . natsu
fall . . . . aki
winter . . . . fuyu

Holidays (American Calendar)

New Year . . . . shin'nen
Easter . . . . fukkatsusai, īsutā
Christmas . . . . kurisumasu

Holidays (Japanese Calendar)

New Years Day, January 1 . . Gantan, Ganjitsu
Adulthood Day, the second Se'ijin no hi
  Monday in January
National Foundation Day, . . Kenkoku-kinenbi
  February 11
Vernal Equinox Day, ... Shunbun no hi
  March 20 or 21
Greenery Day, April 29 . . . . Midori no hi
Constitution Day, May 3 . . . Kenpō-kinenbi
Children's Day, May 5 . . . . Kodomo no hi
Respect for the Aged Day, . Keirō no hi
  the third Monday in
  September
Autumnal Equinox Day, . . . Shūbun no hi
  September 23 or 24
Health-Sports Day, the . . . . Tai·iku no hi
  second Monday in October
Culture Day, November 3 . . Bunka no hi
Labor Thanksgiving Day, . . . Kinrō-kansha no hi
  November 23
Emperor's Birthday, ... Tennō-tanjōbi
  December 23

The Date

What's today's date?
Kyō wa nan'nichi desu ka?

Today is August 4.
Kyō wa hachigatsu yokka desu.

Weather

The climate in Japan is much like that in southern United States, with extremely high humidity in summer (but with a rainy season in June and July).
Most conversations in Japan begin with a discussion of the weather.

What wonderful/terrible weather!
Nan' te subarashii/hidoi otenki deshō!

It's very cold/hot/hot and humid.
Totemo samui/atsui/mushiatsui desu.

It's foggy./It's windy.
Kiri de bonyari shite imasu./Kaze ga arimasu.

Good/bad weather will continue.
Yoi tenki/warui tenki ga tsuzukimasu.

It'll get warmer/colder.
Motto atatakaku/samuku narimasu.

It'll rain/snow.
Ame/Yuki ga furimasu.

The roads are icy.
Dōro ga kootte imasu.

Visibility is only 20 meters/less than 50 meters.
Shikai wa nijū mētā nomi desu./gojū mētā ika desu.

You'll need snow chains.
Sunōchēn ga hitsuyō desu.

air	kūki
calm	nagi
clear/fine/fair	hareta/harete/hare
cloud	kumo
cloudy	kumori
cold	samui
damp/wet	shimetta/nurete
earthquake	jishin

> The island nation of Japan is frequently shaken by (mostly mild) earthquakes. Therefore, the building codes are very strict, and most tremors are barely perceptible.

ebb tide	hikishio
fog	kiri
frost	shimo
frozen	tōketsu
gust of wind	toppū
heat	atsusa, nekki
high tide	michishio
hot	atsui
hot and humid	mushiatsui
hot days	atsui hibi
ice	kōri
lightning	inazuma
possibility of rain	ame moyo
rain	ame
shower	niwaka ame
snow	yuki
storm	arashi
sun, sunshine, sunlight	taiyō, hi, nikkō
temperature	ondo
thunder	kaminari
thunderstorm	raiu
typhoon	taifū
variable/unstable	kawari yasui
warm	atatakai
weather forecast	tenkiyohō
weather report	kishō-tsūhō
wind	kaze
wind velocity	hūryoku

Colors

beige . . . . bēju-iro
black . . . . kuro
blue . . . . ao
brown . . . . cha-iro
colored . . . . iro no tsuita
gold-colored . . . . kin-iro
gray . . . . nezumi-iro/hai-iro
green . . . . midori-iro
orange . . . . orenji-iro
pink . . . . pinku
plain . . . . muji no
purple . . . . fuji-iro, murasaki-iro
red . . . . aka
silver-colored . . . . gin-iro
turquoise . . . . sora-iro
white . . . . shiro
yellow . . . . ki-iro

dark blue/dark green . . . . . . kon-iro/anryokushoku
light blue/light green . . . . . usu-aoi/usu-midori

Personal Contacts

The Western custom of shaking hands is not popular in Japan. People bow to each other, with the depth of the bow reflecting the depth of the respect being shown. Japanese would never hug or kiss one another in public.

Saying Hello

Good morning.
Ohayō gozaimasu!

Good afternoon.
Kon'nichi wa!

Good evening.
Konban wa!

Hello! (male)/Hello! (female)/good afternoon.
Yā/Arā/kon'nichi wa!

Can you tell me your name?
Anata no o-namae o oshiete kudasai?

What's your name?
O-namae wa?

Your name? (male)
Kimi no namae wa?

I am …. (Polite)
Watashi wa … to mōshimasu.

I am ….
Watashi wa … desu.

How are you? (Polite)
O-genki desu ka?

How are you?
O-genki?

Fine, thank you. And you?
Ē, okagesama de, anata/kimi wa?

Introductions

Mr., Mrs., Miss are all expressed in Japanese by *san,* which is placed after either the family name or the given name. A name is never spoken without being followed by *san,* with the exception of your own name, to which it would be a serious error to attach *san.* Thus Mrs. Müller would be *Myurā-san,* and Mr. Müller would also be *Myurā-san.* If you address a female friend by her given name, you would say, for example, *Hiroko-san.* Siblings do not use each other's given names when talking to one another; instead, they use a title, such as "elder sister" or "younger brother." (See also Short Grammar.)

I'd like you to meet (someone).
Goshōkai shimasu.

This is ....
Kochira wa...

Mrs. X.
... X-san desu.

Mr. X.
... X-san desu.

my husband/wife.
shujin/kanai desu.

my son/daughter.
musuko/musume desu.

my friend.
watashi no tomodachi desu.

Saying Good-bye

Good-bye.
Sayōnara!

See you.
Jā mata!

See you later.
Mata ato de!

See you tomorrow.
Mata ashita!

Take care.
Genki de nē!

Good night!
Oyasumi nasai!

Bye!
Jā nē!

Have a good trip!
Yoi tabi o!

To a great extent, the Japanese try to avoid expressing direct judgments about good and bad. People respect their partners in conversation and do not want to hurt their feelings. In Japan, it is considered a sign of strength of character to adapt and subordinate oneself, and this entails no loss of self-respect. Thus apologies—**sumimasen**—are very widely used in Japan. Exchanging apologies represents a good opportunity to leave mistakes behind and to strengthen the relationship.

Requesting and Thanking

Please(permission)./Please(request).
Dōzo./Dōka.

Yes, please.
Hai, dōzo.

No, thank you.
Iie, kekkō desu.

Excuse me, but ....
Sumimasen ga ...?

I'm sorry to bother you.
Ojama shite, sumimasen.

Excuse me, may I ask you some questions?
Sumimasen ga, sukoshi ukagatte mo, yoroshii desu ka?

Can you help me?
Tasukete kuremasen ka?

May I ask you a favor?
Onegai shite mo, yoroshii deshō ka?

Pardon me, but ...?
Osore irimasu ga ...?

Thank you very much. It was such a help to me.
Dōmo/Dōmo-dōmo arigatō, totemo tasukarimashita.

It's very kind of you.
Goshinsetsu ni.

Please tell me ....
... o oshiete kudasai.

Would you recommend ....
... suisen shite kudasaimasu ka?

Thanks.
Arigatō!

Thanks, I'm very happy.
Arigatō, totemo yorokonde!

Thanks. It's very kind of you.
Goshinsetsu ni, arigatō!

You're welcome./With pleasure.
Dō itashimashite!/Yorokonde!

Apologies

I'm sorry.
Sumimasen!

I'm very sorry.
Dōmo sumimasen!

I didn't mean it.
Sōyū imi de wa nakattan' desu!

It's all right./It doesn't matter.
Daijōbu./Kamaimasen!

I'm sorry, but I can't do it.
Zan'nen desu ga, sore wa dekimasen.

Congratulations/Wishes

Congratulations!
Omedetō!

Congratulations on your new baby!
Go-shussan ...

Congraturations on your marriage!
Go-kekkon ...

Happy birthday!
O-tanjōbi ...

Happy New Year!
Akemashite ...

Congratulations for passing the exam!
Gōkaku ...

Congratulations for ..../Happy ....
... omedetō gozaimasu!

Happy birthday!
Otanjōbi omedetō!

I wish you happiness./I wish you success.
Oshiawase ni!/Goseikō o inorimasu!

I wish you success.
Anata no seikō o inorimasu.

(Bless you!) (*after sneezing*)
(Odaiji ni.)
(*In this situation, Japanese actually say nothing at all.*)

I hope you get well soon.
Odaiji ni

36

Opinions and Feelings

Agreement and Conversational Responses

Yes.
Hai.

That's right.
Tadashii desu.

Certainly.
Shōchi shimashita!

No, thank you.
Yoroshii desu!

Okay.
Okē!

Yes, it is.
Sō desu!

Oh!
Ara!

Is that so!
Ara sō!

Is it true?
Hontō desu ka?

Interesting!
Omoshiroi!

How beautiful!
Kirei nē!

I understand.
Wakarimasu.

No choice.
Shō ga nai.

It's exactly right.
Sono tōri desu.

It's true.
Hontō desu.

It's (very) good.
Kore wa (totemo) ii desu nē.

With pleasure.
Yorokonde.

Refusal

There isn't enough time.
Jikan ga arimasen.

I'm not interested in such a thing.
Son'na mono ni wa kyōmi ga arimasen.

I can't agree with that.
Sore ni wa sansei dekimasen.

It won't be a problem at all.
Sore wa mattaku mondai ni narimasen!

Definitely not.
Keshite nai desu!

Not for me.
Watashi wa gomen da!

I don't like it at all.
Sore wa zenzen ki ni irimasen.

Preferences

I like it./I don't like it.
Sore wa suki desu:/Sore wa kirai desu.

I prefer ....
... no hō ga ii desu.

What I like most is ....
Ichiban ii no wa ...

I'd like to know more about it.
Kono koto ni tsuite motto iroiro shiritai desu.

Expressing Ignorance

I don't understand.
Wakarimasen.

I don't understand at all.
Mattaku wakarimasen.

Indecision

Whatever.
Dō demo ii desu.

I still don't understand.
Mada wakarimasen.

Maybe./By chance./Possibly./It may be.
Tabun/Hyotto shitara./Moshika shitara./Sō ka mo shiremasen.

Maybe./Perhaps.
Osoraku.

Delight—Enthusiasm

Terrific!
Sugoi!

Wonderful!
Subarashii!

Awesome!
Monosugoku suteki!

Super!
Monosugoi!

Bad!/Terrible!
Hidoi!/Monosugoi!

Contentment

I'm totally satisfied.
Watashi wa mattaku/jūbun manzoku desu.

Well, I can't complain.
Mā, monku wa iemasen.

It went especially well.
Kore wa tokubetsu umaku itta.

Boredom

How boring!
Nan' te taikutsu nan' darō!

... is boring, isn't it?
... taikutsu nē.

Astonishment—Surprise

Oh, is that so! Now I see.
Āa, sō ka, wakatta yō!

Is that true?
Hontō desu ka?

I can't believe it.
Sore wa shinjiraremasen!

Unbelievable!
Shinjirarenai!

Relief

It's fortunate that ..../Luckily ....
... to yū saiwai!/... no wa saiwai ...!

Aah!/Thank God!
Yare yare/Arigatai!

At last!/Finally!/At long last!
Yatto/Tōtō/Tsui ni!

Composure

Stay calm!/Calm down!
Ochitsuite!/Reisei ni!

Don't worry.
Shinpai shinaide.

Annoyance

It's really terrible.
Kore wa shikashi hidoi, nē!

Damn!
Imaimashii!

I've had enough!/Enough is enough!
Mō jūbun/takusan da!

... Is irritating./... is maddening.
... iraira shimasu/... atama ni kuru wa/yo.

What shameless behavior!/What a nerve!
Nan' te hajishirazu na okonai!/Nan' te atsukamashii!

Could it be real?/That couldn't have happened!
Kon'na koto 'te arun' darō ka!/Kon'na koto wa aru hazu ga nai!

Rebuking

How can you do such a terrible thing!
Dōshite son'na koto suru no!

Keep away!
Chikazukanaide kudasai!

That's absurd!
Tonde mo nai!

Regret – Disappointment

Oh, my!
Kore wa, kore wa!

I'm sorry.
Zan'nen desu.

I feel sorry for ....
... ni totte mattaku zan'nen desu.

That's too bad!/I feel really sorry for him/her!
Zan'nen!/O-kinodoku ni!

Expression and eye contact
Smiling: The Japanese are alleged to wear an inexplicable grin, known as the "Japanese smile." It is "put on" even when a situation is not funny at all. Frequently the smile conceals pain and embarrassment or is an attempt to spare the other person the need to feel sympathy.
Eye contact: It is not customary in Japan to meet the eyes of your partner in conversation and maintain eye contact. Especially when dealing with superiors, one should lower one's eyes to keep from seeming defiant or provocative.
Surreptitious glances from a Japanese are to be interpreted as a sign of respect.

Gestures
To wave someone over, make a downward motion with your hand. To indicate which person you mean, stretch out your arm and, keeping your palm flat, move your hand up or down in the direction of the person in question.
If you want to draw someone's attention to you, wave with your entire hand; never use your index finger to point at a person.
If the person being signaled is not certain whether he's the one you mean, he will point to his nose with his index finger: "Do you mean me?"
If someone scratches the back of his head, it means: "I'm embarrassed."
Crossing your index fingers means: "not allowed"/"no."
If someone makes a fist and stretches out the little finger: "wife" or "girlfriend."
Making a little circle with thumb and index finger stands for: "money." (Rubbing thumb and index finger together is not often understood in Japan.)

How deeply must I bow?
An inclination of 15 degrees is exactly right for those of equal rank or subordinates. With superiors or in a formal situation—when first meeting, for example—an inclination of 30 degrees is appropriate.

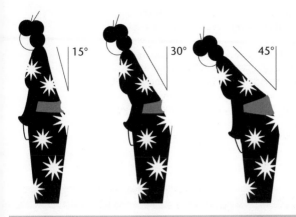

15° 30° 45°

Compliments

How beautiful!
Nan'te kirei deshō!

Oh, wonderful!
Wā, subarashii!

Thank you for your kindness.
Go-shinsetsu ni arigatō!

You're so nice./You're so kind.
Anata wa totemo kanji ga yoi./Anata wa totemo shinsetsu na kata desu.

It was a wonderful meal.
Oshokuji wa subarashikatta desu!

This was one of the best meals I've ever had.
Kon'na subarashii o-shokuji wa metta ni tabeta koto ga arimasen.

This is like a dream world.
Koko wa hontō ni yume no sekai no yō desu!

It looks great.
Sore wa rippa ni miemasu!

The dress looks great on you.
Doresu wa anata ni totemo o-niai desu. /
Doresu wa kimi ni yoku niaimasu.

beautiful	utsukushii
comfortable *(place)*	igokochi ga yoi
delicious	oishii
excellent	batsugun no
friendly	shinsetsu na
impressive	kan'mei o ataete
kind	shinsetsu na
pleasant	kimochi no yoi
pretty	kirei na
wonderful	subarashii

Conversation

Personal Information

How old are you?
O-ikutsu desu ka?

I'm 39 years old.
Sanjū kyūsai desu.

What do you do?
Go-shokugyō wa?

> In Japan it is less customary to mention your profession or occupation. Instead, you should introduce yourself as a member of the company you work for.

I am ....
Watashi wa ... desu.

I work for ....
... ni tsutomete imasu.

I'm living on a pension.
Watashi wa nenkin-seikatsu o shite imasu.

I'm still going to school.
Watashi wa mada gakkō e itte imasu.

I'm a student.
Watashi wa gakusei desu.

Place of Origin and Stay

Where are you from?
Dochira kara irasshaimashita ka?

I'm from Stuttgart.
Shututtogaruto kara kimashita.

Have you been in ... for a long time?
... ni wa mō nagaku irasshaimasu ka.

I have been here since ....
... kara koko ni orimasu.

How long are you going to be here?
Dono kurai irasshaimasu ka?

Is it the first time you've been here?
Koko wa hajimete desu ka?

Do you like Japan?
Nihon wa ki ni itte imasu ka?

Yes, very much.
Hai, totemo.

Family

If you are invited to a private home in Japan, a souvenir from your own country makes a good gift for the host or hostess. Alternatively, you should bring fruit, flowers, or candy. This is customary even among good friends.

When you enter a Japanese home, you should take off your shoes. Usually house slippers are provided at the entrance. If you go into a tatami room, do so only in your stocking feet. To go to the toilet, you need to change to different slippers. You will find them at the toilet door. Don't forget to take these special slippers off again afterwards.

Are you married?
Kekkon shite irasshaimasu ka?

Do you have children?
Kodomo-san wa irasshaimasu ka?

Yes, but they're already grown.
Ē, demo mō seijin shite orimasu./Ē, demo mō otona desu.

How old are your children?
Kodomo-san-tachi wa o-ikutsu desu ka?

My daughter is 8 years old, and my son is 5 years old.
Musume wa hassai de musuko wa gosai desu.

When you say good-bye to the family, you say *itte kimasu* ("I'm going and coming back"). When you return, you say *tadaima* (roughly, "I'm back home"). Those you left at home respond by saying *itte'rasshai* ("So long") or *o-kaerinasai* ("Welcome home").

Hobbies > also Active Vacations and Creative Vacations

What is your hobby?
Shumi o o-mochi desu ka?

I spend a lot of time with my children.
Ōku no jikan o kodomotachi to issho ni sugoshimasu.

I like reading very much.
Watashi wa yomu no ga totemo suki desu.

I surf the internet a lot.
Watashi wa intānetto o kanari shimasu.

I like gardening.
Watashi wa niwa de hataraku no ga suki desu.

I do some painting.
Watashi wa sukoshi e o kakimasu.

I collect antiques/stamps.
Watashi wa kottōhin/kitte o atsumete imasu.

What are you interested in?
Nani ni kyōmi o o-mochi desu ka?

I'm interested in ....
... ni kyōmi ga arimasu.

I'm taking an active interest in ....
Watashi wa yoku ... o shite imasu.

... is one of my favorite activities.
... wa watashi no dai-suki na katsudō no hitotsu desu.

cooking	ryōri
handicraft	kōsaku
learning foreign languages	gaikokugo o narau no
listening to music	ongaku o kiku no
painting	e o kaku no
playing a musical instrument	gakki o hiku no
pottery	tōki o tsukuru no
reading	dokusho
relaxing	kutsurogi
sketching	sukkechi
traveling	ryokō

Fitness ➤ also Active Vacations

How are you keeping in shape?
Dono yō ni shite karada no kondishon o totonoete imasu ka?

I jog./I swim./I do bicycling.
Jogingu o shimasu./Suiei o shimasu./Jitensha ni norimasu.

I play tennis/volleyball once a week.
Shū ni ichido tenisu/barēbōru o shimasu.

I go to a fitness center regularly.
Teiki-teki ni fitonessu-sentā ni kayotte imasu.

What kind of sports do you do?
Donna supōtsu o shimasu ka?

I play ....
... o shimasu.

I'm a ... fan.
Watashi wa ... no fan desu.

I go to ... often.
... ni yoku ikimasu.

Can I play with you?
Issho ni yatte mo yoroshii desu ka?

Do you have anything planned for tomorrow night?
Asu no yoru mō nanika yotei ga arimasu ka?

Would you like to come with me?
Issho ni ikimasen ka?

Would you like to do something together this evening?
Konban nanika issho ni shimasen ka?

May I invite you to dinner tomorrow night?
Asu no yoru shokuji ni shōtai shite yoroshii desu ka?

When shall we meet?
Itsu aimashō ka?

Let's meet in front of .../at ... at 9 o'clock.
Ku-ji ni ... no mae de/... de aimashō.

I'll come to pick you up.
Anata/Kimi o mukae ni kimasu.

Can I see you again?
Anata/Kimi ni mata aemasu ka?

I had such a great time.
Totemo tanoshikatta desu.

Flirting

You have really beautiful eyes.
Kimi wa subarashiku utsukushii hitomi o shite iru.

I love your smile.
Kimi no warai-kata ga suki desu.

I like you.
Kimi ga suki desu.

You're very lovely.
Kimi wa totemo suteki!

I love you.
Kimi o ai-shite imasu!

Do you have a steady boyfriend/girlfriend?
Dareka tokutei no otoko-tomodachi/Dareka tokutei no onna-tomodachi ga imasu ka?

Do you live with anyone?
Dareka to issho ni kurashite imasu ka?

Are you married?
Kekkon shite imasu ka?
  I'm divorced.
  Rikon shimashita.
  I'm separated.
  Bekkyo shite imasu.

Do you want to move in with me?
Watashi no tokoro ni issho ni kimasen ka?

No, it's too soon.
Iie, hayasugimasu!

Let's snuggle.
Pittari yorisoimashō.

Please leave right now.
Sugu kaette kudasai!

Leave me alone.
Kamawanaide kudasai!

Stop it right now.
Sugu son'na koto yamete kudasai!

Communication Problems

What is it?/What did you say?
Nan desu ka?/Ē, nan to osshaimashita ka?

I don't understand.
Wakarimasen.

Could you repeat it, please?
Sore o mō ichido kurikaeshite kudasaimasen ka?

Speak a bit slower, please.
Mō sukoshi yukkuri hanashite kudasaimasen ka?

Yes, I understand.
Hai, wakarimasu.

Do you speak …?
… o hanashimasu ka?

German
Doitsugo …

English
Eigo …

French
Furansugo …

I can speak a little ….
… o sukoshi dake hanashimasu.

Would you write it down, please?
Sore o kaite kudasaimasen ka?

Do you know someone who can interpret from English to Japanese?
Dareka Eigo kara nihongo ni tsūyaku dekiru kata o shitte imasu ka?

How do you say … in Japanese?
Kore wa nihongo de nan' to iimasu ka?

What do these *kanji (Chinese characters)* mean?
Kono kanji wa dō yū imi desu ka?

What does it mean?
Kore wa don'na imi desu ka?

How do you read it?
Kore wa nan to yomimasu ka?

Please write it down.
Dōzo kami ni kaite kudasai!

Please write it in *Romaji*.
Rōmaji de kaite kudasai.

Could you translate this sentence?
Dōzo kono bun o yaku shite kudasaimasen ka?

City maps and maps of the countryside, which have both
Japanese and Roman print, will make it considerably easier for
you to get your bearings.

To help tourists find their way around in this environment,
which is hard to access through reading and speaking, the
Tourist Information Center (TIC) provides many services free of
charge. (It does not handle reservations, however.)

Tōkyō

10th Floor, Tōkyō Kōtsū Kaikan Bldg., 2–10–1, Yūrakuchō,
Chiyodaku, Tōkyō (03) 3201–3331. Business hours:
Mon.–Fr. 9–5, Sat. 9–12.

Narita

**Narita Tourist Information Center (TIC) (New Tōkyō
International Airport Narita).** Arrival Floor, Passenger
Terminal 1 Bldg., New Tōkyō International Airport Narita.
(0476) 30-3383. Business hours: 8–8 (open year-round).
Narita Tourist Information Center (TIC) (New Tōkyō
International Airport Narita). Arrival Floor, Passenger
Terminal 2 Bldg., New Tōkyō International Airport Narita.
(0476) 34-5877. Business hours: 8–8 (open year-round).

Kansai

**Kansai Tourist Information Center (TIC) (Kansai
International Airport).** Arrival Floor, Passenger Terminal Bldg.,
Kansai International Airport. Tel. (0724) 56–6025. Business
hours: 9–9 (open year-round).

Kyōto

Kyōto Tourist Information—operated by Kyōto Prefecture.
9th Floor, JR Kyōto Station, Shimogyō-ku, Kyōto-shi, KYOTO
600–8216, JAPAN. Tel. 075-344-3300. Open daily 10–6,
except on the 2nd and 4th Tuesdays of each month, as well as
at the end of the year and on the New Year's holidays.
Kyōto City Tourist Information: 2nd Floor, JR Kyōto Station,
Shimogyō-ku, Kyōto-shi, KYOTO 600-8216, JAPAN. Tel. 075-
343-6655. Open daily 8:30–7.

Asking for Directions

Useful Phrases

across from . . . . mukai-gawa
after . . . . ato de
back . . . . ushiro
curve . . . . kābu
distant *(= great distance)* . . tōi

far	tōi
front	mae
here	koko
intersection	jūjiro
left	hidari
near	chikai
right	migi
road/street	dōro/michi
side/next	yoko/tonari
straight	massugu
street corner	machi-kado
there/over there	soko/asoko
traffic signal	shingō

Japanese addresses do not follow a linear principle based on streets, but an area principle based on neighborhoods. Street names are virtually nonexistent, apart from a few for especially large streets. The smallest unit of area, the *chōme,* usually consists of a few blocks. Every building within such a *chōme* has a single number (*banchi* = plot number), or a hyphenated double number, such as 16–6, with the first number designating the *banchi,* and the number following the hyphen denoting the *go* (the next-lowest subunit after *banchi*). Since these are not house or building numbers in the American sense, you can't assume that they are sequential, as they are in our country. These numbers have something to do with the construction date of the particular building and refer to the plot of land on which it stands. If you run across three numbers connected by hyphens, the first number gives the *chōme.* Thus 1–16–6 would be *chōme* 1, *banchi* 16, *go* 6. The next-larger unit after chōme has various names: *chō, machi,* or sometimes none at all. Above that level is the *–ku,* which means roughly "section of town". *Higashinada-ku* thus would be the eastern section of town. *Chuō-ku* will take you to the center of town. *Minato-ku* tells you that you need to go in the direction of the port. With the help of a small dictionary, you can figure out the meaning of the word preceding *–ku.*
In addresses, city names are given the ending *–shi,* which means "city" or "town" and serves to differentiate the place name from the prefecture of the same name, *-ken*: *Okayama-shi, Okayama-ken.*
For Ōsaka and Kyōto, *-fu* (not *–shi*) is used, and for Tōkyō, *-to.* Towns in the country are called *mura,* "village." The word *gun,* which also appears on occasion, refers to the next-smaller administrative unit after the *ken.*

Excuse me, but I'd like to go to ....
Sumimasen, ... e ikitain' desu ga?

Go straight ahead to ....
... made zutto massugu ikinasai.

Turn left/right at the traffic light.
Shingō o hidari/migi e magarinasai.

Follow the signs.
Hyōshiki dōri ni itte kudasai.

Could you write this Japanese in *Romaji*?
Kono nihongo o rōmaji de kaite kudasaimasen ka?

Could you write this *Romaji* in Japanese?
Kono rōmaji o nihongo de kaite kudasaimasen ka?

Is it far from here?
Koko kara tōi desu ka?

It's very close.
Sugu chikaku desu.

Excuse me, but is this the street to ...?
Sumimasen ga, kore wa ... e no michi desu ka?

Excuse me, but where is ...?
Sumimasen, ... wa doko desu ka?

I'm sorry, but I don't know.
Zan'nen desu ga, wakarimasen.

I'm a stranger around here.
Watashi wa kono atari no mono de wa arimasen.

Go straight/left/right.
Massugu/hidari e/migi e ikinasai.

Turn left/right at the first/second street.
Saisho no/niban-me no michi o hidari/migi e.

Go across ....
... watarinasai.

54

bridge
Hashi
square/plaza
Hiroba
road/street
Michi

It's best to take a No. ... bus.
...-ban no basu ni noru no ga ichiban desu.

At the Border

To enter Japan, you need a valid passport and a visa, if you are working there. Travelers from the U.S., Canada, Australia and New Zealand can stay in Japan without a visa for up to 90 days, but only as tourists. United Kingdom citizens can stay for up to 6 months (also, only as tourists).

No vaccination certificate is required, nor is there any need for special inoculations.

If you are fingerprinted, it is not because you are thought to be a criminal, but because the Japanese authorities need your fingerprints so that you can be issued a Japanese identification card. This pleasure—probably a one-time occurrence—will be yours only if you will be making a lengthy stay in Japan.

Passport Check

Show me your passport, please.
Pasupōto/Ryoken o misete kudasai!

Do you have a visa?
Biza ga arimasu ka?

Can I get a visa here?
Biza o koko de toremasu ka?

Customs

Do you have anything to declare?
Nanika shinkoku suru mono ga arimasu ka?

Get closer to the right/left.
Migi/Hidari e chikazukinasai.

Open the trunk/suitcase.
Kuruma no toranku/sūtsukēsu o akete kudasai!

Do I have to pay duty for this?
Kore ni kanzē o shiharawanakereba narimasen ka?

Personal Data

address	jūsho
birthdate	sēnen-gappi
birthplace	shussēchi
family name/last name	sē, myōji
given name	na
maiden name	kyūsē
marital status	kazoku-jōkyō
married	kikon
single	mikon
widow	yamome
nationality	kokuseki
personal information	jinbutsu ni kan suru koto

Border

a border entry point	kokkyō-tsūkaten
a national of an EU country	EU-kamēkoku no kokumin
amount of duty	kanzei no kakaru
arrival	nyūkoku
auto insurance card	kokusai jidōsha hokensho
border/national border	sakai/kokkyō
customs clearance fee	tsūkan-tesūryō
departure	shukkoku
driver's license	unten-menkyoshō
duty	kanzei
duty-free	muzei
I.D.	mibun-shōmē-sho
International Certificate of Vaccination	kokusai-shutōtechō
international signs	kokuseki hyōjiban
license plate	nanbā-purēto
passport	pasupōto/ryoken
passport inspection	pasupōto-kensa/ryoken-kensa
valid	yūkō
visa	biza

In Japan, as in Great Britain, vehicles drive on the left. The international traffic signs are in use.

It's not easy to get road maps showing the place names in both Japanese characters and Roman letters. (Such maps are available from the Japanese Automobile Club.)

Expressways are always marked in Roman letters as well as Japanese characters. Since the same is not true of all highways or main roads, it is advisable to compare the characters on your map with the signposts you see before you.

Signs and Information

停車禁止	teisha-kinshi	No Parking
工事現場	kōji-genba	Construction Site
悪路	akuro	Rough Surface
危険	kiken	Danger
横滑りの危険	yoko-suberi no kiken	Slippery
高度の傾斜	kōdo no keisha	Steep Grade
迂回	ukai	Detour
学童児注意	gaku-dōji-chūi	School
乗り入れ禁止	nori-ire-kinshi	No Entry
駐車禁止の終わり	chūsha-kinshi no owari	End of No Parking
砕石	saiseki	Gravel Surface
高圧	kōatsu	High Voltage
病院	byōin	Hospital
緑の矢印は先行の意味ではない／緑の矢印は優先の意味ではない	Midori no yajirushi wa senkō/yūsen no imi de wa nai	The green arrow does not mean right of way.
トラック	torakku	Trucks
右先行／右優先	migi-senkō/migi-yūsen	The right has the right of way.
注意	chūi	Caution
スピード落とせ	supīdo otose	Slow Down
右側（左側）運転	migigawa (hidarigawa) unten	Keep Right/Left
高速道路の出口	kōsokudōro no deguchi	Highway Entrance
出入り口につき駐車お断り	de-iriguchi ni tsuki chūsha o kotowari	Entrance—No Parking

GETTING AROUND

駐車禁止	chūsha-kinshi	No Parking
悪路	akuro	Rough Surface
危険なカーブ	kiken na kābu	Dangerous Curve
バイパス	baipasu	Bypass
短時間駐車圏	tan-jikan chūsha-ken	Short-Time Parking Zone

Roadways, Regulations

Expressways in Japan are toll roads.
The speed limits are 100 km/h on expressways, 50 km/h or often only 40 km/h on highways. The roads are very narrow in Japan. Even when driving between towns, it will be hard to travel at a speed exceeding 40 km per hour.
For information: JAF (Japanese Automobile Federation), 3-5-8, Shiba Park, Minato-ku, 105–0011 Tōkyō; Tel.: (03) 3436-2811.
Business hours: 9:00 – 5:45. www.jaf.or.jp/e/index_e.htm

back street	ura-dōri	裏通り
drive-in	doraibu-in	ドライブイン
entrance	nori-ire/shinyū	乗り入れ／進入
entry/exit	shin'nyūro/deguchi	進入路／出口
fine	bakkin	罰金
highway	kōsoku-dōro	高速道路
highway toll	kōsoku-jidōshadōro-ryōkin	高速道路料金
hitchhike	hittchihaiku	ヒッチハイク
hitchhiker	hittchi haikā	ヒッチハイカー
local express	jun-kōsoku-dōro	準高速道路
main street	menuki-dōri	目抜き通り
maximum blood alcohol content	ketsuekichū no arukōru nōdo no jōgen	血液中のアルコール濃度の上限
national highway/ prefectual highway	kokudō, kendoō	国道／県道
radar check	rēdā-kontorōru	レーダーコントロール
rest area	kyūkei-basho	休憩場所
road signs	michi-shirube	道標
toll	tsūkō-ryōkin	通行料金
traffic jam	jūtai	渋滞

At the Gas Station ➤ also At the Garage

At gas stations, you will be served very obligingly indeed. The station attendant always will fill the tank for you with the right type of fuel, wash the windshields, and empty the ashtrays. Bowing politely in farewell, the attendant also will help you re-enter the traffic on the roadway.

Gas stations are usually closed on Sunday.

Where is the nearest gas station from here?
Koko kara ichiban chikai gasorin-sutando wa doko desu ka?

… liters, please.
… rittoru irete kudasai.

unleaded
Gasorin (namari no hairanu)

super unleaded
Supā (namari no hairanu)

super plus unleaded
Supā-purasu

diesel
Dīseru

Fill it up, please.
Mantan onegai shimasu!

Check the oil, please.
Oiru o shirabete kudasaimasen ka?

Give me a local map, please.
Kono chihō no dōro-chizu o kudasai.

Parking

Finding places to park in Japan is difficult. If you are illegally parked, your car will be towed, and the fines are quite high. Therefore, use parking garages, even if waiting lines are the rule.

Parking places—near temples, for example—are marked on maps. Here you have a real chance to find a spot. Overall suggestion: use public means of transportation.

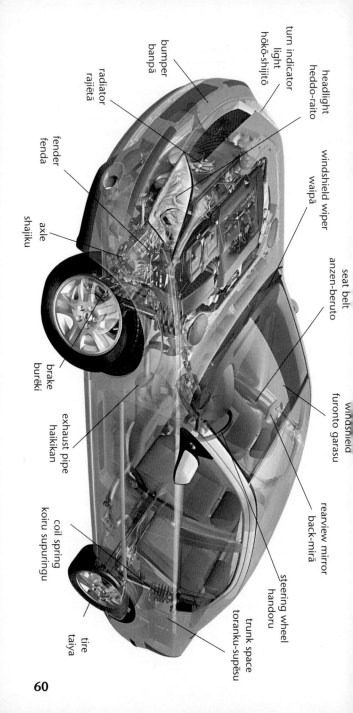

headlight
heddo-raito

turn indicator light
hōkō-shijitō

bumper
banpā

radiator
rajiētā

fender
fenda

axle
shajiku

windshield wiper
waipā

seat belt
anzen-beruto

windshield
furonto garasu

rearview mirror
back-mirā

brake
burēki

exhaust pipe
haikikan

coil spring
koiru supuringu

steering wheel
handoru

trunk space
toranku-supēsu

tire
taiya

60

Excuse me, is there parking nearby?
Sumimasen ga, kono chikaku ni chūsha dekiru tokoro ga
arimasu ka?

Is it okay to park my car here?
Kuruma o koko ni tomete oite mo yoi desu ka?

How much is the parking fee per hour?
Chūsha-ryōkin wa ichijikan ikura desu ka?

Is the parking garage open all night?
Chūsha-jō wa hitobanjū aite imasu ka?

A Breakdown

My car has broken down.
Kuruma ga koshō shimashita.

Is there a repair shop near here?
Kono chikaku ni shūri-jō ga arimasu ka?

Could you call a repair service for me?
Koshō-sābisu ni denwa o shite kudasaimasen ka?

Could you give me some gas?
Gasorin o sukoshi kudasaimasu ka?

Could you help me change the tire?
Taiya-kōkan o tetsudatte kudasaimasu ka?

breakdown	koshō
emergency blinkers	keikokuyō-tenmetsu-sōchi
emergency telephone	hijō-renrakuyō-denwa
flat tire	(taiya no) panku
gas canister	gasorinkan
jack	jakkī
jumper cable	janpā kēburu
repair service	koshō-sābisu
spare tire	yobi-taiya
tools	kōgu/dōgu
tow truck	rekkāsha
tow, to	ken'in suru
towing rope	hikizuna
towing service	rekkāsha-sābisu
triangle warning sign	sankakkei-keikokuhyōji-ki

The engine won't start.
Enjin ga kakarimasen.

There's something wrong with the engine.
Enjin ga nanika okashii desu.

... is not working.
... ga koshō shite imasu.

Oil is leaking.
Oiru ga moremasu.

When will the car/motorcycle be ready?
Itsu kuruma/mōtābaiku wa dekiagarimasu ka?

How much is the repair going cost?
Ikura gurai desu ka?

accelerator	akuseru	アクセル
air filter	eā-firutā	エアーフィルター
alarm system	keihō-sōchi	警報装置
antifreeze	futōeki	不凍液
automatic	ōtomachikku(giā)	自動制御ロック
automatic shift lock	jidō-seigyo-rokku	オートマチック（ギアー）
back light	bakku-raito	バックライト
blinker	meimetsu shingōtō	明滅信号灯
brake	burēki	ブレーキ
brake light	burēkiraito/seidōtō	ブレーキライト／制動灯
brake oil	burēki-oiru	ブレーキオイル
bumper	banpā	バンパー
clutch	kuratchi	クラッチ
damage	hason	破損
defect	koshō	故障
engine	mōtā/enjin	モーター／エンジン
engine oil	oiru, abura	オイル、油
exhaust	haiki	排気
gas tank	tanku	タンク
gear	giā	ギアー
first	fāsuto	ファースト
idling	kara-unten	空運転
reverse	kōshin/bakkugiā	後進／バックギアー
generator	hatsudenki	発電機
hand brake	hando-brēki	ハンドブレーキ
hazard lights	keihō-tenmetsu-sōchi	警報点滅装置
headlight	heddo-raito	ヘッドライト

high beam	hai-bīmu	ハイビーム
hood	bonnetto	ボンネット
horn	kēteki/kurakushon	警笛／クラクション
ignition	sutātā	スターター
low beam	heddoraito-shōmei/	ヘッドライト照明／
	hikari o yowaku suru	光りを弱くする
oil change	oiru-kōkan	オイル交換
oil pump	oiru ponpu	オイルポンプ
parking lights	chūsha-tō	駐車灯
radiator	rajiētā	ラジエーター
radiator water	reikyakusui	冷却水
rearview mirror	bakku-mirā	バックミラー
repair shop	shūri-kojō	修理工場
screw	neji	ねじ
seat belt	anzen-beruto	安全ベルト
short circuit	shōto	ショート
speedometer	sokudokei	速度計
tachometer	takomētā	タコメーター
taillight	tēru-raito	テールライト
tire	taiya	タイヤ
transmission	dendō-sōchi/giā	伝動装置／ギアー
trunk space	toranku-supēsu	トランクスペース
wheel	sharin	車輪
windshield	furonto-garasu	フロントガラス
windshield wiper	waipā	ワイパー
winter tire	fuyu yō taiya	冬用タイヤ

Accident

The legal blood alcohol level in Japan is 0.0%.

I was in an accident.
Jiko ga okimashita!

Call … immediately, please.
Sugu … o yonde kudasai.

  ambulance
  kyūkyūsha
  police
  keisatsu
  fire engine
  shōbōsha

Do you have a first-aid kit?

Kyūkyū-bako o motte imasu ka?

You …

Anata wa …

didn't yield to the car that had the right of way.

yūsen-sha ni chūi shimasen deshita.

didn't use your turn signal.

hōkō-shijitō o tsukemasen deshita.

You …

Anata wa …

were driving too fast.

supīdo o dashisugite hashirimashita.

crossed the intersection while the light was red.

akashingō de kōsaten o watarimashita.

Give me your name and address, please.

Namae to jūsho o oshiete kudasai.

First, get me an interpreter, please.

Mazu tsūyaku o yonde hoshii no desu ga.

handlebar
handoru

gear changer
gia-chenji

bicycle seat
sadoru

headlight
furonto-raito

bicycle pump
kūki-ponpu

rear light
bakku-raito

brake
burēki

inner tube
chūbu

tire
taiya no
sotogawa no
bubun

chain
chēn

pedal
pedaru

wheel
sharin

spoke
supōku

hub
habu

First, I have to call my company.
Mazu watashi no kaisha ni renraku shinakereba narimasen.

Thank you very much for your help.
Tasukete kurete arigatō gozaimasu!

Car, Motorcycle, and Bike Rental

Foreigners are not allowed to drive with an international driver's license in Japan if they are living there for a long period of time. You can obtain a Japanese driver's license, however, without having to take a driving test again. (For information, contact the Japanese Automobile Federation.) For shorter stays, an international driving permit is sufficient, and it also is all you need to rent a car. You rent the car with a full tank and return it the same way. The prices are calculated by the day or hour, independently of the number of kilometers you drive (except on Hokkaido, where the charge is determined by time and number of kilometers driven). Renting a car is expensive. Campers are not yet available for rental.

I'd like to rent ... for two days/one week.
Futsukakan ... karitai desu/isshūkan ... karitai desu

a jeep
jīpu

a motorcycle
ōtobai/baiku

a scooter
sukūtā

a moped
mopetto

a bicycle
jitensha

What's the rate for a day/a week?
Ichi-nichi/Isshūkan ikura desu ka?

You don't charge for mileage, do you?
Kiromētā wa museigen desu ka?

What's the rate per kilometer?
Sōkō-kyori ichi kiro ni tsuki ikura desu ka?

Does the insurance cover the entire car?
Norimono wa zenshatai hoken ga kekerarete imasu ka?

Can I leave the car in ...?
... de norisute wa dekimasu ka?

auto insurance card	jidōsha-hokensho
child seat	Kodomo yō shīto
comprehensive insurance	zenshatai-hoken
deposit, to	kyōtaku suru
driver's license	unten-menkyoshō
helmet	herumetto
ignition key	igunisshon-ki
papers	shorui
partial coverage insurance	bubun-shatai-hoken
seat belt	shīto-beruto
security deposit	hoshōkin
sunroof	sanrūfu
weekend package rate	shūmatsu-ikkatsu-ryōkin

Airplane

All the signs at Japanese airports are in English too.
Announcements are made in both Japanese and English.
At the passport check area, you should join the line marked
"Aliens." At the baggage inspection area, you should look for
the "Non-Residents" sign.

Making a Flight Reservation

When is the next available flight to ...?
Tsugi no ... iki wa nanji desu ka?

Are there seats still available?
Mada seki ga arimasu ka?

One one-way ticket to ..., please.
... iki katamichi ichimai onegai shimasu.

I'd like to reserve one round-trip ticket to ....
... iki ōfuku ichimai yoyaku onegai shimasu.

How much is an economy/a first class ticket?
Ekonomi-kurasu/fāsto-kurasu wa ikura desu ka?

Is it a smoking or nonsmoking section?
Kitsuen mata wa kin'en desu ka?

I'd like ..., please.
... o onegai shimasu.
  a seat by the window
  Madogawa no seki
  a seat by the aisle
  Tsūrogawa no seki

I'd like to cancel my reservation.
Kono furaito o kyanseru shimasu.

I'd like to change my ticket to this flight.
Kono furaito ni henkō shimasu.

At the Airport

Where is the ... airlines counter?
... kōkūgaisha no madoguchi wa doko desu ka.

Show me your ticket, please.
Anata no kōkūken o misete kudasai!

Can I take this as a carry-on?
Kore wa tenimotsu ni dekimasu ka?

On Board

Can I have some water, please?
O-mizu o itadakemasu ka?

Can I have one more pillow/blanket, please?
Kusshon mō hitotsu/mōfu o mō ichimai kashite kudasaimasen ka?

If you wouldn't mind, could we exchange seats?
Moshi yoroshikereba, watashi to seki o kaete kuremasen ka?

Arrival ➤ also Lost-and-Found Office

My luggage is lost.
Watashi no nimotsu ga nakunarimashita.

My suitcase was damaged.
Watashi no sūtsukēsu ga hason shimashita.

Where does the bus to … depart?
… hōkō e no basu wa doko kara demasu ka?

➢ also Train

airlines	kōkū-gaisha	航空会社
airport	kūkō	空港
airport bus	kūkō-basu	空港バス
airport duty	kūkō-shiyōryō	空港使用料
arrival	tōchaku	到着
arrival time	tōchaku-jikan	到着時間
baggage	nimotsu	荷物
baggage cart	nimotsu kāto	荷物カート
baggage check-in	chekkuin	チェックイン
baggage claim	tenimotsu-hikitorijo	手荷物引取り所
boarding pass	tōjō-ken	搭乗券
cancel, to	torikesu	取り消す
change, to	henkō suru	変更する
check in, to	chekkuin suru	チェックインする
connection	setsuzoku	接続
delay	okure	遅れ
departure gate	tōjō-guchi	搭乗口
domestic flight	kokunai-sen	国内線
duty-free shop	menzei-ten	免税店
emergency chute	hijō-dasshutsushūto	非常脱出シュート
emergency exit	hijō-guchi	非常口
emergency landing	fuji-chaku,	不時着、
	kinkyū-chakuriku	緊急着陸
flight	hikō	飛行
international flight	kokusai-sen	国際線
landing	chakuriku	着陸
layover	tochū-chakuriku	途中着陸
life jacket	kyūmē-dōgi	救命胴着
overweight	chōka-jūryō	超過重量
passenger	jōkyaku	乗客
pilot	pairotto	パイロット
security check	sekyuritī-chekku	セキュリティーチェック
security fee	anzen-ryōkin	安全料金
steward/stewardess	suchuwādo/	スチュワード／
	suchuwādesu	スチュワーデス
takeoff	ririku	離陸
terminal	tāminaru	ターミナル

The fare schedules shown on ticket-vending machines are given only in Japanese. It is best to ask what the fare is. Express trains, which stop at only a few stations, usually are marked with a red badge. Local trains lack the badge. Tourists may obtain a Japan Railpass, which allows you to travel at reduced cost. This pass is not sold in Japan; you must bring it with you from your country of origin, where it is available from a Japan Airlines office or a travel agency. You can use it to travel on all the lines in the JR network, including the *Shinkansen,* the Japanese high-speed ("bullet") train. Such a ticket is worthwhile, even if you don't use the train all the time.

Buying Tickets

Two one-way tickets to ..., please.
... e kippu nimai, katamichi kudasai.

regular class/first class
futsū/gurīn

smoking/nonsmoking
kin'en/kitsu-en

A round-trip ticket to ..., please.
... e ōfuku-kippu kudasai.

Round-trip tickets are not cheaper in Japan.

Is there a discount for children/students/seniors?
Kodomo/Gakusei/Nenchōsha waribiki ga arimasu ka?

Nonsmokers need to make reservations early, because there is only one nonsmoking car per train.

I'd like to reserve two nonsmoking seats, please:
Kin'en-seki futatsu yoyaku onegai shimasu:
   Shinkansen to ....
   ... iki Shinkansen.
   at ... (time), on ... (date)
   ...nichi ...ji ni
   in a private compartment
   koshitsu

GETTING AROUND

69

in a sleeping car
shindaisha
in a dining car
shokudōsha

At what time do you have a connecting train for ... at ...?
Nanji ni ... de ... iki ni setsuzoku ga arimasu ka?

How many times do you have to change trains?
Nankai soko de norikaenakereba ikemasen ka?

At the Train Station

I'd like to check in this suitcase as passenger baggage.
Kono sūtsukēsu o ryokyaku te-nimotsu to shite okuritai no desu ga.

Excuse me, which track is for the train to ...?
Sumimasen ga, ... iki ressha wa nanban-hōmu desu ka?

Is this a *Shinkansen* train?
Kore wa shinkansen desu ka?

The *Shinkansen* from ... will be 10 minutes late.
... kara kuru shinkansen ... wa juppun okureru mikomi desu.

On the Train

Is this seat free?
Kono seki wa aite imasu ka?

Would you mind if I open/close the window?
Mado o akete/shimete yoroshii desu ka?

Train station names such as Shin-Ōsaka or Shin-Kōbe denote *Shinkansen* stations. The bullet train, or *Shinkansen,* runs only in the daytime. It covers the 1,181 Km from Tōkyō to Hakata on Kyūshū in 5 hours and 50 minutes. It also operates between Tōkyō and Morioka, far in the north of Japan's main island, Honshu, and between Tōkyō and Niigata, on the Sea of Japan. *Nozomi* (Hope) is the name of the fastest train, which has operated on the Tōkyō-Hakata line since March 1993. *Hikari* (Lightning) and *Kodama* (Echo), the two somewhat slower trains, stop more frequently. There are both reserved and non-reserved seats. The non-reserved ones are usually in the first car. At the train stations in the larger cities, tickets for reserved seats on the shinkansen and express trains, as well as tickets for couchette cars, are sold or reserved in advance at counters marked with green (*midori-no-madoguchi*).

Excuse me, this is my seat.
Sumimasen ga, koko wa watashi no seki desu.

It's my reserved seat.
Koko wa watashi no zasekishitei desu.

Signs and Information

列車ダイヤ案内	resshadaiya-annai	Train Timetable
出発／到着	shuppatsu/tōchaku	Departure/Arrival
案内	annai/	Information/
新聞売り場	shinbun uriba	Newsstand
ポーターサービス	pōtā-sābisu	Porter Sevice
女性用トイレ	joseiyō-toire	Ladies' Room
男性用トイレ	danseiyō-toire	Men's Room
使用中／空き	shiyōchū/aki	Occupied/Vacant
おむつ取り替え室	omutsu-torikae-shitsu	Diaper Change
旅行センター／	ryokō-sentā/	Travel Center/
旅行社	ryokōsha	Travel Agency
禁煙の駅	kin'en no eki	Smoke-free Station
タクシー乗り場／	takushī-noriba	Taxi Stand
タクシースタンド	chikatetsu/	Subway/
地下鉄／	kaisoku densha	Rapid Transit Train
快速電車	koinrokkā	Coin-operated Locker
コインロッカー	nimotsukāto	Baggage Cart
待合室	machiai-shitsu	Waiting Room
鉄道公安部	tetsudō-kōanbu	Transit Police

➤ also Airplane

aisle	tsūro	通路
arrival	tōchaku	到着
baggage	nimotsu	荷物
baggage check-in	nimotsu-ichiji-azukair-sho	荷物一時預かり所
baggage check-in counter	tenimotsu-toriatsukai madoguchi	手荷物取扱 窓口
buffet car	byuffe sha	ビュッフェ車
car number	sharyō-bangō	車両番号
car without booths	shikirinonai-zaseki-ressha	仕切りのない座席列車
central station	chūō-eki	中央駅
coin-operated locker	koin-rokkā	コインロッカー
companion	dōhansha	同伴者

compartment	shashitsu	車室
conductor	shashō	車掌
departure	shuppatsu	出発
dining car	shokudō-sha	食堂車
discount	waribiki	割引
extra charge	warimashi-ryōkin	割増し料金
fare	jōsha-ryōkin	乗車料金
get off, to	oriru	降りる
get on, to	noru	乗る
inspection of tickets	jōshaken-kensa	乗車券検査
nonsmoking car	kin'en no shashitsu	禁煙の車室
onboard vendor	shanai hanbaiin	車内販売員
punch, to (a ticket)	kaisatsu suru	改札する
reservation	yoyaku	予約
reserved seat	zasekishitei	座席指定
round-trip ticket	ōfuku-jōsha-ken	往復乗車券
seat by the window	mado-gawa no seki	窓側の席
severely handicapped	jūdo-shōgaisha	重度障害者
Shinkansen		新幹線
(bullet train)		
(train name)	Hikari	ひかり
(train name)	Kodama	こだま
smoking car	kitsuen you shashitsu	子供用乗車券
station	eki	喫煙用車室
stop	teisha	駅
ticket counter	jōshaken-hatsubaiguchi	停車
ticket for a child	kodomo yō jōsha-ken	乗車券発売口
ticket for a sleeping car	shindaisha no ken	寝台車の券
toilet	toire	トイレ
track	densha no noriba	電車の乗場
train	kisha	汽車
train crew	jōmuin	乗務員
train schedule	jikoku-hjō	時刻表
train ticket	jōsha-ken	乗車券
waiting room	machiai-shitsu	待合い室
weekday	heijitsu	平日

Arrival

When does the next ship/ferry to ... leave?
Tsugi no ... e iku fune/ferī wa itsu demasu ka?

How long does the crossing take?
Wataru no ni wa dono kurai jikan ga kakarimasu ka?

When do we arrive at ...?
... ni wa nan-ji ni tsukimasu ka?

How long do we stay in ...?
... ni dono kurai no jikan orimasu ka?

I'd like ...
... o kudasai.
　a ticket for ....
　... iki jōsenken ...
　a first class ticket.
　Ittō-seki
　a second class ticket.
　Nitō-seki
　a private cabin.
　Koshitsu
　a cabin for two.
　Futari yō senshitsu

I'd like one ticket for the ... o'clock excursion boat.
... ji no yūran-sen no jōsen-ken o ichi-mai onegai shimasu.

On Board

Excuse me, but where is the dining room/lounge?
Sumimasen ga, shokudō/raunji wa doko desu ka?

I don't feel well.
Kibun ga warui no desu ga.

Would you get a doctor on board for me?
Sen'i o yonde kudasaimasen ka?

Could you give me medicine for seasickness?
Yoidome o kudasaimasen ka?

cabin	senshitsu	船室
captain	senchō	船長
continent	tairiku	大陸
cruise	kurūzu	クルーズ
deck	dekki	デッキ
excursion	shūyū	周遊
ferry	ferī	フェリー
get seasick, to	funayoi suru	船酔いする
harbor	minato	港
hovercraft	hobākurafuto	ホーバークラフト
hydrofoil	suichū-yokusen	水中翼船
life belt	kyūmē-ukiwa	救命浮き輪
life jacket	kyūmē-dōgi	救命胴着
life raft	kyūmē-bōto	救命ボート
ocean surface	nami no yōsu	波の様子
pier	futō	埠頭
port of call	kikōchi	寄港地
reservation	yoyaku	予約
seashore	kaigan	海岸
steamboat	kisen	汽船
ticket	jōsen-ken	乗船券

Local Public Transportation

Using a bus is not so easy, since the destinations are written only in Japanese.

Excuse me, but where is the nearest ...?
Sumimasen ga, ichiban chikai ... wa doko desu ka?
  bus stop
  basu no teiryūjo
  train station
  densha no eki
  subway station
  chikatetsu no eki

Which line is the train for ...?
... iki wa dono sen desu ka?

Can I take a bus tour/a day trip from here?
Koko kara basu tsuā/higaeri tsuā ga demasu ka?

What time is the first/last subway for ...?
... iki no shihatsu/saishū chikatetsu wa nan'ji desu ka?

Excuse me, is this the bus for ...?
Sumimasen ga, kore wa ... iki no basu desu ka?

How many stops to ...?
... made wa teiryūjo wa ikutsu desu ka?

Excuse me, but where should I get off/change?
Sumimasen ga, watashi wa doko de
orinakereba/norikaenakereba narimasen ka?

If I have to get off, could you tell me when?
Moshi orinakereba naranu nara, oshiete kudasaimasen ka?

I'd like a ticket for ... .
... iki no jōsha-ken o ichi-mai kudasai.

You can't use a bill for a fare machine.
Jidō-hanbaiki ni wa osatsu wa tsukaemasen.

book of tickets	kaisūken	回数券
bus	basu	バス
bus terminal	basu-tāminaru	バスターミナル
conductor	shashō	車掌
departure	shuppatsu	出発
direction	hōkō	方向
fare	jōsha-ryōkin	乗車料金
get on, to	noru	乗る
last stop	shūten	終点
local bus	shibasu	市バス
local streetcar	shiden	市電
local train	kinkyori-ressha	近距離列車
long-distance bus	chōkyori-basu	長距離バス
mountain railway	aputoshiki-tetsudō	アプト式鉄道
punch a ticket, to	kokuin o osu	刻印を押す
rapid transit train	kaisoku-densha	快速電車
schedule	jikoku-hyō	時刻表
security officer	kōan-kan	公安官
stop	tēryūjo	停留所
subway	chikatetsu	地下鉄
ticket	jōshaken/kippu	乗車券／切符
ticket machine	jōshaken-jidōhanbaiki	乗車券自動販売機
ticket valid for a week	isshūkan-yūkōna-jōshaken	一週間有効な乗車券
ticket valid for a day	ichinichi-ken	一日券
ticket-canceling machine	jōshaken-kokuinki	乗車券刻印機
trolley bus	tororībasu	トロリーバス

To hail a taxi, stretch out your arm and, keeping the palm flat, make a downward motion with your hand. This motion looks more like warding something off than waving it to come closer. Beckoning a taxi with an outstretched index finger is considered decidedly impolite in Japan. Taxi doors open and close automatically. It is advisable always to have somebody write down your desired destination in Japanese or to carry with you a Japanese business card, on the back of which is usually printed a tiny city map. Taxi drivers, too, can find their way around better with such a map to guide them. Tipping is not practiced, unless the driver has gone to special trouble for some reason.

Excuse me, but is there a taxi stand around here?
Sumimasen ga, kono chikaku ni takushīsutando ga arimasu ka?

To a station, please.
Eki e onegai shimasu.

To … Hotel, please.
… hoteru e onegai shimasu.

To … Avenue, please.
… dōri e onegai shimasu.

To …, please.
… made onegai shimasu.

How much will it cost to go to …?
… made o-ikura desu ka?

I'd like a receipt, please.
Reshīto o itadakemasen ka?

cab driver	takushī-untenshu	タクシー運転手
fasten a seat belt, to	beruto o shimeru	ベルトを締める
flat rate	ikkatsu-ryōkin	一括料金、均一料金
	kin itsu-ryōkin	
house number	banchi	番地
rate per kilometer	kiromētā-ryōkin	キロメーター料金
receipt	reshīto	レシート
safety belt	anzen-beruto	安全ベルト
stop, to	tomeru	止める
taxi stand	takushī-noriba	タクシー乗場
tip	chippu	チップ

Traveling with Children

In general, Japan is a very child-friendly country. Because of the Japanese mentality, daily life is attuned to spending time with small children. Thus there are plenty of facilities for children, including play corners and other things.

Many items for children are available in the department stores, and child seats are provided in restaurants everywhere. There are even special child-friendly places to eat.

Children are always welcome in Japan, and they play an important role in the family.

Useful Questions

Excuse me, is there a playground here?
Sumimasen ga, koko ni wa kodomo no asobiba ga arimasu ka?

Do you have babysitting service?
Koko de kodomo o azukeraremasu ka?... o azukatte kuremasu ka?

From what age do you accept children?
Nansai kara desu ka?

Do you know someone who can babysit?
Bebī-shittā o shite kureru hito o gozonji desu ka?

Do you have a baby monitor?
Bebīmonitā ga arimasu ka?

Do you have a program for children?
Kodomo yō puroguramu ga arimasu ka?

Do you have a discount for children?
Kodomo-waribiki ga arimasu ka?

Could you tell me where I can change diapers?
Doko de omutsu o kaeru ka oshiete itadakemasen ka?

On the Road

I'm traveling with small children. Could I have a front seat?
Chiisa na kodomo zure de ryokō shite orimasu. Ichiban mae no seki o itadakemasu ka?

Do you have a seat belt for a child?
Kodomo yō anzen-beruto ga arimasu ka?

Do you have some paper and a pencil/a coloring book?
Kami to enpitsu/nuriechō ga arimasu ka?

Could you lend me a child seat?
Chairudo-shīto o kashimasu ka?

In a Restaurant

Could you bring us a high chair, please?
Kodomo yō isu o motte kite itadakemasen ka?

Do you have a children's menu?
Kodomo yō menyū mo arimasu ka?

Can you warm a feeding bottle?
Honyūbin o atatamete kudasaimasen ka?

Is there a place near here where I can change diapers?
Kono atari ni omutsu o torikaeru basho ga arimasu ka?

Can you tell me where I can nurse a baby?
Kono atari de junyū dekiru basho o oshiete itadakemasen ka?

amusement park	yūenchi
baby food	bebī-fūdo
baby monitor	bebī-monitā
babysitter	bebī-shittā
babysitting	bebī-shittā, komori
bib	yodarekake
bottle	honyū-bin
bottle warmer	honyūbin no ho'onki
boy	otoko no ko
canteen	suitō
cap	bōshi
child seat	kodomo yō shīto
child seat cushion *(for the car)*	kodomo yō shīto-kusshon
children's clothing	kodomo-fuku
coloring book	nuri·e-chō
crib	bebī-betto
diaper	omutsu, oshime
diaper change	omutsu-kōkandai
discount for children	kodomo-waribiki
flipper	sui-ei yō uingu
girl	onna no ko
infant car bed *(for the car)*	nyūji yō bebī-shīto
pacifier	chikubi
playground	asobiba

playmate	asobi-tomodachi
sand castle	suna no shiro
sandbox	suna-ba
sunshade	hiyoke
swimming lane	sui-ei-kōsu
swimming pool for children	kodomo yō pūru
swimming ring	ukiwa
teething ring	oshaburi
toy	omocha

Health

Could you tell me if there is a pediatrician around here?
Kono atari ni shōnika'i ga iru ka oshiete itadakemasen ka?

My child has ....
Watashi no kodomo wa ... ga arimasu

He/she is allergic to ....
... no arerugī desu.

He/she vomited.
Hakimashita.

He/she has diarrhea.
Geri shite imasu.

He/she was stung by an insect.
Sasaremashita.

allergy	arerugī
certificate of vaccination	yobōsesshu-techō
chicken pox	mizu-bōsō
children's disease	kodomo no byōki
children's hospital	shōnika-byōin
cold	kaze
electrolyte solution	denkai-shitsu no yōkai
fever	netsu
German measles	hūshin
inflammation of the middle ear	chūjien
insect bite	mushisasare
measles	hashika
mumps	otafuku-kaze
rash/hives	hasshin/jin'mashin
running nose	hanakaze
scarlet fever	shōkōnetsu
whooping cough	hjakunichi-seki

Travelers with Disabilities

In the past few years, many improvements have been made for people with disabilities in Japan, in both the public and the private spheres. An infrastructure that takes their needs into account now exists. Nonetheless, it is advisable to contact the Tourist Office about these facilities before starting your trip. There are city guides for people with disabilities in Tokyo, Kyoto, and Kamakura: *Guide for People with Disabilities.* If you have problems, people in Japan will be glad to help you. Specialized information on travel arrangements for those with disabilities is also available on the internet.

I'm ....
Watashi wa ... desu.

physically handicapped/physically disabled
karada ga fujiyū/shintai shōgaisha

not able to see well/totally blind
me ga fujiyū/me ga miemasen

I have ....
Watashi wa ... desu.

leg problems/trouble walking
ashi ga warui/ashi ga fujiyū/arukemasen

muscular dystrophy
kin'i-shukushō

On the Road

Can I bring my folding wheelchair on the airplane?
Watashi no oritatamishiki-kurumaisu o hikōki (no naka) ni mochikonde mo ii desu ka?

Can I get a wheelchair for departure/arrival at the airport?
Kurumaisu wa shuppatsu/tōchaku no hikōjō de yōi saremasu ka?

Can I get a seat by the aisle?
Tsūrogawa ni zaseki o itadakemasu/kudasaimasu ka?

Are there toilets for the physically handicapped?
Shōgaisha yō no toire ga arimasu ka?

Is there a washroom for the physically handicapped?
Shōgaisha yō no senmenjo ga arimasu ka?

Is there a bathroom for the physically handicapped?
Shōgaisha yō no yokushitsu ga arimasu ka?

Can somebody help me when I change cars?
Dareka norikae no toki ni watashi o tetsudatte kudasaimasen ka?

Is the entrance to the car level with the ground?
Kuruma no noriguchi wa dōitsu heimen desu ka?

Are there kneeling busses?
Yuka no hikui basu wa arimasu ka?

Is there a ramp for wheelchairs at the platform?
Eki no hōmu wa kurumaisu yō ni surōpu ni natte imasu ka?

Is there a rental car with an accelerator lever for the physically handicapped?
Shintai-shōgaisha yō ni kasoku–rebā no rentakā ga arimasu ka?

I'd like to rent a wheelchair-accessible camping car.
Kuruma-isu yō no kyanpingukā o kashite kuremasu ka?

Can I rent a bicycle for the physically handicapped?
Dokoka kono atari de shōgaisha yō no jitensha o kariremasu ka?

Accommodations

Could you send me some information on hotels in ... suitable for the physically handicapped?
Dono hoteru ga ... de shōgaisha ni teki shite iru ka shiryō o watashi ni okutte kudasaimasen ka?

Could you tell me which hotels and camping sites have facilities for the physically handicapped?
Dono hoteru to kyanpujō ga shōgaisha yō no setsubi o motte iru ka watashi ni oshiete kudasaimasen ka?

What kind of floor does the room have?
Heya wa donna yukabari ni natte imasu ka?

Museums, Sights, Theater ...

Can someone with walking problems get to the exhibition by elevator?
Tenjikai wa ashi no warui hito demo erebētā de ikemasu ka?

Do you have a special guide for the handicapped?/ Do you have a city tour for the deaf?
Shōgaisha ni tokubetsu na annai ga arimasu ka?/Rōasha ni shinaikankō-annai ga arimasu ka?

Can we bring in a guide loop for the deaf?
Yūdōrūpu o mimi no kikoenai hito no tame ni ireraremasu ka?

Do you have a museum guide /a theater schedule for the blind/the deaf?
Me no mienai hito/rōasha yō hakubutsukan/engeki jōen no annai ga arimasu ka?

accelerator lever *(car)*	te no akuseru
access without stairs/steps	dan no nai tsūro/dan no nai iriguchi
accessibility	hairiyasusa/noboriyasusa/ chikazukiyasusa/...
association for the handicapped	shōgaisha-renmei
attendant	tsukisoinin
automatic door	jidō-doa
automatic door opening	jidōteki na doa no kaikōbu
barrier-free	bariafurī
blind	shikakushōgai
blind (person). He/she is blind.	me no mienai (hito)/(ano hito wa) me ga miemasen.
blind person	shikakushōgaisha
braille	tenji
braillewriter	tenjitaipu
cabin suitable for a wheelchair (ship)	kurumaisu yō senshitsu
car accommodating a wheelchair (train)	kurumaisu ga haireru sharyō
care service	fukushi-sābisu
crutch	matsubazue
deaf	tsunbo
deaf person	mimi no kikoenai hito, rōasha
deaf-mute	rōa/tsumbo to oshi
doorsill	shikii
epilepsy	tenkan
equipped for the handicapped	shōgaisha yō ...
guide loop	yūdōrūpu
hand grip	te no nigiri/totte
hand-driven bicycle	handobaiku
handrail	tesuri/rankan
hard of hearing	nanchō
headphone/earphone	heddo-hōn, iyahōn
height	takasa
help for boarding	jōshaji no tetsudai

ID for the handicapped	shōgaisha techō
level with the ground	(jimen to) onaji takasa no
lift	rifuto
mentally handicapped	seishinshōgai/shintekishōgai/ chitekishōgai
movement-impaired	kadōshogai/katsudōshogai
mute	oshi
outpatient care facilities . . .	gairai kaigo-sutēshyon
paralysis of one side of the . body	hanshinfuzui
parking space for the . . . . . handicapped	shōgaisha yō no chūshajō
physical disability	shintaishōgai
ramp	surōpu/keishahōmu, sakamichi
requiring care	sewa no hitsuyō na/kaigo ga hitsuyō na
sanitation facilities	ēsei setsubi
seeing-eye dog	mōdōken
severely handicapped	jūdoshōgaisha
shower stool	shawā yō isu
shuttle bus service	kuruma de no sōgei-sābisu
sign language	shuwa
social assistance officer	sōsharusutēshon
social assistance programs .	shakaikyūsaijigyō
stair/step	kōbai/katamuki
steering wheel knob *(car)* . .	handoru no (kirikae) botan/handoru no (kirikae) suichi
step	dan
suitable for a wheelchair . . .	kurumaisu yō
toilet for the handicapped .	shōgaisha yō toire
wheelchair	kurumaisu
collapsible wheelchair	oritatamishiki kurumaisu
electronic wheelchair	denki-kurumaisu/denki jikake no kurumaisu
onboard wheelchair	sennai/kinai yō kurumaisu
wheelchair user	kurumaisu no riyōsha
white cane	(mōjin yō) tsue
width	haba
width of a door	doa no haba
width of the corridor . . . . . . /entrance hall	rōka no haba/genkan no haba

Accommodations

The Japan National Tourist Organization (JNTO) can provide you with hotel addresses (with the exception of love hotels and temples). The office in Tōkyō can supply you with the addresses of the branch offices in other towns. You can get information there in English.

10th Floor, Tōkyō, Kōtsū Kaikan Bldg. 2–10–1, Yūrakuchō, Chiyoda-ku. Tōkyō 100–0006. Tel.: (03) 3201-3331. Business hours: 9–5 (Monday to Friday), Saturday 9–12, closed on Sunday and on national holidays.

Information

Could you recommend a ...?

... o watashi ni shōkai kudasaimasen ka?

nice hotel

Yoi hoteru

simple hotel

Kantan na hoteru

pension

Penshon

room in a private home

Kojin no heya

Is it in the center of the city/in a quiet area/near a beach?

Sore wa chūshin ni/shizuka na tokoro ni/hamabe no chikaku ni arimasu ka?

Is there also ...?

Koko ni mo ... ga arimasu ka?

a campsite

kyampujō

a youth hostel

yūsuhosuteru

How can I get there?

Soko e wa dono yō ni ittara ii desu ka?

Business hotels: Western style, that is, they conform to our ways of life. They are available in every city of any size. Admittedly, they are not cheap, but they offer the advantage of allowing you to relax in the evening without having to adapt to a strange culture.

Ryokan: Japanese style, with futons as beds. There is no Western-style bathroom, but a Japanese bath (*furo*). Breakfast consists of rice and soup, and green tea is drunk. Breakfast and dinner are included in the price. A *ryokan* is usually quite expensive.

Minshuku: The furnishings and food are the same as at a *ryokan*. The difference is that here you lay out your futon yourself, and in the morning you straighten it up yourself as well. A *minshuku* is much cheaper than a *ryokan*. You pay not for the room, but for the futons you have used. Breakfast and dinner are included. The first night's stay entails more stress than relaxation (communication problems, finding your way around in the room, the bathroom, the toilet, etc.). In a *minshuku* you are treated like a family member, and you are also expected to behave as if you were a family member.

Pension/boardinghouse: Similar to a *minshuku*. Not so traditionally Japanese. Usually run by young people.

Love hotels (*rabu hoteru*): This name does not conceal a bordello. Love hotels are houses — frequently recognizable by their exterior (Disney castles, medieval fortresses, etc.)—in which couples rent a room in order to spend a few hours in an undisturbed atmosphere. Japanese houses, with their paper doors, do not muffle sounds. Since love hotels are visited only during the day, you can stay there sometimes more cheaply than anywhere else. Not until after 10 P.M., however.

You can even spend the night in many temples — this is a special pleasure for those with artistic interests. A vegetarian meal is served in your room, and it is a delight for eyes and palate alike.

Hotel—Pension—Bed-and-Breakfast

At the Reception Desk

I have a reservation. My name is ….

Watashi wa hito-heya yoyaku shimashita. Watashi no namae wa … desu.

Do you still have vacancy for ...?
... mada heya wa aite imasu ka?

a night
Hitoban

two days
Futsuka

a week
Isshūkan

We're sorry, but we don't.
Iie, zannen desu ga, arimasen.

Could you recommend some other hotels?
Dokoka hoka no hoteru o oshiete kudasaimasen ka?

Would you call there for me?
Soko ni denwa o kakete kudasaimasen ka?

Yes. What kind of room would you like?
Ē, donna heya ga yoroshii desu ka?

..., please.
... o kudasai./onegaishi masu.

A single room
Hitori yō no heya hitotsu

A twin room
Futari yō no heya isshitsu

A quiet room
Shizuka na heya o hitotsu

A room with a shower
Shawā tsuki de

A room with a bath
Furo tsuki de

A room with a balcony/ a terrace
Barukonī/Terasu tsuki de

A room with the view of the ocean
Umi ga mieru heya

A room facing a courtyard
Uchi-niwa ni men shita heya

Is it okay if I look at the room?
Heya o mite mo yoi desu ka?

Is it okay if I look at another room?
Hoka no heya o mite yoroshii desu ka?

I'll take this room.
Kono heya ni shimasu.

90

Can you bring in a third bed/a bed for a child?
Mata mitsume no betto/kodomo yō betto o sara ni irete
kudasaimasen ka?

How much will it be including ...?
... tsuki de o-ikura desu ka?

breakfast
Chōshoku

two meals
Nikai-shokuji

three meals
Zen-shokuji

Fill in the registration, please.
Todoke de yōshi ni kinyū shite kudasai?

Show me your passport/ID, please.
Anata no ryoken/mibunshōmeisho o misete kudasai?

Could you bring my baggage to my room?
Watashi no nimotsu o heya ni hakobasete kudasaimasen ka?

Where can I park?
Doko ni chūsha dekimasu ka?

In the garage, please.
Watashitachi no shako ni oite kudasai.

In the parking lot.
Watashi domo no chūsha-jō ni oite kudasai.

Asking for Service ➤ also Breakfast

From what time can we eat breakfast?
Chōshoku wa nan-ji kara dekimasu ka?

When are the hours for meals?
Shokuji no jikan wa nan-ji desu ka?

Where is the dining room?
Shokudō wa doko desu ka?

Where is the breakfast room?
Chōshoku no heya wa doko desu ka?

Can you call at 7 o'clock tomorrow morning?
Ashita asa hayaku shichiji ni okoshite kudasaimasen ka?

Please bring me ....

... o motte kite kudasai?

a bath towel

Basu-taoru

one more blanket

Mōfu o mō ichimai

How does the ... work?

... wa dono yō ni ugokimasu ka?

Room 24, please.

Nijū-yon-gō shitsu onegai shimasu!

Is there mail for me?

Watashi-ate ni yūbinbutsu ga todoite imasu ka?

Where can I ...?

Doko de watashi wa ... ga dekimasu ka?

drink something

nanika nomu koto

rent a car

kuruma o ichidai kariru koto

make a telephone call

denwa o suru koto

Can I put my valuables in your safe?

Watashi no kichō-hin o sēfutī-bokkusu ni azukeru koto ga dekimasu ka?

Can I leave my baggage here?

Watashi no nimotsu o koko ni oite mo yoi desu ka?

How many sets of futon do you need?

Futon wa nan-kumi irimasu ka?

Could you tell me how to lay out the futon?

Futon o dono yō ni shiku no ka oshiete kudasaimasen ka.

Excuse me, can I have some hot water/hot tea?

Sumimasen ga, atsui oyu/ocha o itadakemasu ka?

Tatami: Rice straw mats of a standard size. Even in modern homes, at least one room has these rice straw mats on the floor, and you step on them only in your stocking feet. Tatami rooms are usually furnished in traditional Japanese style: paper sliding doors, a scroll, beneath it an ikebana arrangement on a small table, and a little home shrine in one corner. Japanese homes generally contain far less furniture and other things than ours.

Futon: The Japanese bed, which in no way resembles our beds. The somewhat harder part is the mattress, the softer, the comforter. Futons are stored in closets (*oshiire*) in the daytime, and in the evening they are spread out in the same place where people live, eat, and work during the day. In the morning everything is first aired on the balcony and then stowed away once more.

Furo: The Japanese bath, which is also available in a ryokan or a minshuku, is used only in the evening. In a *ryokan,* a cotton kimono (*yukata*) will be provided in your room. You change into it in your room and, wearing the *yukata,* go into the bathroom. The water is already in the tub and is usually quite hot. Don't make the mistake of climbing into it to wash your body. The Japanese *furo* is used for relaxation, not for getting clean. In the bathroom, you will find plastic bowls with which you scoop water out of the tub. Soap your body down outside the tub, and then—in the area designated for this purpose in the bathroom—rinse the soap off thoroughly by pouring water over yourself. Now you can slip into the tub. Don't let the water out when you have finished bathing. After you, all the other guests and all the family members will bathe in the same water. Then there will be fresh, hot water again the following evening.

Kotatsu: Traditional and modern Japanese houses have no central heating. In winter, it often is uncomfortably cold in Japanese homes. To get warm, people creep under the *kotatsu.* A space is built into the floor under the dining table, provided with heating elements. The family members gather around the table and put their legs in this space. A cloth that reaches all the way to the floor ensures that the heat does not escape. The disadvantage of this spot-heating system is that your feet and legs are almost roasted, while your back and upper body remain in the cold air of the room.

Complaints

This room wasn't cleaned today.
Kono heya wa kyō o-sōji sarete imasen.

The air conditioning doesn't work.
Kūrā wa kikimasen.

The faucet doesn't close properly.
Jaguchi ga umaku shimarimasen.

There's no water.
Mizu ga demasen.

There's no hot water.
Oyu ga demasen.

The toilet/sink is stopped up.
Toire/Sen'mendai ga tsumatte imasu.

I'd like another room.
Hoka no heya ga hoshiin' desu ga.

Departure

I'm checking out at … o'clock tonight/tomorrow.
Watashi wa konban/asu …-ji ni shuppatsu shimasu.

By what time should I leave the room?
Itsu made heya o karani shinakereba ikenai no deshō ka?

Would you please have my bill ready?
Seikyūsho o yōi shite kudasaimasen ka?

Do you take a credit card?
Kurejitto-kādo o uketsukemasu ka?

Could you get me a taxi?
Takushī o ichidai yonde kudasaimasen ka?

Thank you very much. Good-bye.
Iroiro arigatō gozaimashita!
Sayōnara!

94

Typically Japanese

low Japanese table	tsukue
depression under the table for feet and legs	hori-gotatsu
seat with backrest but no legs (semi-Western)	za-isu
charcoal brazier *(heating in old Japanese houses)*	hibachi, robata
closet with painted sliding door for storage of household objects	oshi-ire
Japanese paper	washi
sliding paper screen (unpainted)	shōji
sliding paper door (painted)	fusuma
tatami	tatami

adapter	adaputa
air conditioning	eakon
apartment	apāto
armchair	āmu-cheā
arrival day	tōchakubi
ashtray	haizara
balcony	barukonī
bathroom	basu-rūmu, furoba

The electrical current is 110 volts. Electric shavers that can be switched to 110 volts will work to some extent. The plugs do not conform to the European standard; you will need an adapter. If you want to use your electrical appliances in Japan, you can do so with the help of a transformer.

bathtub	yokusō
bed	betto
bed linen	shiitsu-kabā
bedroom	shinshitsu
bidet	bide
blanket	mōfu
breakfast	chōshoku, asagohan
buffet	byuffe
chair	isu
changing sheets	shītsu-kōkan
clean, to	kurīningu suru
closet	todana, tansu
comforter	kakebuton
cup	koppu

dining room	shokudō
dinner	yūshoku
door code	doa no angō
electric fan	senpūki
elevator	erebētā
entrance hall, lobby	genkan-hōru, robī
farmhouse	nōka
faucet	jaguchi
floor	kai
futon	futon
garage	shako
glass	gurasu
hand brake	hando-burēki
hanger	hangā ...
heating	danbō
key	kagi
lamp	ranpu
lamp for a night table	naito-tēburu no rampu
light	hikari, akarusa, akari
lightbulb	denkyū
long weekend	enchō sareta shūmatsu
lounge	danwa-shitsu
lunch	chūshoku, hiru gohan
maid	meido
mattress	mattoresu
memo pads	memo-yōshi
minibar	minibā
mirror	kagami
motel	mōteru
night table	naito-tēburu
off-season	shīzun-offu
parking lot	chūsha-jo
pension	penshon
pillow	makura
plug	puragu
preseason	shīzun-mae
price list *(for example, for the minibar)*	nedan-hyō
radio	rajio
reception	uketsuke
registration	todokede, shinkoku
repair, to	shūri suru
reservation	yoyaku
room	heya
safe	kinko/seifutī-bokkusu
season	shīzun

security guard	shuē
shoeshine cloth	kutsu-migaki no dogu
shower	shawā
shower curtain	shawā yō kāten/shikirido
shower head	shawā-guchi
shuttle bus	sōgei-basu
stationery	binsen
stay	shukuhaku
swimming pool	pūru
switch	suitchi
table	tsukue, tēburu
tableware *(for breakfast)*	(chōshoku yō) shokki-setto
telephone	denwa
terrace	terasu
three meals included	Sanshoku-tsuki
toilet	toire
toilet paper	toiretto-pēpā, toire no kami
towel, bath towel	taoru, basu-taoru
TV	terebi
TV room	terebi-shitsu
two meals included	Nishoku-tsuki
vacation facilities	kyūka yō setsubi
wall outlet	konsento, sashikomi
washbasin	senmen-dai
wastebasket	gomibako
water	mizu
cold water	mizu
hot water	oyu
window	mado

Youth hostels usually have very strict regulations concerning evening curfew and the time to get up in the morning. Meals are often eaten jointly.
There are no age restrictions, and the youth hostels are very inexpensive.

Camping

Is there a campsite near here?
Kono chikaku ni kampujō ga arimasu ka?

Is there still a space for pitching a tent?
Tento no basho ga mada arimasu ka?

How much is the charge per person per day?

Ichinichi no ryōkin wa ikura desu ka/mata hitori ni tsuki ikura desu ka?

How much is the charge for ... ?

... ryōkin wa ikura desu ka?

  a car
  Kuruma
  a tent
  Tento

Where is ...?

... wa doko desu ka?

  a toilet
  Toire
  a washroom
  Senmenjo
  a shower
  Shawā

camping	kyampu
camping permit	kyampingushō
camping site	kyampu-jō
clothes dryer	kansō-ki
drinking water	nomimizu
electrical outlet	sashikomi
electricity	denki
gas canister	gasu-bonbe
gas cartridge	gasu-kātūshe
gas cooker	gasu-konro
guidebook for camping sites	kyampu-jō gaidobukku
hammer	hanmā
oil lamp	sekiyū-ranpu
plug	puragu
pole for a tent	tento no pōru
portable cooking stove	konro
propane gas	puropangasu
reservation	yoyaku
rope for a tent	tento yō rōpu
sink	nagashi-dai
sleep in a tent, to	tento ni netomari suru
tent	tento
wall outlet	konsento, sashikomi
washroom	senmen-jo
water	mizu
water tank	mizu-tanku

Eating and Drinking

Eating out and shopping are among the favorite pastimes of the Japanese.

Japanese restaurants usually serve one or two specialties. Wax models of the dishes on the menu are displayed in the front window.

You can order by pointing to the dish of your choice and saying *kore o kudasai.*

Or you can simply say ... *o kudasai,* for example:

Bīru o kudasai (A beer, please)

Supageti o kudasai (Spaghetti, please)

Eating Out

Could you recommend me a Japanese restaurant?
Wafū resutoran o oshiete kudasaimasen ka?

Could you recommend me a restaurant where I can eat a western meal?
Yōshoku ga taberareru resutoran o oshiete kudasaimasen ka?

Could you recommend me a Chinese restaurant?
Chūka-ryōri no resutoran o oshiete kudasaimasen ka?

You can eat Western-style meals in the large hotels or in international restaurants.

Where is ... around here?
Koko de wa ... wa doko ni arimasu ka?

a good restaurant
oishii resutoran

an inexpensive restaurant
amari takakunai resutoran

a diner/ a fast food restaurant
keishokudō, fāsuto fūdo no mise

Where can I have a good (inexpensive) meal nearby?
Kono chikaku no doko de oishiku/(tegoro ni) taberaremasu ka?

I'd like to invite you for a meal.
Shokuji ni go-shōtai shitai no desu ga.

In a Restaurant

I'd like to make a reservation for four for tonight.
Konban yonmei de tēburu o yoyaku shitai desu.

Is this table still free?
Kono tēburu wa mada aite imasu ka?

Table for two/three, please.
Futari/san'nin yō ni tēburu o onegai shimasu.

Where is the restroom?
Toire wa doko desu ka?

Is it okay to smoke?
Tabako o sutte mo ii desu ka?

Ordering

Table customs: Once the first dish is on the table, you can start to eat. Just say *itadakimasu* — whether your neighbor at the table is eating or not.
Slurping while you eat is not considered ill-bred, but quite normal, in Japan. However, blowing your nose is taboo.
After the meal, bow slightly and say *gochisō sama deshita,* or "thank you for the meal."

Waiter/waitress ...
Bōisan/Wētoresu-san

show me the menu, please.
menyū o misete kudasai!

show me the drink menu, please.
nomimono no menyū o misete kudasai!

Saying "Waiter" or "Waitress" is not customary. Instead, people say *sumimasen* ("Excuse me!" "Pardon me!") when they want something.

What would you recommend?
Osusume-hin wa nan desu ka?

Do you have vegetable dishes/diet dishes?
Yasai-ryōri/daietto-ryōri ga arimasu ka?

Do you also have a children's menu?
Kodomo yō menyū mo arimasu ka?

Have you decided?
Okime ni narimashita ka?

…, please.
… o onegai shimasu.

For an appetizer/ the main course/dessert, …, please.
Zensai ni/Mein ni/dezāto ni … o onegai shimasu.

No appetizer, thank you.
Zensai wa kekkō desu.

Come with me and I'll show you what we'd like to eat.
Nani o tabetai ka, omise shitai no de issho ni kite kudasai.

We're sorry, but … is sold out.
Sumimasen ga, … wa (mō) arimasen.

This dish is available only with an advanced order.
Kono ryōri wa yoyaku o ukete nomi tsukurimasu.

Can I get … instead of …?
… no kawari ni … o onegai dekimasu ka?

I don't like …, so can you cook without …?
… ga sukidewanai no de, … nashi de ryōri shite itadakemasu ka?

How would you like your steak cooked?
Dono-yō ni sutēki o oyaki itashimashō ka?
  well-done
  ueru-dan
  medium
  midiamu
  rare
  nama

What would you like to drink?
Nani o nomitai desu ka?

A glass of ..., please.
... o ippai onegai shimasu.

A bottle/a half bottle of ..., please.
... o botoru de ippon/hāfusaizu-botoru ippon kudasai.

With ice, please.
Kōri mo onegai shimasu.

Enjoy your meal!
Itadakimasu!

Cheers!
Kanpai!

> **Drinking customs:** Many an evening ends with drinking beer or sake, frequently with singing as well. Glasses are continually refilled, even if they are not empty yet, so it is easy to lose track of things. When your neighbor picks up the bottle to top up your glass, he does not do the same for himself; that would be bad manners. You're responsible for doing that! When it's time to leave, it's no problem simply to leave behind a full glass. That is more polite than impolite, since it gives the hosts the feeling that the quantity offered was ample in any event.

Do you have anything else to order?
Nani-ka hoka ni go-chūmon ga gozaimasu ka?

Would you bring me ..., please.
... o motte kite kudasai.

Chopsticks, please.
O-hashi o onegai shimasu.

Can I get more bread/water/rice?
Pan/O-mizu/Gohan no okawari ga dekimasu ka?

Complaints

You probably will have no opportunity to complain about anything, since you will be treated with the utmost courtesy in Japan. That is true even if you behave incorrectly out of ignorance or mischance.

I don't have ....
... arimasen.

Did you forget my ...?
Watashi no ... o o-wasure desu ka?

I didn't order this.
Kore wa chūmon shite imasen.

The soup is cold./The soup is too salty.
Sūpu ga hiete imasu./Sūpu ga shio-karai desu.

The meat is too tough/too fatty.
Niku ga katai/aburami-bakari desu.

This fish is not fresh.
Kono sakana wa shinsen dewa arimasen.

Would you take this back, please?
Kore o modoshite kudasai.

Would you get the manager, please?
Shihai-nin o yonde kudasai.

The Bill

The bill: In Japanese restaurants, when each dish is served, a coupon or a covered bill is placed on the table. You pay at the cash register. Tipping is not customary in Japan.

Check, please.
O-kanjō o onegai shimasu!/O-kaikei o onegai shimasu!

One check, please.
Zenbu issho ni onegai shimasu.

Separate checks, please.
Betsubetsu ni o-kaikei o onegai shimasu.

Is the service charge included?
Sābisu wa komi desu ka?

I don't think the bill is correct.
Kono o-kanjō wa chigau yō ni omoimasu.

I didn't have this. I had ....
Kore wa ukete imasen. ... o moraimashita.

How was it?
Ikaga deshita ka?

It was a wonderful meal.
O-ryōri wa totemo subarashikatta desu.

I'll give it to you.
Kore wa anata ni sashiagemasu.

Please take it.
Dōzo, o-tori kudasai.

Invitation to Dinner

I would like to invite you to a meal.
Shokuji ni go-shōtai shitai no desu ga.

Cheers!
Kanpai!

How does it taste?
O-aji wa ikaga desu ka?

Yes, very good.
Hai, totemo oishii desu.

Please take some more.
Dōzo motto otori kudasai.

Yes, thank you.
Arigatō, itadakimasu.

No, thank you.
Iie, kekkō desu.

What is this dish called?
Kono ryōri wa nan' to iimasu ka?

Can you use chopsticks?
O-hashi ga tsukaemasu ka?

No, not yet.
Iie, mada tsukaemasen.

Show me that, please.
Sore o misete kudasai.

Try this dish, please.
Kono o-ryōri o tameshite mite kudasai.

➢ **also Groceries**

appetizer	zensai
artificial sweetener	jinkōkanmiryō
ashtray	haizara
bone	hone
bowl	hachi, bōru
breakfast	chōshoku, asagohan

Breakfast—*asa gohan*

The typical Japanese breakfast is an ample meal. It includes a dish of rice, a bowl of *miso soup* (made of soy paste), *tsukemono* (radishes or other vegetables pickled in brine), fresh or cooked vegetables, a portion (usually small) of dried fish or meat, and a cup of green tea.

Many families, however, have the kind of breakfast customary in the U.S.: coffee or tea with bread (toast), butter, and jam, boiled eggs, cheese, ham, and fruit.

When you spend the night in a hotel, breakfast may be either Western or Japanese. In a Japanese *ryokan,* of course, a Japanese breakfast is served.

---

carafe	garasu-sei mizusashi
children's menu	okosama yō menyū
chopsticks	hashi, o-hashi

106

cook	kokku
corkscrew	koruku-sen·nuki
course	kōsu, zen
cup, bowl	kappu, chawan
saucer	uke-zara
dessert	dezāto
diabetic	tōnyōbyō-kanja
diet food	daietto-shoku
dinner	yūshoku
dish	ryōri
dish cooked in a frying pan	furaipan-ryōri
draft beer	nama-bīru
dressing	doresshingu
drink	nomimono
dry (wine)	karakuchi
fish bone	sakana no hone
fork	fōku
glass	gurasu
cup	koppu
wineglass	wain-gurasu
grill	guriru
homemade	hōmumēdo no
hot	atsui
hungry	onaka no suita
ketchup	kechappu
knife	naifu
lunch	chūshoku, hiru gohan
main dish	mein-disshu
mayonnaise	mayonēzu
menu	menyū
mustard	karashi
napkin	napukin
nonalcoholic	arukōru nuki
oil	oiru, abura
order	chūmon
pepper	koshō
pepper mill	koshō-ire
plate	sara
portion	ichininmae
refreshment stall (simple restaurant in a public park)	chamise
rice (boiled)	gohan
salad buffet	salada-byuffe
salt	shio
salt shaker	shio-ire
sauce	sōsu

107

seasoning	chōmiryō
slice	suraisu
soup	sūpu
soup dish	sūpu-zara
specialty	mēbutsu
spoon	supūn
teaspoon	tī-supūn
stain	shimi
straw	sutorō
sugar	satō
sweet *(wine)*	amakuchi
table setting	naifu, fōku to supūn
tablecloth	tēburu-kake
tableware	shokki
tea-ceremony house	chashitsu
teapot	kyūsu, tī-potto
tip	chippu
to season	aji o tsukeru
today's special	honjitsu no o-susume-ryōri
toothpick	tsumayōji
tough	katai
vegetarian	saishoku-shugi no
vinegar	su
waiter/waitress	uētā *(m)*, uētoresu *(f)*
water	mizu

Preparation

baked	yaketa
cooked	ryōrishita
hot	karai
low-fat	abura no sukunai, tēshibōno
melted	toketa
raw	nama no
roasted, broiled, grilled	yaketa
on a skewer	kushiyaki
on a grill	guriru de
in a frying pan	furaipan de
roasted, fried	itta, itameta
simmered	terobi de nita
smoked	kunsei no
soft	yawarakai
sour	suppai
steamed	mushita
stuffed	tsumeta
succulent	mizuke no ōi
sufficiently cooked	hi ga tōtta
sweet	amai
to bake ... in an oven	tenpi de yaku
tough	katai
well-done	jūbun ni yaketa

cooked
ryōrishita

boiled
nita

steamed
mushita

prepared in a double boiler
oyu de atatameta

broiled
yaketa, yaita

fried
abura de ageta

grilled
guriru de yaita

109

I would like ...
... o kudasai

Menu

A Japanese meal consists of:
a dish of rice, a bowl of *miso-shiru* soup (based on soybeans
and protein-rich ingredients), pickles (radishes or other
vegetables preserved in brine), one or more types of
vegetables, a (usually) small portion of fish or meat, and a cup
of green tea.
Beer or sake (rice wine, served either cold or warm) is drunk
with the meal. Wine made from grapes is rare in Japan. There
is not yet a long tradition of viticulture. Only the prefectures of
Yamanashi near Tōkyō and Ikeda on the island of Hokkaido are
known in Japan as wine-growing areas.

Typical Japanese Dishes

sashimi	various sorts of raw fish
(o)sushi	raw or cooked fish with vegetables in or on rice
Tempura	small pieces of fish and vegetables, battered and fried in deep fat
sukiyaki	vegetables, meat, glass or cellophane noodles cooked in a mixture of soy sauce, sugar, water, and rice wine. It is prepared at your table.
donburi	simple one-dish meal of rice with various toppings, such as chicken, egg, meat, etc.
okonomiyaki	"Japanese pizza." A kind of omelet prepared at the table by the guests themselves. Vegetables, meat, shrimp, and squid are stirred into the batter before it is fried.
shabu-shabu	very thin slices of beef and vegetables, briefly cooked at the table in a pot of boiling water
ramen	Chinese noodles in broth
soba	thin buckwheat noodles
yakisoba	fried noodles with soy sauce, vegetables, and meat
udon	thick wheat noodles

115

| onigiri | rice balls wrapped in seaweed |
| tofu | custard-like soybean curd—Japan's oldest culinary specialty |

Fish and Shellfish

unagi	eel
kaki	oyster
tara	cod
masu	trout
nishin	herring
koi	carp
ebi	shrimp
sake	salmon
saba	mackerel
kai	shellfish
harako	roe
maguro	tuna
ika	squid
kujira	whale

Vegetables

nasu	eggplant
takenoko	bamboo shoot
hakusai	Chinese cabbage
mame, gurinpīsu	peas/green peas
kyūri	cucumber
meron	melon
shōga	ginger
ninjin	carrot
jagaimo	potato
retasu	lettuce
negi	onion
hasu	lotus
wasabi	horseradish
pīman	green pepper
kinoko	mushroom
gobō	burdock
nori	seaweed
serori	celery
daizu	soybean
moyashi	bean sprouts

asuparagasu	asparagus
hōrensō	spinach
satsumaimo	sweet potato
suika	watermelon
kyabetsu	cabbage

Fruit

painappuru	pineapple
ringo	apple
anzu	apricot
banana	banana
yō-nashi	pear
ichigo	strawberry
kuri	chestnut
ichijiku	fig
kaki	persimmon
sakuranbo	cherries
mikan	mandarin orange
orenji	orange
gurēpufurūtsu	grapefruit
momo	peach
budō	grapes
remon	lemon

Beverages

Nonalcoholic Beverages

koka-kōra	Coca-Cola®
aisu-kōfī	iced coffee
aisu-tī	iced tea
gurēpu furūtsu-jūsu	grapefruit juice
ryokucha	green tea
remonēdo	lemonade
gyūnyū, miruku	milk
mineraru-wōtā	mineral water
orenji-jūsu	orange juice
mizu	water

Alcoholic Beverages

bīru	beer
sake	sake *(rice wine)*
shōchū	shochu (vodka-like liquor)
umeshu	plum wine *(plums, sugar, and shochu)*
wain (aka, shiro)	wine
uisukī	whiskey

Sightseeing and Excursions

The Tourist Information Center offers a guide program, **Goodwill Guide**, with volunteer guides. These are usually university students; they will guide you through the city and answer your questions. The program is available in Tōkyō, Yokohama, Ōsaka, Kōbe, Kyōto, Nara, Sapporo, Kagoshima, Nagoya, Hiroshima, Fukuoka, and Beppu.

At the Tourist Information Office

Are there city maps of ...?
... no shigai-chizu o kudasai.

Do you have a schedule of events for this week?
Konshū no moyōshimono no puroguramu ga arimasu ka?

Are there sightseeing buses in the city?
Shinai-kankō-basu ga arimasu ka?

How much is the sightseeing bus in the city?
Shinai-kankō wa ikura desu ka?

I'm sorry to bother you, but could you call there for me?
Sumimasen ga, watashi no tame ni soko e denwa o kakete kudasaimasen ka?

Places of Interest—Museums

Opening Hours, Guided Tours, Admission

Can you tell me what places of interest there are?
Donna meisho ga aru ka oshiete kudasai.

You should see ....
Kanarazu ... o minasai/otozure nasai.

Could you take me to the places of interest in the city?
Machi no omo na meisho e tsurete itte kudasai.

We would like to see the ....

Watashitachi wa ... o kenbutsu shitai no desu ga.

exhibitions

tenrankai

museum, museum of art

hakubutsu-kan, bijutsu-kan

castle

o-shiro

temple, shrine

o-tera/jinja

Shintoism is the native religion of Japan. Little is known about its origin and founders. What is certain is that this religion was already in existence before the sixth century. To this day, Shintoism continues to be characterized by worship of nature (for example, holy trees) and respect and veneration of ancestors. There are two very famous shrines that are said to have been erected in the age of the gods: the Ise Shrine in Ise and the Izumo Taisha Shrine near Matsue.

In the sixth century, Buddhism was introduced to Japan via Korea and China. During this period, Japan acquired its first constitutional government with Prince Regent Shōtoku, an enthusiastic advocate of the Buddhist teachings. Numerous temples were built at this time. The most famous is the Hōryūji Temple, which is said to be the oldest wooden structure in the world.

Is there also a guided tour in English?

Eigo no annai mo arimasu ka?

What kind of place/temple is this?

Koko wa donna basho/o-tera desu ka?

What time does the museum open?

Hakubutsukan no kaikan wa nan-ji desu ka?

When is the next guided tour?

Tsugi no annai wa itsu desu ka?

Is it okay to take pictures?

Koko de shashin o totte mo ii desu ka?

Two admission tickets, please.
Nyūjōken o ni-mai kudasai!

Two adults and one child.
Otona futari to kodomo hitori.

Is there a discount for ...?
... no waribiki ga arimasu ka?

  children
  Kodomo
  students
  Gakusei
  seniors
  Nenchōsha
  groups
  Gurūpu

Is there a catalog for the exhibition?
Tenjikai no katarogu ga arimasu ka?

Sightseeing

Is this ...?
Kore wa ... desu ka?

When was this building constructed/ restored?
Kono tatemono wa itsu tateraremashita/naosaremashita ka?

Who painted this picture?
Kono e wa dare no desu ka?

Is there a poster/a picture postcard/a slide?
Kono e no posutā/ehagaki/suraido ga arimasu ka?

Azuchi-Momoyama period	Azuchi-Momoyama-jidai
Buddhist	bukkyō-to
china	tōki
Chinese ink	sumi
customs	fūshū
Edo period	edo-jidai, tokugawa-jidai
gong/bell	kane, beru
Heian period	heian-jidai
influence	eikyō
Kamakura period	kamakura-jidai
lantern	tōrō
lantern (paper)	chōchin
lantern (streetlight)	gaitō, chōchin

Brief Outline of Japanese History

Nara Period: The emperor's seat of government is in Nara. This is the age of the flowering of Buddhism, a time when many temples were built and art objects were influenced by Buddhism. The largest statue of Buddha in Japan, which is in the Todaiji Temple in Nara, dates from this period.

Heian Period: The capital is moved from Nara to Kyōto. After the Chinese model, the city is laid out in a chessboard arrangement. With the introduction of a new Japanese writing system, literature and poetry experienced a golden age.

Kamakura Period: In 1192, a military government in Kamakura assumed power. There followed a 700-year period of military rule in Japan.

During this era, the doctrines of Buddhism were formulated. The four principal sects were Jōdo Shinshu, Shingon, Zen, and Nichiren. Today only Jōdo and Nichiren still play a role. Zen Buddhism was the religion of the warrior class. Its maxims taught that life is simple and hard.

Muromachi and Azuchi-Momoyama Period: The new military government has its seat in Muromachi, Kyōto. The gold and silver pavilions, the former villas of the military rulers, still testify to their wealth. In Zen art, the rock garden of the Ryōanji Temple dates from this period.

Although the Azuchi-Momoyama Period meant a century of civil war, artistic and creative life flourished. The nō theater, the tea ceremony, ikebana, and garden architecture came into being during this era.

Edo Period: In 1603 the military ruler Ieyasu Tokugawa moved his capital to Edo, which today is Tōkyō. It was a peaceful time. In art, high-quality woodcuts and works in stone, porcelain, and lacquer were created. The kabuki theater, colorful and cheerful, also arose at this time.

Birth of Modern Japan: In 1853 the American naval officer Matthew C. Perry, with his fleet near Tōkyō, landed in Japan. He compelled Japan to enter into trade with the United States. The Edo Period ended with this forced meeting of Eastern and Western culture.

Meiji Period (1868-1912): In 1868, the capital of the imperial Meiji government was Tōkyō. This was the age of the Industrial Revolution. Japan developed into a democracy and adopted its constitution on May 3, 1947.

The Meiji Period was followed by the Taishō Period (1912-1925), the Showa Period (1926-1988), and the Heisei Period (1989 to the present).

Meiji period	meiji-jidai
Muromachi period	Muromachi-jidai,
Nara period	Nara-jidai
pagoda	pagoda
palace	kyūden
pavillion	pabirion
Peace Memorial Museum (Hiroshima)	genbaku-hakubutsukan
pilgrim	junrei-sha
pilgrimage	junrei no tabi
place of worship	reihai-jo
Sakyamumi/Buddha	shaka, hotoke-sama
school	gakkō
Shintoism	shintō
Showa period	shōwa-jidai
shrine	jinja
sketch	suketchi
statue of Buddha	butsuzō, daibutsu
stone garden (in a Buddhist temple)	sekitei
straw festoon (in a shrine)	nawa
Taisho period	taishō-jidai
tea ceremony	sadō
temple	o-tera
temple gong	o-tera no kane
theater	geki, geki-jō, shibai
vase	kabin
well/fountain	ido, funsui
Zen Buddhism	zen-shū

General

alley	roji
art	gējutsu
birthplace	shusseichi
business hours (business)	eigyō-jikan
car-free zone	hokōshā-tengoku
changing of the guard	eihei-kōtai
city area	machi no ikkaku
discovery	hakken
downtown	hankagai
emperor/empress	tennō, kōtē/kōgō, jotē
folk museum	minzokugaku-hakubutsukan
guidance	annai
historic site	iseki
history	rekishi
house	ie, uchi

king/queen	ō/ōhi
landmark	mejirushi
market	ichiba
museum	hakubutsu-kan, bijutsu-kan
museum schedule	kaikan-jikan
park	kōen
place of interest	midokoro, mēsho
protection of cultural assets	bunkazai-hogo
religion	shūkyō
restore, to	shūfuku suru
sightseeing by bus	shinai-kankō-basu
street	michi
suburbs	kōgai
tour	kengaku
tour guide	gaido, annai-nin
tourist bureau	kankō-kyoku

Architecture

arch	āchi, yumigata
archaeology	kōko-gaku
architect	kenchiku-ka
architecture	kenchiku
bridge	hashi
building	kenchiku-butsu
castle	shiro
ceiling	tenjō
cemetery	bochi
church	kyōkai
city hall	shiyakusho
city wall	shiheki
courtyard	uchi-niwa
excavation	hakkutsu
facade	fassādo
fortress	yōsai
fountain	funsui
gate	mon
inscription	mei
market	māketto
mausoleum	otamaya
memorial	kinen no basho
monastery *(Buddhist)*	sōin
monument	kinen-hi, kinen-butsu
old district	kyū-shigai
palace	kyūden
place, seat, plaza	basho, seki, hiroba
reconstruct, to	fukkō suru

roof	yane
ruins	haikyo
steeple	kyōkai no tō
structure	tatemono
temple	o-tera, shinden
theater	geki, geki-jō, shibai
tomb	haka
ancient tomb	kofun
tombstone	haka-ishi
tower	tō, yagura
treasure house	hōbutsuden
university	daigaku
wall, castle wall	kabe, jōheki
well, fountain	ido, funsui
window	mado
wing	sode

Visual Arts

art gallery	gyararī, garō
art jewelry	chōkin-gējutsu
arts and crafts	kōgei
bronze	seidō
ceramic art	tōgei
ceramics	tōjiki
copy	mosha
cross	jūji
crucifix	kirisuto-jūjika
etching	etchingu
exhibit	chinretsu-hin
exhibition	tenji-kai, tenran-kai
graphic art	gurafikku āto
lithograph	ritogurafu
model	moderu
mosaic	mozaiku
nude	ratai
original	orijinaru, genbutsu, gensaku
painter	e-kaki, gaka
painting	kaiga
painting, photograph	e, shashin
portrait	shōzō
poster	posutā
pottery	tōki
sculptor	chōkoku-ka
sculpture	chōkoku
silk screen	shiruku sukurīn

sketch	suketchi
stained glass	sutendo-gurasu
statue	ritsuzō, chōzō
still life	seibutsu
unglazed pottery	suyaki
burial mound figurine	haniwa
vase	kabin
watercolor painting	suisai-ga
wood sculpture	mokuchō
wood-block print	mokahanga
ukiyoe (genre picture)	ukiyo-e

Styles and Periods

bronze age	seidōki-jidai
century	seiki
Christianity	kirisuto-kyō
dynasty	ōchō
expressionism	hyōgenshugi
golden age	zenseiki
impressionism	inshō-ha
mannerism	manirisumusu
Middle Ages	chūsei
modern	modan na
Momoyama period	momoyama jidai
("Japanese Rococo")	
period	jidai
prehistoric	senshi, yūshi-izen no
Stone Age	sekki-jidai
style	yōshiki

Excursions

Where shall we start?
Doko kara shuppatsu shimashō ka?

What time shall we meet?
Nan-ji ni aimashō ka?

Do we pass by ...?
... no tokoro o toorimasu ka?

Do we also see ...?
... mo kengaku shimasu ka?

Where is the temple/shrine?
O-tera/Jinja wa doko ni arimasu ka?

amusement park	yūenchi
astrological observatory	tenmondai
bird sanctuary	chōrui-hogo-chiiki
botanical garden	shokubutsu-en
canyon	keikoku
cave	dōkutsu
cherry blossoms	sakura no hana
day trip	higaeri-ryokō
fishing village	gyoson
forest	mori
forest fire	yama-kaji
hot spring	onsen
Japanese garden	nihon-teien
lake	mizuumi
lava	yōgan
limestone cavern	shōnyūdō
market	ichiba
marshland	numachi
mineral spring	kōzen
mountain	yama
mountain pass	komichi, tōge
mountain range	sanmyaku
mountain village	sanson
national park	kokuritsu-koen
nature conservation area	shizen-hogo-chiiki
observation platform	tenbō-dai
outdoor museum	yagai-hakubutsukan
outing	ensoku, kōraku
pavilion	pabirion
remote area	kōhaichi
river	kawa
rock wall	ganpeki
sacred place (Buddh.)	seichi, junreichi
safari-style zoo	shizen-dōbutsuen
scenery	hūkei, keshiki
spring	izumi, wakimizu
summit	chōjō
surroundings	shūi, shūhen
tour	shūyū
tour of islands	shima-meguri
valley	tani
volcano	kazan
waterfall	taki
zoo	dōbutsuen

Active Vacations

Excuse me, but is there … here?
Sumimasen ga, koko ni … ga arimasu ka?

a swimming pool
pūru

an outdoor swimming pool
okugai-pūru

an indoor swimming pool
okunai-pūru

Is there a sauna here?
Koko ni sauna ga arimasu ka?

Give me one admission ticket, please.
Nyūjōken ichimai kudasai!

Could you tell me where … is?
… ga doko ni aru ka oshiete kuremasu ka?

a shower
Shawā

a changing room
Kōi-shitsu

泳げる人だけ。	Oyōgeru hito dake!	For swimmers only!
飛込み禁止	Tobikomi-kinshi!	No diving allowed!
水浴び禁止/水浴禁止	Mizuabi-kinshi!/ suiyoku-kinshi!	No swimming allowed! (at the lake)
水泳禁止	Suiei-kinshi!	No swimming allowed! (at the river or at the seaside)

Is it … beach?
Hamabe/Kaigan wa … desu ka?

a sandy
suna-ji

a pebble
ishi ga ōi

Are/Is there sea urchins/jellyfish/seaweed?
Koko ni wa uni/kurage/kaiso ga arimasu ka?

Is the current strong?
Nagare ga hayai desu ka?

Is it dangerous for children?
Kodomo ni wa kiken deshō ka?

When is the high tide/low tide?
Michishio/hikishio wa itsu desu ka?

I'd like to rent ....
Watashi wa ... o karitai desu.

  a deck chair
  dekki-chea

  a parasol
  higasa

  a boat
  bōto

  a set of water skis
  suijō-sukī ichisetto

How much is it per hour/day?
Ichi-jikan/ichi-nichi ikura desu ka?

air mattress	kūki-matto
beach volleyball	bīchi-barēbōru
children's pool	kodomo yō pūru
fins	suiei yō hire-ashi
jet ski	suijō-sukūtā
lifeguard	pūru/kaisuiyokujō no kanshinin
paddle boat	ashibumi bōto
sauna	sauna
sunbathing lawn	nikkō-yoku yō shibafu
swim, to	oyogu, suiei suru
swimmer	oyogeru hito
wading pool	mizuasobi yō pūru
water ski	suijō-sukī
waterski, to	suijō-sukī o suru
water wings	ude ni maku ukiwa
wind screen	kaze-yoke

Other Activities and Sports

What kind of sports can I play here?
Koko de donna supōtsu ga dekimasu ka?

Is there ... here?
Koko ni ... ga arimasu ka?

  a golf course
  gorufu-jō
  a tennis court
  tenisu-jō

Could you tell me a good place for fishing/hiking around here?
Kono atari de wa doko de tsuri/haikingu ga yoku dekiru ka
oshiete itadakemasu ka?

Where can I rent ...?
Doko de ... ga kariraremasu ka?

I'd like to try a beginner's/an advanced course.
Shoshinsha/Jōkyūsha yō kōsu o shitai desu.

Water Sports

boat operating license	bōto-untenmenkyoshō
canoe	kanū
houseboat	yakata-bune
life raft	kyūmei-bōto
motorboat	mōtā-bōto
paddle boat	paderu-bōto
paddle, to	kanū o kogu
rafting	rafutingu
regatta	regatta
return service	hikitori-sābisu
row, to	fune o kogu
rowboat	kogibune
rudder	kaji
sailboat	yotto
sailing excursion	yotto-asobi
sailing, to sail	sēringu, hansō suru, yotto ni noru (koto)
surfboard	sāfin-bōdo
surfing	sāfin
tour on a houseboat	yakatabune ni noru
wind direction	kaze-muki
windsurfing	kaze-sāfin

Diving

dive, to	moguru
diving equipment	sensui-dōgu
diving mask	sensui-megane
harpoon	mori
neoprene wetsuit	neopren-sensui-fuku
oxygen inhalator	sanso-kyūnyūki
scuba dive, to	sensui-dōgu o tsukete sensui suru
snorkel	sunōkeru
snorkel, to	sunōkeru suru

Fishing

closed season	kingyōki
deep-sea fishing	enkai-tsuri
fish, to	tsuri o suru
fishing	tsuri
port authority	kōmubu

Ball Games

ball	bōru, tama
basketball	basuketto-bōru
goal	gōru, (shūto)
goalkeeper	gōru-kīpā
goalpost	gōru no shichū
halftime	hāfu-taimu
handball	hando-bōru
net	ami, netto
rugby	ragubī
soccer	sakkā
soccer field	sakkā-jō
soccer game	sakkā-gēmu, sakkā-kyōgi
team	chīmu
volleyball	barēbōru

Tennis and Badminton

badminton	badominton
doubles	daburu
ping-pong	takkyū
racket	raketto
shuttlecock	badominton
singles	shinguru

squash	sukkashu
tennis	tenisu
tennis racket	raketto

Fitness and Strength Training

aerobics	aerobikku
bodybuilding	bodībirudingu
fitness center	fittonesu-sentā
fitness training	kondishon-torēningu
gymnastics	taisō
jazz aerobics	jazu-taisō
jog, to	jogingu o suru
jogging	jogingu
judo	jūdō
karate	karate
spinal exercise	sekichū-taisō
stretching	shūshiku-undō

Sumō wrestling is Japan's national sport. It is not comparable with any of our sports, since sumō wrestling is a profound part of Japanese culture. The origins of sumō date back more than one thousand years. According to myth, it is a pastime that the Shintō gods themselves invented and prescribed for humans. Originally these wrestling matches were held in Shintō temples, and the first tournaments were jointly organized by the priests and the authorities. Form and ceremony play a determining role in a sumō wrestling match, as in most Japanese art forms. Western observers sometimes wonder why the show is so slow to start, but the stamping of feet, clapping of hands, sprinkling of salt in the ring, staring at the opponent, and other things are all part of the event. The ritual lasts four minutes, the match itself, one minute. The sumō wrestlers, who weigh 440 pounds and more, are not simply fat, however, but also athletes. The fat increases their striking power. The purpose of the match is to force the opponent to touch the ground with some body part—other than his feet—or to push him out of the ring. Everything is allowed except boxing, kicking, pulling hair, choking, and other rough behavior of that sort.

sumo	sumō
taiko (drum)	taiko

Wellness

Bathing in hot springs (*onsen*) is very popular in Japan. There are around 13,000 such springs, and owing to the healing power attributed to the thermal springs, these resorts are a popular vacation destination and are also significant as medicinal spas. The best-known spa resort is Beppu, located on Japan's southernmost peninsula of Kyūshū.

massage . . . . massāji
sauna . . . . sauna
solarium . . . . sorarium
steam bath . . . . mushiburo
swimming pool . . . . pūru
whirlpool . . . . wirupūru
yoga . . . . yoga

Biking

air pump . . . . kūki-ponpu
bicycle . . . . jitensha
bicycle race . . . . jitensha-kyōgi, saikuringu
bike helmet . . . . jitensha yō herumetto
bike path . . . . jitensha-dō
cycling tour . . . . jitensha-ryokō
mountain bicycle . . . . mauntenbaiku
racing bicycle . . . . keirin yō jitensha
repair kit . . . . shūri-dōgu
ride a bicycle, to . . . . jitensha ni noru
scooter . . . . sukūtā
trekking bicycle . . . . turekkingu-jitensha
tube . . . . chūbu

Hiking and Mountain Climbing

I'd like to do a mountain-walking tour.
yama no tabi o shitai no desu ga.

Can you suggest an interesting route for me, please?
Chizu de omoshirosō na rūto o oshiete kudasai.

Bergwandern . . . . yama-aruki
day trip . . . . higaeri-tsuā
duration of hike . . . . aruku-jikan

135

free climbing	furīkuraimingu
hiking	haikingu
hiking course	haikingu-kōsu
hiking map	haikingu yō chizu
long-distance route	chōkyori-yūhodo
mountain climbing	tozan
route	rūto
safety rope	anzen yō rōpu
shelter	hinan-goya
trekking	torekkingu

Horseback Riding

horse	uma
polo	poro
ride	tōnori
ride a horse, to	jōba o suru
riding school	jōba-gakkō
stable	jōba yō kyūka

Golf

18-hole golf course	jūhachiban-hōru-jō
club (meeting place)	kurabu
clubhouse	kurabu no ie
course	pā no kōsu
golf	gorufu
golf club (implement)	gorufu-kurabu
greens fee	purei-hi
hit, to	utsu

Flying Sports

around-the-world trip	sekai-isshū
ascent	jōshō
gliding	guraidingu
parachuting	rakkasan-kōka
paraglider	paraguraidā
paragliding	paraguraidingu
pilot a hang glider, to	hanguguraidā ni noru
thermal	netsu-kikyū

Give me a day ticket, please.
Ichinichi-ken o kudasai.

How many points do you charge for a skilift ride?
Sukī no rifuto wa nan-ten ni narimasu ka?

What time is the last lift going up/going down?
Saigo no nobori/kudari rifuto wa nanji desu ka?

baby lift	bebīrifuto
base station	fumoto-eki
binding	bindingu, tomegu
cable railway	kēburu-kā
chairlift	rifuto
cross-country skiing	kurosu kantorī sukī
curling	kāringu
day ticket	ichinichi-ken
downhill skiing	arupen-sukī
ice hockey	aisu-hokkē
ice skate, to	sukēto o suru
ice skating	sukēto
ice-skating boot	sukēto-gutsu, sukēto
ice-skating rink	sukēto-rinku
long-distance course	chōkyori-kōsu
middle station	chūkan no eki
powder snow	kona-yuki
ride on a sled, to	sori ni noru
ski	sukī
ski pole	sukī-sutokku
ski, to	sukī o suru
skiing goggles	yuki-megane
skiing instructor	sukī no shidō-in
skiing school	sukī-gakkō, kōsu
sled	sori
snowboard	sunōbōdo
summit station	yama no eki
tow lift	ken'in-rifuto
weekday pass, week-long pass	uīkudē-pasu, heijitsu yūkō no isshūkan-pasu

Other Sports

athletics	rikujō kyōgi
boules game	būru-asobi

ACTIVE VACATIONS

137

bowling	bōringu
bungee jumping	banji-jampu
do inline skating, to	inrain-sukēto o suru
inline skating	inrainā
miniature golf	mini-gorufu
roller-skating	rōrā-sukēto
rollerskate, to	rōrā-sukēto o suru
skateboard	sukēto-bōdo
skateboard, to	sukēto-bōdo o suru
skittle	sukittoru (kyūchūgi)

Sporting Events

Could you tell me what kind of sports events you have here?
Koko de dono yō na supōtsu no moyōshi-mono ga aru ka oshiete kudasai.

I'd like to see a soccer game.
Sakkā-gēmu o mitai no desu ga.

I'd like to see sumo/baseball.
Sumō/Yakyū ga mitai no desu ga.

When/where is it held?
Itsu/Doko de okonawaremasu ka?

Baseball means to the Japanese what football means to Americans. A modern, well-heeled Japanese plays golf, even if lack of space allows him to play only in a gigantic cage next to an urban expressway and with no real greens. The Japanese adore this sport, to which they have even devoted a day: October 10.
In addition to all the Western sports, traditional sports such as jūdō, yoga, karate, and *aikidō* are highly cherished. *Kendō,* the art of swordsmanship, is a required subject at many schools. This martial art originated during ancient Japan's samurai era. The form of it practiced today is more athletic than martial. Bamboo swords are used in *kendō,* and the fighters wear protective clothing.

How much is an admission ticket?
Nyūjō-ken wa o-ikura desu ka?

What's the score?
Nan'tai nan' desu ka?

two to one
Ni-tai ichi.

one to one
Ichi-tai ichi.

Foul!
Fauru!

Nice shot!
Umai shūto!

Goal!
Gōru

admission ticket	nyūjō-ken
athlete	supōtsu-senshu
championship	senshuken
competition	kyōgi, shiai
crossing pass	yokogawa/kyōgijō o naname ni kiru sō kyū
cycle racing	kērin
draw	hikiwake
free kick	furī-kikku
game	gēmu
kickoff	kikku-ofu
lose, to	makeru
loser	haisha
offside	ofusaido
pass	pasubōru
penalty	penarutī
penalty area	penaruti-eria
playing field	undō-jō
program	puroguramu
race	kyōsō, kēba (horse); kērin (bike); rēsu (car)
sports arena	kyōgi-jō
ticket booth	kippu-uriba
umpire, referee	shinpan
victory	shōri
win, to	katsu

139

Creative Vacations

I'd like to apply for....
Watashi wa ... ni mooshikomitai.
  a pottery class
  tōkō-kōza
  a Japanese language class
  nihongo-kōza
  a beginner's class
  shoshinsha yō
  an advanced class
  jōkyūsha yō

How many hours are scheduled per day?
Ichi-nichi nan'jikan no yotei desu ka?

Do you have a limit for the number of participants?
Sankasha-sū wa kagirarete imasu ka?

Do I need background knowledge?
Yobichishiki wa hitsuyō desu ka?

When is the deadline for the application?
Mooshikomi wa itsu made desu ka?

Is the cost of materials included in the tuition?
Zairyōhi wa fukumarete imasu ka?

What should I bring with me?
Nani o motte konakereba narimasen ka?

cooking	ryōri
course	kōsu
dance performance	dansu-jōen
drama workshop	engeki-kenshūkai
language course	gogaku-kōsu
make jewelry, to	kinzaiku suru
nude sketch	rataidessan
oil painting	abura-e
paint watercolors, to	suisaiga o kaku
paint, to	e o kaku
play drums, to	taiko o utsu
silk dyeing	kenpu-zome
take photographs, to	shashin o toru
theatrical company	geki-dan
wood workshop	mokuzai-kōsaku-jo
workshop	wākushoppu, kenshūkai
yoga	yoga

140

Entertainment

Traditional Japanese Musical Instruments

Shamisen: Three-stringed musical instrument comparable to a balalaika. The sound of this instrument is "typically Japanese."

Koto: A 13-stringed musical instrument that is plucked. It is chiefly women who have always played this instrument for entertainment—today, mostly for solo pieces.

Shakuhachi: A bamboo flute that is played vertically. The purpose of the playing was to focus the mind in order to look from the transitory present into the mysteries beyond this world. The tone is reminiscent of wind and bamboo.

Taiko: Japanese drum. The Japanese love festivals—and drumming is a part of them. The drummers have the rhythms in their heads in the form of syllables, such as ten-te-ka, ten-te-ka to-to ten-ten. Even if your stay in Japan is only a brief one, you will surely have an opportunity to hear these drummers at a shrine or on the street.

Theater—Concert—Movies

What play is being performed in the theater tonight?
Konban dono sakuhin ga gekijō de jōen sareru ka oshiete kudasaimasu ka?

What movie can I see tomorrow night?
Asu no ban nan no eiga ga miremasu ka?

Could you recommend a good play?
Nanika yoi shibai o susumete kudasaimasu ka?

What time does the performance start?
Nanji ni moyōshimono ga hajimarimasu ka?

Where can I buy a ticket?
Chiketto wa doko de kaemasu ka?

Give me two tickets for tonight, please.
Konban yō kippu (o) nimai kudasai.

Two seats for ..., please.
... no seki futaribun kudasai!

May I have a program, please?
Puroguramu o moraemasen ka?

Nō: The *nō* theater came into being about 700 years ago. Originally it was a lyric drama that was presented at Shintoist festivals between religious rites. Even today, the stage continues to resemble a Shintoist shrine. The text is presented rhythmically, to the accompaniment of classical Japanese music. Instead of make-up, the actors wear masks symbolizing certain characters. The costumes correspond to the clothing of the fifteenth century.

Kabuki: Perhaps because it is more cheerful, *kabuki* theater is more popular than *nō.* It is a combination of rhythmically spoken verses and dances accompanied by *shamisen* music. The costumes and stage sets are very colorful. In *kabuki,* all the women's roles are played by men. The big *kabuki* stages include a brief English-language summary of the pieces in their program booklets.

Bunraku: Bunraku is a kind of puppet theater, in which romantic ballads are sung to the accompaniment of *shamisen* music. The major puppet figures are controlled so deftly by three puppeteers that their movements seem almost real.

admission ticket	nyūjō-ken
advance ticket	maeuri
box office	kippu-uriba
cloakroom	kurōku
festival	fesutibaru, gējutsu-sai
intermission	kyūkei
performance	jōen, jōē, ensō, moyōshimono
program	puroguramu

Theater

actor/actress	haiyū/joyū
ballet	barē
box seat	bokkusu, shikiri-seki
bunraku	bunraku
cabaret	yose
chorus	gasshōdan, kōrasu
comedy	komedī, kigeki
curtain	maku
dancer	dansā, odoriko
direction	enshutsu
drama	shibai, gikyoku, dorama
first balcony	nikai shōmen sajikiseki
kabuki	kabuki
koto	koto
musical	myūjikaru

143

opera	opera
operetta	operetta
orchestra (seat)	paruketto
outdoor theater	yagai-gekijō
performance	jōen *(theater)*, joeī *(film)*, ensō *(music)*
play	shibai, geki
popular play	minzoku-geki, taishū-geki
premiere	shoen
shakuhachi	shakuhachi
shamisen	shamisen
theater	geki, geki-jō, shibai
theater program	jōen-puroguramu
tragedy	higeki
vaudeville	yose, engekijō
vaudevillian	komedian

Concert

blues	burūsu
chorus	gasshōdan, kōrasu
classical	kurashikku
composer	sakkyoku-ka
concert	konsāto, ongakkai
chamber music	shitsunai ~
church music	kyōkai ~
symphony orchestra	sinfonī ~
conductor	shikisha
folk	minzoku
jazz	jazu
orchestra	ōkesutora, kōkyōgaku-dan
pop	poppu
popular music	minshū-ongaku
rap	rappu
reggae	regei
rock	rokku
singer	kashu, sēgaku-ka
soloist	sorisuto
soul	souru
techno	tehino

Movies

direction	enshutsu
leading role	shu-yaku

movie	eiga
action film	akushiyon-eiga
animation film	manga-eiga
black-and-white film	shiro-kuro-firumu
classic film	koten-eiga
comedy	komedī, kigeki
documentary film	dokyumentari, kiroku-eiga
drama	dorama
science-fiction film	kūsō-kagaku-shōsetsu-eiga
short film	tanpen-eiga
thriller	surira-shōsetsu-eiga
Western	seibu-geki
movie actor/actress	eiga-haiyū *(m)*/ēga-joyū *(f)*
movie theater	eiga-kan
outdoor movie theater	yagai-eigakan
original script	genpon, orijinaru-tekisuto
special effects	tokubetsu-kōka
subtitles	sabu-taitoru, jimaku

Nightlife

What's there to do around here at night?
Yoru koko de nani ga dekimasu ka?

Are there nice places to have a drink around here?
Koko ni ii nomiya ga arimasu ka?

Where can you go dancing around here?
Koko de wa doko de dansu ga dekimasu ka?

Shall we dance (again)?
(Mō ichido) odorimashō ka?

band	bando
bar	bā
casino	tobakujō, kajino
dance band	dansu no bando
dance, to	odoru
discotheque	disuko
drinking place	nomiya
folk concert	minzoku buyō no yoru/fōkudansu no yoru
folklore	minzoku no ongaku ya dansu
formal attire	yoru no ifuku
gambling	kakegoto
go out, to	soto e iku

live music	nama-ensō
nightclub	naito-kurabu
party	pātī
show	shō

Festivals and Events

Could you tell me when the ... festival is?
... -fesutibaru wa itsu okonawareru ka oshiete kudasai.
  It's from ... to ....
  ... kara ... made.
  It's in August every year.
  maitoshi hachigatsu ni
  It's every other year.
  ni-nen-goto

Can anyone take part?
Daredemo sanka dekimasu ka?

Typical Festivities and Events

Boys' Festival (May 5)	tango no sekku
Daimonji Bonfire (in Kyoto)	daimonji
Doll Festival (March 3)	hinamatsuri
Dolls for the Doll Festival	hinaningyō
evening fair stall	yomise
Fall Festival	aki matsuri
festival	fesutibaru, gējutsu-sai
fireworks	hanabi
New Year	o-shōgatsu
procession, float	gyōretsu, dashi
The day before the beginning of spring (February 3)	setsubun
The bean-throwing ceremony	mame maki
To chase out demons	oni o oidasu
The God of Fortune	fuku no kami
sacred Shinto music and dance	okagura
Star Festival (July 7)	tanabata
Summer Festival	natsu matsuri
year-end fair	toshi no ichi

Shopping

Shopping is a favorite activity in Japan. The numerous small stores are open seven days a week, 24 hours a day. The large department stores close in the evenings, but are open on Sundays.

Questions

I'm looking for ...
... o sagashite imasu.

I'd like to get to ...
... ga hoshī desu.

Is somebody helping you?
Mō tei'in ga ōtai shite imasu ka?

Just looking, thank you.
Chotto mite iru dake desu.

Do you have ...?
... ga arimasu ka?

Do you have something else?
Hoka ni nanika gozaimasu ka?

Making Purchases

How much is this?
Kore wa ... ikura desu ka?

That's expensive!
Kore wa takai desu nē!

Can you discount it a little?
Sukoshi yasukushite kuremasu ka?

That's okay. I'll take it.
Ii desu, sore o kudasai.

Do you take credit cards?
Kurejittokādo de yoi desu ka?

Stores and Shops

Excuse me, where is the ...?
Sumimasen ga, ... wa doko desu ka?

business hours
Eigyō-jikan

antique shop	kottōya
art gallery	gashō
bakery	panya, bēkarī
bookstore	honya
boutique	butikku
butcher	nikuya
candy store, pastry shop	okashi-ya, kēki-ya
catering service	pātī-sābisu
ceramics store	tōjiki-ten
cigar and tobacco store	tabakoya
confectionery	okashiya
cosmetics shop	keshōhin-ten
delicatessen	kōkyū-shokuryōhin-ten
department store	hyakka-ten, depāto
drugstore	doraggu sutoā
dry cleaners	kurīningu-ya
electrical appliance store	denkiya
fish market	sakanaya
flea market	nomi no ichi
florist	hanaya
grocery store	shokuryōhin-ten
hairdresser, barber	biyō-shi, tokoya
hardware store	kanamono-ya
health food store	kenkō-shokuhin-ten
jewelry store	hōseki-shō
laundromat	koin-randorī
laundry shop	sentaku-ya
leather goods store	kawaseihin-ten
liquor store	sakaya
market	ichiba
natural food store	shizen-shokohin-ten
newspaper distributor	shinbun-hanbaiten-shu
optician	megane-ya
pharmacy	kusuriya, yakkyoku

photo store	shashin-ya
sausage shop	sōsēji-rui-shokuhin-ten
second-hand store	furudōgu-ya
shoe repair shop	kutsu-shokunin
shoe store	kutsuya
souvenir shop	miyagemono-ten
sporting goods store	supōtsu-yōhin-ten
stationery shop	yōsai-shi, shitate-ya
supermarket	sūpā-māketto
tailor	bunbōgu-ten, bunbōgu-ya
toy store	omochaya
travel agency	ryokō-sha
vegetable store	yaoya
watchmaker's	tokei-ya
wine store	wain-ya

Books, Magazines, and Stationery

..., please.
... o kudasai.

A map written with romaji
Rōmaji de kaite aru chizu

A German-Japanese dictionary
Dokuwa-jiten

An English-Japanese dictionary
Eiwa-jiten

An English newspaper
Eigo no shinbun

A magazine
Zasshi

A travel guidebook
Ryokō-gaidobukku

A hiking map for this area
Kono chihō no haikingu yō chizu

Do you have a Japanese-English dictionary written with romaji?
Rōmaji de kakareta waei-jiten ga arimasu ka?

I'd like to get an easy book for studying Japanese.
Nihongo ga benkyō dekiru kantan na hon ga hoshii no desu ga.

Do you have a guidebook in English?
Eigo no gaido-bukku ga arimasu ka?

Books, Magazines, and Newspapers

book	hon
city map	shigai-chizu
comic book	manga no shōsatsu
cookbook	ryōri no hon
daily newspaper	shinbun
detective story	suiri-shōsetsu
guidebook	gaido-bukku
illustrated magazine	zasshi
map	chizu
newspaper	shinbun
novel	shōsetsu
paperback	poketto-bukku
road map	dōro-chizu
textbook	kyōkasho
women's magazine	fujin-zasshi

Stationery

air mail paper	kōkūbin yō binsen
ballpoint pen	bōrupen
colored pencil	iro-enpitsu
coloring book	nuri-e-chō
envelope	fūtō
notepad	memo-yōshi
paper	kami, yōshi
pencil	enpitsu
picture postcard	e-hagaki
stationery	binsen, bunbōgu

CDs and Cassettes

> ➢ also Electrical Goods and Concert

Do you have a ...'s CD/cassette?
... no CD/kasetto ga arimasu ka?

I'd like a CD with ... music.
... no ongaku no CD o kudasai.

May I listen?
Shichō shite yoi desu ka?

cassette	kasetto
CD	CD (kogata-rekōdo)
CD player	CD-pureiyā
portable CD player	keitai yō CD-pureiyā
DVD	DVD (dējitaru bideo disuku)
headphone	heddo-hōn
speaker	supīkā
Walkman®	wōkuman

Drugstore Items

aftershave lotion	higesori yō keshōsui
Band-Aid®	bando-eido
bathtub mat	surippu no patto
body shampoo	shawā yō ekitai-sekken
brush	burashi
comb	kushi
contraceptive device, condom	hiningu, kondōmu
cotton	wata
cotton swab	menbō
cream	kurīmu
dental floss	ha no te-ire yō kenshi
deodorant	deodoranto
dish towel	fukin
dishwashing liquid	senzai (shokki arai yō)
drugstore item	nichi yō zakka keshōhin
face powder	paudā
hair clip	kamidome
hair gel	heāgeru
hand cream	hando-kurīmu
laundry detergent	senzai (sentaku-yō)
lip cream	rippu-kurīmu
lipstick	kuchibeni
lotion	nyūeki
manicure	manikyua
mascara	masukarā
maxi pad	sēri-yōhin, napukin
mirror	kagami
nail clipper	tsumekiri
nail polish remover	jokō-eki
night cream	naito-kurīmu
perfume	kōsui
pot cleaner	tawashi
razor blade	kamisori no ha
razor, electric razor	kamisori, denki-kamisori (el.)
rubber band	gomu-wa

I would like
... o kudasai

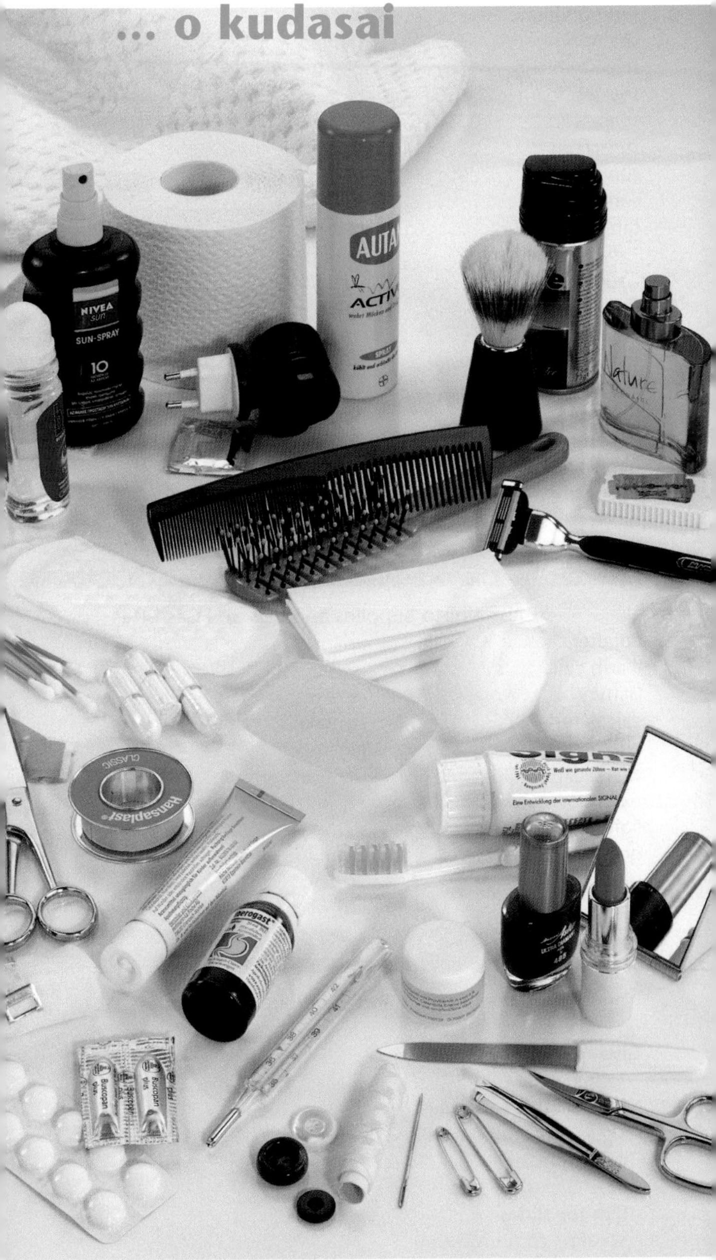

setting lotion	setto-rōshon
shampoo	shanpū
shaving brush	higesori yō hake
shaving foam	higesori yō awajō no sekken
soap	sekken
sunscreen	hiyakedome-kurīmu
suntan lotion	hiyakedome-nyūeki
suntan oil	san-oiru
tampon	tanpon
mini/regular/super/ super plus	mini/nōmaru/sūpā/sūpā purasu
tissue	chirigami, tisshu
toilet paper	toiretto-pēpā
toothbrush	haburashi
toothpaste	hamigaki
toothpick	tsumayōji
tweezers	pinsetto
ultraviolet ray protection	shigaisen yobō
washcloth	tenugui

Electrical Goods

> ➢ also Photo Supplies and CDs and Cassettes

adapter	adaptā
alarm clock	mezamashi-dokei
battery	denchi
calculator	dentaku
charger	jūdensōchi
dryer	doraiyā
extension cord	enchō-kōdo
lightbulb	denkyū
notebook	nōtobukku
plug	puragu

Photo Supplies

> ➢ also Filming and Photographing

Give me some..., please.
... o kudasai.

film for this camera
Kono kamera yō no fuirumu

color film
Karā fuirumu

film for slides
Suraido yō no fuirumu

154

film with 36/24/12 exposures
Sanjū-roku/Nijū-yon/Jū-ni mai dori no fuirumu

... doesn't work at all.
... wa mō ugokimasen.

This is broken. Can you repair it?
Kore ga kowareta no de, shūri o onegai dekimasu ka?

Could you show me the latest camera/video recorder?
Ichiban atarashii kamera/bideo o misete kudasaimasen ka?

black-and-white film	shiro-kuro no fuirumu
digital camera	dejitaru-kamera
DVD	dejitaru bideo-disuku
exposure meter	roshutsu-kei
film speed	kankōdo
flash	furasshu
lens	renzu
objective	renzu
Polaroid® camera	poraroido kamera
rangefinder	faindā
self-timer	serufu-taimā
shutter	shattā
telephoto lens	bōen-renzu
tripod	sankyaku
underwater camera	sui-chū kamera
video	bideo
video camera	bideo-kamera
video film	bideo firumu
video recorder	bideo-rekōdā
videocassette	bideo no kasetto

Hairdresser/Barber

Wash and blow-dry, please.
Aratte doraiyā de kawakashite kudasai.

Cut with/without wash, please.
Kami o aratte/arawazu ni kitte kudasai.

I would like ....
... ga hoshī desu.

Just a trim, please.
Kami no saki dake.

Not too short/very short/somewhat short, please.
Mijika suginai yō ni/Totemo mijikaku/Sukoshi mijikame ni, onegai shimasu.

Show/hide my ears, please.
Mimi wa dashite kudasai./Mimi wa kakureru yō ni shite kudasai.

Shave my beard, please.
Hige o sotte kudasai.

Trim my mustache/beard, please.
Kuchi-hige/Hige o mijikaku kitte kudasai.

Thank you very much. It's wonderful.
Arigatō gozaimasu. Totemo ii desu.

bangs	kirisage-maegami
beard	hige
blond	kinpatsu no, burondo no
blow-dry, to	doraiyā o ateru
color, to	senshoku suru, someru
comb, to	kami o tokasu
curl	kāru
curl, to	uēbu o tsukeru
dandruff	fuke
hair	kami
dry hair	kansōshita-kami
oily hair	aburakkoi-kami
hair color	heā-kārā
hairpiece	heā-pīsu
hairstyle	kamigata
layered cut	dan-katto
mustache	kuchi-hige
part, to	kamino wakeme
perm	pāma
set hair, to	kami o setto suru
shampoo	shanpū
sideburns	momiage
straight, loose hair	tarege
to tint	kami ni iroai o tsukeru
wig	katsura

Household Goods

aluminum foil	arumi-hoiru
bottle opener	sen'nuki
can opener	kankiri
candle	rōsoku
charcoal	guriru yō sumi
charcoal lighter	hi-okoshi
clothesline	monohoshi-zuna
clothespin	sentaku-basami
cooler	reikyaku-bakku
corkscrew	koruku-sen'nuki
fork	fōku
freezer pack	reikyakuzai
fuel alcohol	nenryō yō arukōru
glass	gurasu
grill	guriru
household goods	katei yō hin
knife	naifu
needle	hari
paper napkin	kami-napukin
petroleum	sekiyu
plastic bag	purasuchikku no fukuro
plastic cup	purasuchikku no koppu
pocket knife	poketto-naifu
safety pin	anzen-pin
scissors	hasami
spoon	supūn
string	nizukuri-himo
thermal flask	mahōbin
trash bag	gomi-bukuro
wire	harigane
wrap	rappu

Groceries

What would you like?
Nani ni itashimashō?

I'd like ..., please.
... o kudasai.
  one kilogram of ...
  ... ichi-kiro
  10 sheets of ...
  ... jū-mai

a slice of ...
... hitokire.
a pack of ...
... hito-pakku
a glass of ...
... ippai
a can of ...
... hito-kan
a bottle of ...
... ippon
a shopping bag
Kaimono bukuro ichimai

Is it okay if it's a litte bit over?
Sukoshi ōme demo yoroshii desu ka?

Would you like something else?
Nanika mada yoroshii desu ka?

Could I taste it?
Kore kara chotto ajimi-shite mo yoroshii desu ka?

That's all.
Sore de, zenbu desu.

Fruit

almond	āmondo
apple	ringo
apricot	anzu
banana	banana
blackberry	seiyō-yabuichigo
cherry	sakuranbo, cherī
coconut	kokonattsu
date	natsume
fig	ichijiku
fruit	kudamono
grape	budō
grapefruit	gurēpufurūtsu
lemon	remon
mandarin orange	mikan
melon	meron
watermelon	*suika*
nut	nattsu
orange	orenji
peach	momo
pear	nashi
pineapple	painappuru

158

plum	ume, sumomo
strawberry	ichigo

Vegetables

asparagus	asuparagasu
avocado	abogado
beans	mame
kidney beans	ingen
string beans	saya ingen
bell pepper	pīman(saya)
cabbage	kyabetsu
carrot	ninjin
cauliflower	karifurāwā
celery	serori
corn	tōmorokoshi, kōn
cucumber	kyūri
eggplant	nasu
garlic	nin·niku
green peas	gurinpīsu
leek	negi
olive	orību
onion	tamanegi
parsley	paseri
potato	jagaimo
salad	sarada
lettuce	retasu
spinach	hōrensō
squash	kabocha
tomato	tomato
vegetable	yasai

Bakery Products and Confectionery

Only white bread is available in Japan.
Supermarkets always offer ready-made tempura: pieces of vegetables, chicken, and fish, battered and fried in deep fat. There are not a great many snack bars, but the number of beverage vending machines is enormous.
In smaller restaurants, you can eat *udon* or *soba* (noodles in broth) very inexpensively.

biscuit	bisuketto
bread	pan
white bread	shiropan
cake	kēki
candy	kyandī

chewing gum	chūingamu
chocolate	chokorēto
bar of chocolate	ita-choko
stick of chocolate	bō-choko
cookie	kukkī
honey	hachimitsu
ice-cream	aisukurīmu
jam	jamu
muesli	mūzuri
oatmeal	ōtomīru
rolls (bread)	rōru pan
sandwich rolls	rōru pan no sandoitchi
sweets	o-kashi
toast	tōsuto

Eggs and Dairy Products

butter	batā
buttermilk	batā-miruku
cheese	chīzu
cream cheese	kurīmu-chīzu
goat cheese	yagi-nyū-chīzu
sheep cheese	yōnyū-chīzu
slice of cheese	hitokire goto ni kirareta chīzu
cream	nama-kurīmu
sour cream	sawā-kurīmu
whipped cream	awadate nama-kurīmu
egg	tamago
milk	gyūnyū, miruku
lowfat milk	shibōbun no sukunai gyūnyū
yogurt	yōguruto

Meat and Sausages

beef	gyūniku
chicken	tori-niku, niwatori
cutlet	katsuretsu
frankfurter	sōsēji
goulash	hangarīfū shichū
ground meat	hiki-niku
ham	hamu
boiled ham	yudeta hamu
uncured ham	nama-hamu
lamb	ramu-niku
liver pâté	rebā-iri-pai
meat	niku
mutton	maton, hitsuji no niku
pork	butaniku

rabbit	usagi
salami	sarami
sausage	sōsēji
sliced meat	usukukitta niku
veal	koushi no niku

Fish and Seafood

clam	hamaguri
crab	kani
eel	unagi
fish	sakana
gold carp	kin no funa
herring	nishin
mackerel	saba
mussel	mūrugai
oyster	kaki
prawn	ebi
sea bass	suzuki
shellfish	kai
shrimp	ebi
sole	shitabirame
squid	ika
swordfish	mekajiki
tuna	maguro

Miscellaneous

butter	batā
flour	komugiko
margarine	māgarin
mayonnaise	mayonēzu
mustard	karashi
noodle	men
oil	oiru, abura
olive oil	orību-oiru
rice	kome
cooked rice	gohan
salt	shio
sugar	satō
vegetable bouillon	yasaikonsome-sūpu no moto
vinegar	su

Beverages

apple juice	ringo-jūsu
beer	bīru
nonalcoholic beer	arukōru-nashi no bīru
champagne	shyanpan

coffee	kōhī
decaffeinated coffee	kafein-nashi no kōhī
lemonade	remonēdo
mineral water	mineraru-uōtā
carbonated/not carbonated	tansan iri/tansan nashi
orange juice	orenji-jūsu
tea	kōcha
chamomile tea	kamitsure no hana o senjita yakuyu
fruit-flavored tea	kudamono no ocha
green tea	sencha, ryokucha, ocha
herbal tea	yakusōcha
peppermint tea	pepāminto no ocha
tea bag	tēbakku
wine	wain
red wine	aka-wain
rosé	rose
white wine	shiro-wain

Fashion

➢ **also Colors**

> **Traditional Japanese Clothing:**
> **geta:** Japanese wooden clogs, or platform sandals, with two "heels"
> **pokkuri:** high wooden clogs worn by *maiko*
> **zōri:** shoes made of lighter material with no heel
> **kimono obi:** colored sash worn with the kimono
> **yukata:** light Japanese cotton kimono. It is usually worn in summer and when going to the Japanese bath (*furo*).
> **tabi:** white socks with a separate section for the big toe

Clothing

I'd like to see some ....
... o misete kudasai.

May I try it on?
Shichaku shite yoroshii desu ka?

What is my size?
Ōkisa wa o-ikutsu desu ka?

It's a little too ....
Kore wa chotto ...
  tight/loose
  kitsu/ōki sugimasu.
  short/long
  mijika/naga sugimasu.
  small/large
  chīsa/ōki sugimasu.

It fits well. I'll take it.
Kore ga chōdo aimasu. Kore ni shimasu.

It's a little different from what I want.
Kore wa watashi ga hoshii mono to chotto chigaimasu.

bathing suit	mizu-gi
bathrobe	basu-gaun
bikini	bikini
blazer	burezā
blouse	burausu
bow tie	chōnekutai
brassiere	burajā
briefs	burīfu
cardigan	kādigan
children's socks	chiisa na kodomo yō sokkusu
clothing	ifuku
coat	kōto
costume, suit	kosuchūmu, sūtsu
cotton	men, kotton
geta (Japanese wooden shoes)	geta
gloves	tebukuro
hat	bōshi
sun hat	hiyoke-bōshi
jacket	uwagi
jeans	jīnzu
jogging pants	joggingu-zubon, joggingu-pantsu
jogging suit	joggingu-sūtsu
kimono	kimono
leggings	reginsu
linen	rinneru, asa
muffler	mafurā
national dress	minzoku-ishō
necktie	nekutai
obi	obi
panties	pantī
pantyhose	panti-sutokkingu
parka	anorakku

pokkuri (wooden shoes worn by maiko)	pokkuri
raincoat	rein-kōto, amagappa
scarf	sukāfu, erimaki
shirt	waishatsu, shatsu
shorts	shōtsu
silk	kinu
ski pants	sukī-zubon
skirt	sukāto
sleeve	sode
slip	surippu
socks	sokkusu, kutsushita
stockings	sutokkingu
suit	sūtsu
sweater	sētā
swimming cap	suiei-bō
swimming trunks	suiei-pantsu
T-shirt	tī-shatsu
trousers	zubon
umbrella	kasa
undergarment	dōgi
undershirt	andāshatsu
underwear	shitagi
vest	chokki
western clothes, one-piece dress	yōfuku, wanpīsu
wool	ūru, ke

Cleaning

I'd like to get this dry-cleaned.
Kore o kurīningu shite kudasai.

When will it be ready?
Itsu dekiagarimasu ka?

dryclean, to	dorai-kurīningu suru
iron, to	airon o kakeru
laundry	sentaku

Optician

I'd like to get these eyeglasses/this frame repaired.
Kono megane/Waku o shūri shite kuremasen ka?

I'm near-sighted/far-sighted.
Watashi wa kinshi/enshi desu.

What is my vision?
Shiryoku wa dono kurai desu ka?

The right eye is ..., and the left eye is ....
migi wa ... desu, hidari wa ... desu

When can I pick up my glasses?
Itsu megane o tori ni kitara ii desu ka?

I'd like to get some disinfecting solution for hard/soft contact lenses.
Katai/Yawarakai kontakto-renzu yō hozon-eki o kudasai.

I'd like to get some cleaning solution for hard/soft contact lenses.
Katai/Yawarakai kontakto-renzu yō senjō-eki o kudasai.

I'd like to get some sunglasses.
Sangurasu o kudasai.

I'd like to get a telescope.
Bōenkyō o kudasai.

Shoes and Leather Goods

I'd like to get a pair of shoes for ....
... -gutsu o kudasai.

I'd like to get a pair of slippers.
Surippa o kudasai.

My shoe size is ....
Watashi no kutsu no ōkisa wa ... desu.

It's too tight/big.
Kitsu-/Ōki-sugimasu.

backpack	ryukku-sakku
bag	kaban, fukuro, bakku
bathing shoe, beach shoe	suiei yō kutsu, yoku yō surippa, bīchi-sandaru
belt	beruto
boots	būtsu
briefcase, trunk	kaban, toranku
handbag	hando-bakku

heel	kakato
leather coat	rezā-kōto
leather jacket	rezā-jaketto
leather pants	kawa-zubon
rubber boots	gomu-nagagutsu
rubber sandals	gomuzōri
sandals	Sandaru
shoe brush	kutsu-burashi
shoe polish	kutsu-kurīmu
shoelace	kutsuhimo
shoes	kutsu
shoulder bag	shorudā-bakku
ski boots	sukī-gutsu
sneakers	undō-gutsu
sole (shoe)	soko, kutsuzoko
suspenders	sasupendā
traveling bag	ryokō yō kaban
waistpack	poshetto
wheeled suitcase	tororī

Souvenirs

Souvenirs/Mementos
The road to a temple often will take you down a kilometer-long street of artisans' shops, where many of these items are sold:

bamboo articles	take-zaiku
woodblock prints	hanga
wooden puppets	kibori ningyō
Japanese scrolls	kake jiku
lacquer articles	shikki
origami	origami
porcelain	tōki
dolls	ningyō
silk	kinu
music boxes	orugōru
ink paintings	sumi-e

I'd like to get ....
... o kudasai.
some mementos/a souvenir
Kirei na kinenhin/Kirei na omoi de no shina
something unique to this area
Kono chihōdokutoku no mono

How much would you like to spend?
Yosan wa o-ikura desu ka?

I'd like to get something not too expensive.
Amari takakunai no ga hoshī no desu ga.

It's nice!
Kore wa kawaii desu nē.

Thank you very much. But I can't find exactly what I wanted.
Arigatō gozaimashita. Demo nanimo ki ni itta mono wa arimasen.

ceramics	tōgeihin
doll with national costume	minzoku ishō o tsuketa ningyō
embroidery	shishū
fan	sensu
folkart store	mingeihin no mise
genuine	honmono no
handcrafted	tesei
jewels	kazari akusesarī
kitschy	zokuaku na, inchiki na
pottery	tōki
regional products/specials	chihō no seihin/tokubetsu na mono
sculpture	chōkoku
souvenir	omiyage

Tobacco

A packet/carton...
... hitohako/ichikāton
filter-tipped/without filter, please.
Fuirutā-tsuki/Fuirutā-nashi o kudasai!

Do you have American cigarettes?
Amerika no tabako ga arimasu ka?

Ten cigars/cigarillos, please.
Hamaki/Chigariro o juppon kudasai.

A pack/tin of cigarette/pipe tobacco, please.
Maki-tabako o hitohako/hitokan kudasai.
Paipu yō tabako o hitohako/hitokan kudasai.

ashtray	haizara

cigar	hamaki
cigarette	maki-tabako
cigarette lighter	raitā
cigarillo	chigario
matches	matchi
pipe	paipu

Watches and Jewelry

Do you have cultured pearls?
Yōshoku-shinju ga arimasu ka?

bracelet	buresu retto
brooch	burōchi
chain	kusari
coral	sango
costume jewelry	fasshon-akusesari
crystal	suishō, kurisutaru
earring	mimi-kazari, iyaringu
earstud	piasu
gold	kin, gōrudo
jewel	kazari akusesarī
necktie pin	nekutaipin
pearl	shinju
pendant	pendanto
ring	yubiwa
silver	gin
travel alarm clock	keitai yō mezamashi-dokei/ ryokō yō mezamashi-dokei
waterproof wristwatch	bōsui-dokei
wristwatch	ude-dokei
for a woman/man	fujin yō ~/shinshi yō ~

Health

At the Pharmacy

Japanese physicians act as their own pharmacists. That is, you normally obtain medicines directly from the doctor.

Could you tell me where the nearest pharmacy open late at night is?
Ichiban chikaki (yakintōban no) yakkyoku wa doko ni aru ka oshiete kudasaimasu ka?

Could you give me something for ...?
... tame ni nanika kudasaimasen ka?

You need a prescription for this.
Kore wa shohōsen ga hitsuyō desu.

absorbent cotton	wata
aspirin	asupirin
Band-Aids®	bando-eido
burn ointment	yakedo yō nankō
chamomile solution	kamitsure-chinki
circulation stimulant	kekkōsokushin-zai
condom	kondomu
cough medicine	sekidome-gusuri
disinfectant	shōdoku-yaku
drops	tekizai
drug	kusuri
ear-drops	mimi no kusuri
elastic bandage	shinshukusei no aru hōtai
eye drops	me-gusuri
gauze bandage	gāze no hōtai
headache medicine	zutsū-yaku
insect bite medicine	mushi-sasare yō no kusuri
insulin	inshurin
iodine	yōdo
laxative	gezai
medicine	kusuri
ointment	nankō
painkiller	itamidome
powder	paudā
prescription	shohōsen
sleeping pill	suimin-yaku
sunscreen cream	hiyakedo yō nankō
suppository	zayaku

170

tablet	jōzai
thermometer	taionkei
throat lozenges	nodo no kusuri
tranquilizer	chinseizai
vitamins	bitaminzai

Product Enclosure

seibun	**Ingredients**
ōyō-han'i	uses
shiyōjō no chūi	warnings
fukusayō	side effects
sōgosayō	interaction

yōhō-yōryō	**Directions:**
ichinichi ni ikkai/sūdo ...	once/several times a day
fukuyō suru	take, to
jōzai hitotsu	1 tablet
nijū teki	20 drops
keiryō-kappu hitotsu	1 measuring cup
shokuji no mae ni, shokuzen ni	before a meal
shokuji no ato de, shokugo ni	after a meal
kūfuku-ji ni	on an empty stomach
kamazu ni shōryō no mizu de nomikomu	swallow with a small amount of water without chewing
shōryō no mizu de tokasu	dissolve in small amount of water
kuchi no naka de tokasu	dissolve in the mouth
gaiyō no	for external use
Hifu no ue ni usuku nuri nurikomu	apply thin coat on skin and rub in
nyūji	infants
chiisai kodomo (...-sai made)	small children (up to ... years old)
gakudōji	school-age children
seishōnen	juveniles
otona	adults
kodomo no te no todokanai tokoro ni hokan shite kudasai!	Keep out of reach of children.

At the Doctor's Office

➤ also Traveling with Children

Health care and medical facilities are on a very high level in Japan. Many doctors and dentists understand English. In large cities, foreign patients are also treated in the hospitals operated by religious denominations. English-speaking physicians can also be found in the telephone book under the heading "Medical Care."

If you have an emergency, it is best to contact your embassy:

United States Embassy: 1-10-5 Akasaka, Minato-ku, Tokyo 107-8420 or Box 205, APO AP 96337-5004 Tel. (03) 3224-50001 DSN 224-5000

Canadian Embassy: 7-3-38, Akasaka 7-chome, Minato-ku, Tokyo 107-8503 Tel. (03) 5412-6200

British Embassy: 1 Ichiban-cho, Chiyoda-ku, Tokyo Tel. (03) 5211-1100

Australian Embassy: 2-1-14 Mita, Minato-ku, Tokyo 108-8361 Tel. (03) 5232-4111

Could you recommend ...?
... o suisen shite kudasaimasen ka?
  a doctor
  Isha
  an ophthalmologist
  Me-isha, ganka-i
  a gynecologist
  Fujinka-i
  an ear, nose and throat doctor
  Jibi·inkōka-i
  a dermatologist
  Hifuka-i
  a pediatrician
  Shōnika-i
  a doctor in a private practice
  Kaigyō-i
  a urologist
  Hi·nyōka-i
  a dentist
  Ha-isha, shika-i

Where is her/his clinic?
Kanojo/Kare no shinsatsushitsu wa doko desu ka?

What is bothering you?
Doko no guai ga warui no desu ka?

I have a fever.
Netsu ga arimasu.

I'm often ....
Yoku ... desu.
  not feeling well, feeling sick/feeling nauseated
  guai ga warui/kibun ga warui, hakisō
  dizzy
  memai ga shimasu

I lost consciousness.
Kizetsu shimashita.

I have a terrible cold.
Hidoku kaze o hīte imasu.

My head/throat hurts.
Atama/Nodo ga itai desu.

I have a cough.
Seki ga demasu.

I have a ....
Watashi wa ...
  sting
  sasaremashita.
  bite
  kamaremashita.

I have an upset stomach.
I o kowashimashita.

I'm ....
Watashi wa ... o shite imasu.
  having diarrhea
  geri
  constipated
  benpi

173

I can't bear this food/heat.
Kono shokuji/Atsusa ga taeraremasen.

I'm hurt.
Kega o shimashita.

I've fallen.
Korobimashita.

Could you give me something for...?/Could you prescribe something for ...?
Nanika ... yō ni kudasai./Nanika ... yō ni shohō shite kudasaimasen ka?

I usually take ....
Futsū watashi wa ... o nonde imasu.

I have high/low blood pressure.
Ketsuatsu ga takai/hikui desu.

I'm a diabetic.
Watashi wa tōnyō-byō desu.

I'm pregnant.
Ninshin shite imasu.

Until just recently, I was ...
Sukoshi mae watashi wa ... deshita.

Examination

Is something bothering you?
Dō shimashita ka?

Where does it hurt?
Doko ga itai desu ka?

It hurts me here.
Koko ga itai desu.

Roll up your sleeve, please.
Sode o makuriagete kudasai.

Breathe deeply. Hold your breath.
Shinkokyū o shite. Iki o tomete kudasai.

I want a blood/urine sample.
Ketsueki-/Nyō- kensa ga hitsuyō desu.

174

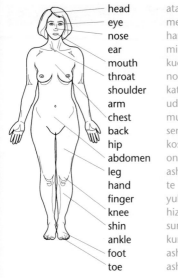

head	atama
eye	me
nose	hana
ear	mimi
mouth	kuchi
throat	nodo
shoulder	kata
arm	ude
chest	mune
back	senaka
hip	koshi
abdomen	onaka
leg	ashi
hand	te
finger	yubi
knee	hiza
shin	sune, keikotsu
ankle	kurubushi
foot	ashi
toe	ashi no yubi

You must have an X-ray taken.

Rentogen o toranakereba narimasen.

You must have surgery.

Shujutsu o shinakereba narimasen.

You should rest for several days.

Sūjitsukan seiyō shita hō ga yoroshii desu.

You don't need to be concerned.

Shinpai suru hitsuyō wa arimasen.

Do you have a certificate of vaccination?

Yobōsesshu-techō o omochi desu ka?

I gave you a vaccine for ....

... no yōbō-chūsha o shimashita.

How long do I have to stay here?
Dono kurai koko ni inakereba narimasen ka?

Can I have a glass of water, please?
(O-)mizu o koppu ippai kudasai.

Could you give me a painkiller?
Itamidomo o kudasai.

Could you give me a sleeping pill?
Nemuri-gusuri o kudasai.

Could you give me a hot-water bottle?
Yutanpo o kudasai.

I can't sleep.
Nemuremasen.

When can I get up?
Itsu okite mo yoroshii desu ka?

Illnesses and Complaints

abscess	nōyō
AIDS	e·izu
allergy	arerugī
angina	angīna, hentōsen-en
appendicitis	mōchō-en
asthma	zensoku
backache	senaka no itami, yōtsū, gikkurigoshi
bleeding	shukketsu
bloated	onaka ga haru
blood poisoning	haiketsu-shō
broken (leg, arm, etc.)	oreta
broken bone	kossetsu
bronchitis	kikanshi-en
burn	yakedo
cancer	gan
cerebral hemorrhage	nōikketsu
chapped	hibi
chill	okan

cholera	korera
circulatory trouble	junkan-shōgai
cold	kaze
colic	sentsū
concussion	nōshintō
constipation	benpi
contagious	utsuriyasui, densensei no
convulsion	keiren
cut	kirikizu
diabetes	tōnyōbyō
diarrhea	geri
diphtheria	jifuteria
dizziness	memai
faint, to	kizetsu suru, ki o ushinau
fever	netsu
food poisoning	shoku-chūdoku
get hurt, to	kega o suru, fushō suru
hard to breathe	kokyū-konnan
head cold	hanakaze
headache	zutsū
heart attack	shinzō-hossa
heart defect	shinzō-kekkan
heart trouble	shinzō-shōgai
heartburn	muneyake
hemorrhoids	ji
hernia	herunia
high blood pressure	kōketsu-atsu
hives	jinmashin
hoarse	shagareta
I'm allergic to	... no arerugī de aru
illness	byōki
impaired balance	heikō-shōgai
impaired vision	shiryoku-shōgai
indigestion	shōka-furyō
infection	densen, kansen
inflammation	enshō
influenza	ryūkan
injury	kega, fushō
insomnia	fumin-shō
internal bleeding	naishukketsu
itch	kayui

177

jaundice	ōdan
kidney stone	jin-seki
malaria	mararia
middle ear inflammation	chūjien
migraine	henzutsū
miscarriage	ryūzan
myocardial infarction	shinkin-kōsoku
nausea	hakike
nephritis	jin-en
nosebleed	hana-ji
pain	itami
painful	itai
palpitations	shinzō no dōki
paralysis	mahi
pneumonia	haien
poisoning	chūdoku
polio	shōni-mahi
rheumatism	ryūmachi
rhinitis	bien
sciatica	zakotsu-shineitsū
side-pain	wakibara no itami
sinusitis	zentō-dōen
sneeze, to	kushami o suru
sore throat	nodo no itami
sprain, to	nenza shite iru
stomachache	itsū
strain	sujichigai
stroke	sotchū
sunburn	hiyake
sunstroke	nisshabyō
swell, to	hareru
swelling	hare
tetanus	tetanusu, hashōhū
tonsillitis	hentōsen-en
tumor	dekimono, shuyō
typhoid	chifusu
ulcer	kaiyō
venereal disease	seibyō
wound	kizu
yellow fever	ōnetsu byō

Body—Doctor—Hospital

abdomen . . . . kafukubu
anesthesia . . . . masui
ankle . . . . kurubushi
appendix . . . . mōchō
arm . . . . ude
artificial limb . . . . gishi
back . . . . senaka
backbone . . . . sebone
bandage . . . . hōtai
belly . . . . onaka
bladder (urinary) . . . . bōkō
bleed, to . . . . shukketsu suru
blister . . . . suihō
blood . . . . chi, ketsueki
blood pressure . . . . ketsu-atsu
blood type . . . . ketsueki-gata
bone . . . . hone
bowel movement . . . . bentsū
brain . . . . nō
breathe, to . . . . iki o suru, kokyū suru
bronchi . . . . kikanshi
bypass surgery . . . . baipasu
certificate . . . . shōmei-sho
certificate of vaccination . . . yobōsesshu-techō, shutō-techō
chest . . . . mune
collarbone . . . . sakotsu
cough . . . . seki
diagnose . . . . shindan
diet . . . . daietto
digestion . . . . shōka
doctor's office hours . . . . . . shinsatsu-jikan
dress, to . . . . hōtai o suru
ear . . . . mimi
eardrum . . . . komaku
esophagus . . . . shokudo
examination . . . . kensa, shinsatsu
eye . . . . me
face . . . . kao
finger . . . . yubi
foot . . . . ashi
gallbladder . . . . tan'nō
hand . . . . te
head . . . . atama

health insurance	kenkō-hoken
health insurance certificate	hoken-shō
hearing	chōryoku
heart	shinzō
heart specialist	shinzō-senmon'i
hip	koshi
hospital	byōin
hospital ward	sutēshon, byōtō
illness	byōki
injection	chūsha
intestine	chō
intravenous drip	tenteki
joint	kansetsu
kidney	jinzō
knee	hiza
leg	ashi
lip	kuchibiru
liver	kanzō
lung	hai
male nurse	kango-nin
medical certificate	shindan-sho
menstruation	gekei, seiri, mensu
mouth	kuchi
muscle	kin·niku
nerve	shinkei
nervous	shinkei-shitsu na
nose	hana
nurse	kango-fu
operation	shujutsu
pacemaker	shinpaku-chōseiki
pregnancy	ninshin
prescribe, to	shiji suru, shohō suru
pulse	myaku
pus	umi
rib	abarabone
scar	kizuato
sex organ	sēki
shinbone	keikotsu, sune
shoulder	kata
skin	hada, hifu
specialist	senmon'i
spine	sebone
splint	soegi
stab wound	sashikizu
sterilize, to	shōdoku suru

stitch, to	nū, hōgō suru
stomach	i
surgeon	geka'i
sweat, to	ase o kaku
throat	nodo, kubi
toe	ashi no yubi
tongue	shita
tonsils	hentōsen
ultrasound examination	chō-onpa-kensa
unconscious	ishiki-fumē
urine	nyō
vaccination	yobōsesshu
virus	bīrusu
visiting hours	hōmon-jikan
vomit, to	ōto suru
waiting room	machiai-shitsu
X-ray	rentogen
X-ray photograph	rentogen-shashin

At the Dentist's

I have a (terrible) toothache.
(Hidoku) ha ga itai desu.

This tooth (top, bottom, front, back) hurts.
Kono ha (ue/shita/mae/oku) ga itai desu.

I've lost a filling.
Ha no tsumemono o naku shimashita.

I've chipped a tooth.
Ha ga kakemashita.

I'm going to give you a temporary treatment.
Karino shochi o shite okimasu.

I'd like an injection, please.
Chūsha o kudasai.

I don't want an injection.
Chūsha wa shinaide kudasai.

bridge	burijji
crown	shikan, kabuse
denture	gishi, purotēze

extract, to	nuku
filling	jūtenzai
gum	haguki, shiniku
hole	ana
incisor	monshi, itokiriba
jaw	ago
molar	okuba
tooth	ha
toothache	haita, ha ga itamu, shitsū
wisdom tooth	oyashirazu

電　話
Telephones

エレベーター裏側の公衆電話もご利用下さい

IC テレホンカード専用機

Essentials from A to Z

Bank

Foreign currencies as well as traveler's checks can be exchanged for Japanese currency only at banks with the sign "Authorized Foreign Exchange Bank." These banks are quite numerous in the large cities, but less common in the countryside. If you are reluctant to carry around large sums of cash at all times, you can open an account at the post office.
In Japan, unlike other Asian countries, you can't pay in dollars. Only the yen is accepted.
The exchange rate alone, however, tells you little about the actual purchasing power of the yen. Items that are everyday needs often cost twice as much as in the United States.

Money Transfers
There are two possibilities:
1. If you're not in a hurry, have someone send you a bank remittance in yen (marked "poste restante" and "special delivery").
2. You can have your money sent directly to a bank, either by a letter of transfer or a wire transfer.

Could you tell me where the nearest bank is?
Kono atari de wa doko ni ginkō ga aru ka oshiete kudasaimasen ka.

I'd like to exchange ... U.S. dollars to yen.
... doru o ... en ni ryōgae shitai desu.

Go to window number ..., please.
... ban no madoguchi e itte kudasai.

What's the exchange rate today?
Kyō no rēto wa ikura desu ka.

I'd like to cash in ....
... o kaetai desu.
  this traveler's check
  Kono toraberāzuchekku

What's the maximum amount I can get?
Saikō ikura made yoroshii desu ka?

Show me ..., please.
... o misete kudasai?

your identification card
Anata no shōmeisho

your passport/ ID
Anata no ryoken/mibunshōmeisho

Would you sign here, please?
Koko ni sain o shite kudasaimasen ka?

The ATM won't return my card.
Genkin-jidō-hikidashi-ki ga watashi no kādo o modoshite kuremasen.

I lost my traveler's checks. What should I do?
Watashi no toraberāzu-chekku o nakushimashita. Dō shitara ii deshō ka?

account	kōza
ATM	genkin-jidō-hikidashi-ki
bank	ginkō
bill	shihei, osatsu
cash	genkin
cent	sento
charge	tesūryō
check	kogitte, chekku
to write out a check	kogitte o kiru/furidasu
coin	kōka, kahei
credit card	kurejitto-kādo
currency	tsūka
euro	yūro
exchange	ryōgae
exchange rate	sōba, rēto
foreign exchange	gaikoku-kawase
form	kinyū-yōshi
IC card	chippukādo
money	okane
money order	sōkin-kawase
pay, to	shiharau
payment	shiharai
PIN	anshō-bangō
receipt	ryōshūsho
signature	shomei, sain
small change	kozeni
Swiss franc	suisu-furan
to change	ryōgae suru
total amount	sōgaku, kingaku

transfer . . . . furikae-sōkin
 wire transfer . . . . denshin-gawase
traveler's check . . . . ryokō-kogitte, toraberāzu-chekku

Filming and Photographing

➢ also Photo Supplies

Could you take my picture?
Watashitachi no shashin o totte kudasaimasu ka?

It's very kind of you.
Go-shinsetsu ni!

Push this button, please.
Kono botan o oshite kudasai.

This is how you can control the distance/aperture.
Kyori/Shibori wa sono yō ni chōsetsu shimasu.

May I take your picture?
Shashin o totte yoroshii desu ka?

It'll be a wonderful memory of my vacation.
Sō sureba kyūka no yoi omoide ni narimasu.

camera . . . . kamera
horizontal shot . . . . yoko-naga(-ban)
picture . . . . shashin
snapshot . . . . sunappu-shashin
take a picture, to . . . . shashin o toru
vertical shot . . . . tate-saizu

Lost-and-Found Office

➢ also Police

Where is the lost-and-found office?
I-shitsu-butsu-tori-atsukai-jo wa doko deshō ka?

I lost ....
Watashi wa ... o nakushimashita.

I left my purse on the train.
Hando-baggu o kisha no naka ni wasuremashita.

Please let me know if it's handed in.
Moshi mitsukarimashitara renraku kudasaimasen ka?

This is the address of my hotel/my parents' home.
Koko ga watashi no hoteru/jikka no jūsho desu.

Police

Japan is a very safe country. Stealing is a rare occurrence. If you've lost something, don't give up hope. As a rule, things that have been found are turned in.

Could you tell me where the nearby police station is?
Moyori no keisatsu-sho wa doko ni aru ka oshiete kudasaimasen ka?

I'd like to report a ....
... o todokemasu.

  theft
  Tōnan
  robbery
  Kishū

My pocketbook was stolen.
Hando-bakku ga nusumaremashita.
  My briefcase was stolen.
  Shorui-ire/Kami-ire ga nusumaremashita.
  My camera was stolen.
  Kamera ga nusumaremashita.
  My car/bicycle was stolen.
  Kuruma/Jitensha ga nusumaremashita.

My car was forced open.
Watashi no kuruma ga kojiakeraremashita.

... was stolen from my car.
Watashi no kuruma kara ... ga nusumaremashita.

I can't find my son/daughter.
Watashi no musuko/musume ga inaku narimashita.

This man is bothering me.
Kono otoko no hito ga watashi o wazurawasemasu.

Could you help me?
Otetsudai itadakemasu ka?

When was it exactly?
Seikaku ni wa sore wa itsu no koto desu ka?

Give me your name and address, please.
Anata no namae to jūsho o onegai shimasu.

Could you contact the American Consulate?
Amerika ryojikan ni renraku o totte kudasai.

Could you tell me how I can find ...?
Dō shitara ... ga mitsukaru ka oshiete kudasai.

I'd like to go to this address. Could you tell me how to get there?
Kono jūsho no tokoro e ikitai no de, dono yō ni ittara ii ka, oshiete kudasaimasen ka?

arrest, to	taiho suru
bother, to	meiwaku o kakeru
break into, to	kojiakeru
briefcase	kami-ire, shorui-ire
car radio	kā-rajio
car registration	jidōsha-tōroku-sho
check	kogitte, chekku
credit card	kurejitto-kādo
crime	hanzai
debit card	kogitte-kādo
document	shorui
drug	mayaku
fight	naguriai
guilt	tsumi, ochido
ID	mibun-shōmei-sho
jail	keimusho
judge	hanji, saiban-kan
key	kagi
lawyer	bengoshi
lose, to	makeru
passport	pasupōto, ryoken
police	keisatsu
police car	patokā
police officer	keisatsu-kan
pretrial detention	kōryū
purse-snatcher, pickpocket	hittakuri, suri
rape	gōkan, bōkō
report, to	todoke deru
robbery	fuiuchi, shin·nyū, shūgeki
seize, to	sashiosaeru, ōshū suru
sexual harassment	seiteki iyagarase

188

smuggling	mitsuyu
theft	tōnan
thief	dorobō
trial	saiban
wallet	saifu
witness, eyewitness	shōnin, mokugeki-sha

Post Office

Use the red mailboxes to mail your letters. You will find them on streets everywhere.

Could you tell me where ... is?
the nearest post office
Moyori no yūbinkyoku ...
the nearest mailbox
Moyori no posuto ...
... wa doko ni aru ka oshiete kudasaimasu ka?

How much is a letter/postcard ...?
Tegami wa/Hagaki wa ... ikura desu ka.
to the United States
Amerika e
to England
Igirisu e
to Australia
Ōsutoraria e

Three ... yen stamps, please.
(Yūbin-)Kitte sanmai ... en no o kudasai!

This letter..., please.
Kono tegami o ... de
by express mail
sokutatsu
by registered mail
kakitome
by air mail
kōkū-bin
by sea mail
funabin

How much is a letter to the United States?
Tegami wa Amerika made dono kurai kakarimasu ka?

189

Are there commemorative stamps?
Kinen-kitte ga arimasu ka?

➤ also Bank

address	jūsho
addressee	uketori-nin
affix a stamp, to	kitte o haru
air mail, via	kōkū-bin de
baggage	nimotsu
collection	kaikan
commemorative stamp	kinen-kitte
customs declaration	tsūkan-shinkoku
declaration of value	kakaku-hyōki
express	sokutatsu
fax	fakkusu
fax machine	fakkusu no kikai
fee	ryōkin
fill in, to	kinyū suru
form	kinyū-yōshi
forward, to	tensō suru
letter	tegami
mailbox	posuto
main post office	honkyoku
package	kozutsumi
post office	yūbin-kyoku
post office savings passbook	yūbin-yokin-tsūchō
postage	sōryō
postcard	yūbin-hagaki
poste restante	kyoku-dome
printed form	kinyū-yōshi
registered mail	kakitome
sender	okurinushi, hassō-nin
shipping tag	nifuda
stamp	kitte
stamp dispenser	kitte-jidō-hanbaiki
telegram	denpō
telex	terekkusu
weight	omosa
zip code	yūbin-bangō

Telephoning to and from Japan
If you want to call Japan from the United States, first dial the
international code, 011, then the country code, 81, and then
the area code (without the 0). Finally, dial the desired telephone number.
To call the United States from Japan, first dial 001 and then 1
for United States. Then comes the appropriate area code, and
finally the desired telephone number.
Keep the time difference in mind: The time in Japan is +14
hours.

Domestic calls in Japan
In Japan, there are public telephones everywhere, but few actual phone booths. You can recognize them by their light
green color. Phone cards are available at the train station kiosk
and in convenience stores (such as Seven-Eleven, Family Mart,
Lawson, etc.). Both the caller and the person called say *moshi-
moshi. watasi wa … desu*. You end the conversation by saying
shitsurei shimasu or *sayōnara*.
Japanese telephone numbers consist of 9 or 10 numerals, usually in three groups. The first group is the prefix for long-distance calls.

Could you tell me where the nearest telephone booth is?
Moyori no denwa-bokkusu wa doko ni aru ka oshiete kudasaimasen ka?

I'd like to get a telephone card, please.
Denwa-kādo o ichimai kudasai.

**Could you give me some change? I'd like to get some 10-yen
and 100-yen coins.**
Okane o kuzushite kudasaimasen ka? Jū-en dama to hyaku-en
dama ga hoshii no desu ga.

What is the area code for …?
… no shigai-kyokuban wa nanban desu ka?

A long-distance call to …, please.
… e no chōkyori-tsūwa o onegai shimasu.

Using a public phone
– Remove the receiver
– Deposit money (10-yen or 100-yen coins)
– Dial the number (rapid series of beeps means the number is
  busy)

Time difference
Japan, including all the islands, is part of one time zone. In winter, clocks are 14 hours ahead of our Eastern Standard Time; in summer (daylight savings time), they are 13 hours ahead.

International calls
In a hotel, you can have overseas calls arranged for you or request them yourself, using the number 0051. After you name the country you are calling plus the telephone number, you will be connected quickly. Some telephones also allow you to dial the overseas number yourself.
Prefixes:

United States and Canada	0 01 1
United Kingdom	0 01 44
Australia	0 01 61

Emergency number for the police: 110
Emergency number in case of an accident: 119

I'd like to make a collect call.
Korekuto-kōru o onegai shimasu.

Go to No. ... booth, please.
...-ban bokkusu e dōzo.

A Telephone Conversation

Hello, this is ....
Kochira wa ... desu.

Japanese telephone users answer by saying *moshi-moshi* and then giving their name.

Hello, who is it, please?
Moshi-moshi, donata desu ka?

Good afternoon, this is ....
Kon'nichi wa, watashi wa ... desu.

192

May I speak to Mr./Mrs./Miss/Ms. ...?
... san to o-hanashi dekimasu ka?

I'm sorry, he/she is not here now.
Zan'nen desu ga, kare/kanojo wa rusu desu.

Should he /she call you?
Kare/Kanojo wa anata ni kochira kara denwa shimashō ka?

May I take a message?
Nanika o-tsutae shimashō ka?

Would you tell him that I called?
Watashi ga denwa shite kita koto o kare ni tsutaete kudasai.

"This number is not in service."
"Kono denwa-bangō wa tsukawarete orimasen."

answer the telephone, to . .	denwa o toru
answering machine	rusuban-denwa
area code	shigai-kyokuban
busy	hanashi-chū
call, to	denwa o suru, denwa o kakeru
cellular (mobile) phone	keitai-denwa
charge	ryōkin
collect call	korekutokōru
connection	setsuzoku, renketsu
dial, to	daiyaru o mawasu
information	infomēshon
international call	kaigai-tsūwa
local call	shinai-tsūwa
long-distance call	chōkyori-denwa, shigai-tsūwa
person-to-person call	tsūwa-mōshikomi
receiver	juwaki
talk	hanashi
telephone	denwa
telephone book	denwa-chō
telephone booth	denwa-bokkusu
telephone call	denwa, yobidashi
telephone card	terefon-kādo
telephone number	denwa-bangō
yellow pages	shokugyo-betsu denwa-chō

Toilet and Bathroom

Where is the restroom?
Toire wa doko desu ka?

May I use your restroom?
Anata no tokoro de toire o karite mo yoroshii deshō ka?

May I have the restroom key?
Toire no kagi o kashite itadakemasu ka?

clean	kirei, seiketsu na
dirty	kitanai
flushing toilet	suisen
Gentlemen	dansei
Japanese-style toilet	nihonshiki toire
Ladies	josei
sanitary napkin	sēri-yōhin, napukin
soap	sekken
tampon	tanpon
toilet	te-arai-ba
toilet paper	toiretto-pēpā
towel	taoru

A Short Guide to Japanese Grammar

Sentence Structure

Japanese follows a simple sentence pattern:

Subject	Object	Predicate
Kore wa This	ringo (an) apple	desu. is.
Watashi wa I	doitsu-jin German	desu. am.

This sentence order can always be retained in Japanese, since grammatical information is given by placing particles after words as markers.

Thus placing the particle **ka** after the predicate turns the sentence into a question:

Kore wa This	ringo (an) apple	desu **ka?** is?

Placing **o** after the noun creates a direct object.

Watashi wa I	ringo **o** the apple	kaimasu. buy.

- The Japanese noun almost always appears with a place marker:
  - either the particle **ga**, if it is the subject, or **wa**, if it is the topic of the sentence,*
  - or a particle (**o, ni, no,** etc.) that makes the grammatical role (case) clear,
  - or **desu**, the equivalent of "is," after the noun.

Sentence order also does not change in the various tenses and in negations.

Anata wa You	ringo o the apple	kaimashita ka? bought?
Watashi wa I	ringo o the apple	kaimasen deshita. not bought.

Interrogative words, prepositions, and even conjunctions have the nature of nouns and are treated as such syntactically. The interrogative word **doko** (where?) is treated like the nouns **Kyōto** and **eki** (train station) in the following sentences:

---

* **wa** can designate both the subject and the direct object as the sentence topic; that is, it can replace the particles **o** and **ga**. If another element of the sentence is the topic, **wa** must follow the appropriate particles, that is: **ni wa, no wa,** etc.

195

Eki wa (the) train station	doko where	desu ka? is?
Anata wa you	doko e where	ikimasu ka? go?
Watashi wa I	Kyōto e to Kyoto	ikimasu. go?
Anata wa you	doko kara from where	kimashita ka? came?
Watashi wa I	eki no mae ni in front of the train station	machimasu. wait.

Nouns

Japanese has neither definite nor indefinite articles. The grammatical information about the way a noun is used is provided by particles that are placed after the noun or pronoun and thus are known as **postpositions**. The nouns themselves are not changed. Since every noun can occupy any position within a sentence, nouns almost always are followed by their appropriate marker in the sentence: either by the appropriate postposition* or by the word **desu** (is).

Cases

wa, **ga**	use the noun in the 1st case (nominative, "who")
no (no wa)	uses the noun in the 2nd case (possessive, "whose")
ni (ni wa)	uses the noun in the 3rd case (indirect object, "to or for whom")
o, wa	use the noun in the 4th case (direct object, "whom")
wa, ga	after a noun or pronoun not only designate use in the 1st or 4th case, but also emphasize the sentence topic, which often, but not always, is the grammatical subject of the sentence. (See also footnote on page 195, on **wa, no wa, ni wa**)
	Ashita wa **Tomorrow**	nani o what	shimasu ka? are you doing?
	Kare wa **He**	hikōki de with (the) airplane	kimasu. comes.

* In a few instances, postpositions are omitted. This book also contains sentences in which the sentence element in question must appear without a postposition; these are idiomatic usages, not mistakes made by the author.

no	The particle **no** after a noun or pronoun indicates that it belongs to a person or thing, that is, it shows possession.		
	The possessor always precedes the particle **no**; the object always follows it.		
	ie no	mado	window of the house
	chichi no	ie	the house of the father
	If the particle **no** follows personal pronouns, it creates possessive pronouns: my, your, his, etc.		
	watashi no my	hon book	(whose book?)
	anata no your	kuruma car	(whose car?)
ni	1.	**ni** stands for the indirect object (dative) and answers the question "to or for whom?"	
		Kare wa He	okāsan ni to the mother	agemasu gives
	2.	**ni** is used to designate the space, place, or point in time at which someone or something is located: **ni** answers the questions "where?" and "when?"	
		Hoteru **ni** tomarimashita. "In a hotel (I) stayed"; I stayed in a hotel.	
		Nanji **ni** kimasuka? "When (you) will come?"; What time will you come?	
o		The particle **o** after a noun has the function of the direct object/accusative ("whom or what?")	
		Tokei o kaimasu. "A clock (I) to buy"; I'm buying a clock.	

Additional Particles

A few other particles are listed below. They function along the same lines as the "case particles."

e (to)	indicates direction in response to the question "where (to)?"
	Depāto **e** ikimasu. I'm going to the department store.
	Doitsu **e** kaerimasu. I'm going back to Germany.
de (in [the])	indicates the place of an action in response to the question "where?"
	Nihon **de** kaimashita Bought in Japan.

SHORT GRAMMAR

de (with, by means of)	de (with, by means of) indicates the means by which something occurs: "with what?"
	Ohashi **de** tabemasu. I eat with chopsticks. Takushi **de** ikimasu. I'm going by taxi.
made (until up to)	made (until, up to) indicates the point in time or space until which an action or a condition continues: "Until when/up to where?"
	Baseru **made** ... As far as Basel ... Kyō **made** ... Until today ... Itsu kara itsu **made** ... ka? From when until when ...?
kara (from)	indicates the point in time or space at which an activity begins: "from/since when/where?"
	Kinō **kara** byōki desu. I've been ill since yesterday. Ima **kara** ginkō ni ikimasu. (Starting) now I'm going to the bank. Itsu **kara** gakkō ni ikimasu ka? How long have you been going to school? Ashita **kara** ikimasu. I'm going as of tomorrow.
ka	at the end of a sentence means the same as a question mark. This particle **ka** is the only difference between a declarative statement and a question.
	Ringo o kaimasu. You're buying an apple. Ringo o kaimasu ka? Are you buying an apple?

Plural

Generally the plural is not indicated through the noun. Usually the meaning is revealed by the context, for example, by the use of designations of quantity such as **takusan** (much) etc. For persons, plural endings are customarily formed by adding –**tachi** or –**gata** (polite) or –**ra** to the end of the noun.

kodomo	child	→	kodomo-tachi	the children
sensei	teacher	→	sensei-gata	the teachers
kare	he	→	kare-ra	they

Personal Pronouns

They are more rarely used in Japanese than in English. Unlike English, Japanese does not require the use of a personal pronoun with the conjugated verb.

| Kyōto e ikimasu. | I'm going to Kyoto. *or* You're going to Kyoto. |
| "go to Kyoto." | *or* He's going to Kyoto. *or* We're going to Kyoto. |

Since the conjugated verb usually is used without a personal pronoun and the conjugational endings give no clue as to the person, because they are the same for all persons, only the context can tell you whether **I** or **you** or **they** is meant.

Pattern

Singular		Plural	
I	watashi / watakushi	we	watashi-tachi / watakushi-tachi
you	anata	you	anata-tachi
he	kare	they *(m)*	kare-tachi
she	kanojo	they *(f)*	kanojo-tachi
		they *(n)*	kare-ra

• Since the personal pronouns generally represent the sentence topic, they are usually followed by the particle **wa**:

| Watashi wa doitsu-jin desu. | I am (a) German. |
| Anata wa nihon-jin desu ka? | Are you (a) Japanese? |

A Japanese does not define himself as an individual, but in his social context. Adults speak differently with children than with other adults, children speak differently with adults than with other children, and men speak with each other differently than with women. Employees speak differently with their bosses than with other employees, etc. This is expressed in the choice of personal pronouns, among other things. Thus the Japanese language has a large number of personal pronouns, in order to express respect or politeness, equal social level, or, for example, to address someone during a dispute. Some examples:

I

watakushi	polite
watashi	neutral, standard
boku	familiar, used only by men
ore	familiar/vulgar, used only by men (to express annoyance, etc.)

you

anata	polite or neutral
anta	familiar (more often used by women, but also by men)
omae	familiar/vulgar, more often used by men, but also by women (corresponds to **ore**)

When addressing someone, the personal pronouns are used more rarely in Japanese than in English. Once you know someone, you prefer to address him by his name or title, even if he is your direct partner in conversation.

Anata wa sensei desu ka? Are you a teacher?
Sumisu-san wa sensei desu ka? Are you (Mr./Mrs. Sumisu) a teacher?

• By the way: Never address someone by his name or talk about him without appending –san (Mr./Mrs./Miss) to his or her given name or family name.

Forms of Address Inside the Family
Younger siblings do not address their older brothers or sisters by their given name, but by their title, which expresses the difference in age:

For example:
onii-san	elder brother
oneˉ-san	elder sister

A distinction is also drawn between speaking about your mother and speaking to your mother, and between speaking about your own children and speaking about those of your partner in conversation.

haha	my mother
chichi	my father
kodomo	my child(ren)
musuko	my son
musume	my daughter
kanai	my wife
shujin	my husband

okāsan	Mother *(as form of address)*
	your mother
otōsan	Father *(as form of address)*
	your father
okosan	your children
musuko-san	your son
musume-san	your daughter
okusan	your wife
goshujin	your husband

he, she

In English, these 3rd person personal pronouns are used when two people are talking about a third. Since a Japanese prefers to use a name or title even when addressing someone (2nd person), the personal pronoun for the 3rd person is even more rarely used. If you don't know the name, you speak in the 3rd person of

> **ano kata** *(polite)*   this person
> **ano hito**   this person

Use of the Personal Pronouns in the Cases

The same rules apply as for nouns: The grammatical information is expressed by the particles. For example, if you add **no** after a personal pronoun, you are expressing the genitive, that is, indicating possession:

> watashi no   my
> anata no   your
> onēsan no   the . . . of the elder sister

Verbs

There are no special forms for number, person, and gender. Verbs frequently are used without personal pronouns.

> kaimasu   I buy, you buy, he/she/it buys, we buy, you buy, they buy

Japanese has only two real tenses: present and past. The future is expressed through other means.

The special feature of Japanese verbs is the multiplicity of endings that can be used to express nuances, such as an invitation to joint action, a wish, disinclination, etc. In addition, there are differences in regard to politeness. The forms differ, depending on whether you are speaking to an equal or to a person in a higher position. Many of these nuances are expressed by special endings that are attached to the verb stem.

Verb Groups

Depending on their infinitive ending, verbs are divided into two groups:

Group 1 (**u**-verbs):	verbs that do not end in –**eru, -iru**
	yom**u** to read kak**u** to write
Group 2 (**ru**-verbs):	verbs that end in –**iru** or –**eru**
	dek**iru** to be able kang**aeru** to think

Formation of the Verb Stem

Group 1:   With this group, the verb stem is obtained simply by dropping the –**u**. To attach the endings, an –**i**- is inserted between the stem and the ending.

verb		stem
yomu	to read	**yom-**
nomu	to drink	**nom-**
kaku	to write	**kak-**
kau	to buy	**ka-**

Group 2:   With this group, the –**ru** is dropped, and the endings are directly attached.

verb		stem
dekiru	to be able (can)	**deki-**
yomeru	to be able to read	**yome-**
taberu	to eat	**tabe-**

Tenses

Present

Japanese has

—an affirmative form of the present and

—two negative forms, one of which is polite, the other, neutral.

The affirmative form of the present is created by attaching the ending **–masu** to the verb stem:

deki**masu** I can, you can, he can, etc.

The negative polite form is derived by adding **–masen** to the verb stem:

deki**masen** I can't, you can't, etc.

The negative neutral form is formed:
for Group 1 by adding **–anai,**

yom**anai** I don't read, you don't read, you (pl.) don't read, etc.
hatarak**anai** I don't work, you don't work, etc.

for Group 2 by adding **–nai.**

deki**nai** I can't, you can't, etc.

verb	stem	affirmative	negative (polite)	negative (neutral)
yomu	yom-i-	yomi**masu**	yomi**masen**	yom**anai**
hataraku	hatarak-i-	hataraki**masu**	hataraki**masen**	hatarak**anai**
dekiru	deki-	deki**masu**	deki**masen**	deki**nai**

Past

Japanese has two affirmative past tenses:
—a compound form, which can always be used
—an abbreviated past tense form, which is more restricted in usage
As with the present tense, there are two negative forms here as well: one polite, the other, neutral.

The affirmative form is created by adding **–mashita** to the stem:

deki**mashita** I was able (could), you were able, he was able, etc.

The abbreviated affirmative past tense form ends in **–ta**/**–da.** This **–ta**/**–da** is attached to the verb stem, which changes in Group 1 verbs, though not always in a regular fashion:

kai**ta** I wrote/have written
yon**da** he read/has read
tabe**ta** I ate/have eaten

The formation of the **–ta** form follows the same rules that apply to the formation of the **–te** form, discussed in the following section.

For the negative polite form, use the negative present tense form of the verb + **deshita**:

> dekimasen deshita   I wasn't able, you weren't able, etc.

For the neutral form, attach –**anakatta** to the stem of the Group 1 verbs:

> yom**anakatta**   I didn't read, etc.

To the stem of the Group 2 verbs, add only –**nakatta**.

> deki**nakatta**   I wasn't able, etc.

verb	stem	affirmative (long form)	affirmative (**ta** form)	negative (polite)	negative (polite)
yomu	yom-i-	yomi**mashita**	yonda	yomimasen deshita	yomanakatta
kaku	kak-i-	kaki**mashita**	kaita	kakimasen deshita	kakanakatta
dekiru	deki-	deki**mashita**	deki**ta**	dekimasen deshita	dekinakatta

The Absolute Present (–te-form)

Japanese has a form to express the absolute present, a momentary state or condition. In English, one could render it by using the words "now", "just", "at the moment". This form corresponds to the English progressive, or –ing, form.

The –**te** form in Japanese is always used in combination with a form of **iru** to be, which is treated like any other Japanese verb:

> imasu   — present
> imashita   — past
> imasen   — present, negated
> imasen deshita   — past, negated

Shinbun o yonde imasu.	I'm reading the newspaper.
Tegami o yonde imashita.	I've read the letter.
Suzuki-san o shitte imasu ka?	Do you know Mr. Suzuki?
Hai/E, shitte imasu.	Yes, I know (him).
Kono koto o shitte imashita ka?	Did you know of this thing?
Hai/E, shitte imashita.	Yes, I knew (it).

The formation of the –**te** form is not quite as regular as the other forms. It is important, since the –**te** form is also used to express the imperative and to link clauses as well.

Verb Group 1: –te is attached to the verb stem, but with a change in the final consonant of each stem.

verb		stem	consonant change	–te form
kaku	to write	kak-	k → i	kaite
kiku	to hear	kik-	k → i	kiite
aruku	to walk	aruk-	k → i	aruite
hanasu	to speak	hanas-	s → shi	hanashite
kasu	to lend	kas-	s → shi	kashite
kaeru	to return	kaer-	r → tt	kaette
shiru	to know	shir-	r → tt	shitte
matsu	to wait	mats-	ts → tt	matte
motsu	to have	mots-	ts → tt	motte
yomu	to read	yom-	m → nd	yonde
sumu	to live	sum-	m → nd	sunde

Verb Group 2: –te is added to the stem. The formation of these forms is quite regular.

verb		stem	–te form
iru	to be	i-	ite
miru	to see	mi-	mite
dekiru	to be able (can)	deki-	dekite
oboeru	to remember	oboe-	oboete
tsutomeru	to be employed	tsutome-	tsutomete

Irregular Forms

kuru	to come	kite
suru	to do	shite
iku	to go	itte
iu	to say	itte

Overview of Forms

Verb Group 1

verbs not ending in -iru, -eru		stem	–te form	–ta form	–anai form
kaku	to write	kak-	kaite	kaita	kakanai
yomu	to read	yom-	yonde	yonda	yomanai
kaeru	to return	kaer-	kaette	kaetta	kaeranai

Verb Group 2

verbs ending in –iru, –eru				–nai-Form
iru to be	i-	ite	ita	inai
miru to see	mi-	mite	mita	minai
dekiru to be able (can)	deki-	dekite	dekita	dekinai
oshieru to teach	oshie-	oshiete	oshieta	oshienai

Irregular Forms

suru to do		shite	shita	shinai
kuru to come		kite	kita	konai

Endings and Sentence Structures for Expressing Nuances

Suggestion for joint action
Expression of future action

"Let's!"

Formation: **verb stem   +   –mashō**

iku to go	iki	-mashō
Yokohama e ikimashō.	Let's go to Yokohama!	
Sukiyaki o tabemashō⁻.	Let's eat sukiyaki!	
Kimono o kaimashō.	Let's buy a kimono!	
Gorufu o shimashō.	Let's play golf!	

Expression of a wish
"I'd like to!"

Formation: **verb stem   +   –tai desu**

taberu to eat	tabe	-tai desu
Sukiyaki ga tabetai desu.	I'd like to eat sukiyaki!	
Kabuki ga mitai desu.	I'd like to see the kabuki theater.	

• Always use the particle **ga** in connection with these –**tai** forms.

"I don't want to"

Polite form:	**verb stem** + **–taku arimasen**
iku to go	iki -taku arimasen
Kyōto e ikitaku arimasen.	I don't want to go to Kyoto.

Neutral form:	**verb stem** + **–taku nai desu**
suru to do	shi -taku nai desu
Kyō wa benkyō shitaku nai desu.	I don't want to work today.

Wish form in the past tense

"I wanted to"

Formation:	**verb stem** + **–takatta desu**
iku to go	iki -takatta desu
Kyōto e ikitakatta desu.	I wanted to go to Kyoto.

Polite Request (imperative/command form)

Polite form:	**–te- Form** + **kudasai**
yomu to read	yonde kudasai
Yonde kudasai!	Please read!
Chotto matte kudasai!	Please wait a moment!

Among friends:	**verb stem** + **–nasai**
kiku to hear	kiki -nasai
kikinasai	Hear!
tabenasai	Eat!

Polite refusal/Negative imperative

"Please don't!"

Formation:	**verb stem** + **naide kudasai**
taberu to eat	tabe naide kudasai
Kore o tabenaide kudasai!	Please don't eat this!
Kore o wasurenaide kudasai!	Please don't forget this!

Brusque refusal

Formation: **–te-Form + wa ikemasen**

terebi o miru to watch television	mi-te	wa ikemasen
Terebi o mite wa ikemasen!	Watching television is out of the question!	

• Another way to express a brusque refusal is to use the words **-wa dame desu** no way.

Polite inquiry
"May I?" "Is it all right if I ...?"

Formation: **–te-Form + mo ii desu ka?**

Terebi o mite mo ii desu ka?	May I watch television?
Itte mo ii desu ka?	May I say?

Polite refusal in response to a polite inquiry

In Japan, people are very careful about declining or even saying "no." They paraphrase this in order to avoid being overly familiar. A simple **chotto**, which means a little, is adequate. Saying **chotto komarimasu** or **muzukashii desu ne** is more straightforward and means that embarrasses me.

To have to (must)

Formation: **–ta-Form + –nakute wa narimasen***
–ta-Form + –nakute wa ikemasen*

Yūbinkyoku ni ika-nakute wa narimasen.	I have to go to the post office.
Narande mata-nakute wa narimasen deshita.	I had to wait in line.
Genkin-futo o tsukawa-nakute wa ikemasen.	You have to use the cash envelope.

* The hyphen is used between the stem and the ending here only to make things clearer. Normal spelling: ikanakute, matanakute, tsukawanakute.

• When referring to yourself, use **narimasen;** when referring to other people, use **ikemasen**.

To not have to, not need to

Formation: **nai-Verbstamm + nakute mo ii**

matsu to wait, nai-Form: matanai I'm not waiting.
Matanakute mo ii desu.   You don't have to wait.

"It is better if . . ."

Formation: **–ta-Form + hō ga ii (desu)**

literally:	"Direction if good"
Watashitachi wa kaetta hō ga ii desu.	It's better if we go home.

"It is better if . . . not . . ."

Formation: **nai-Form + hō ga ii (desu)**

Osake wa nomanai hō ga ii desu.	It's better not to drink sake.

- **hō** is a noun and means "one of two sides, possibilities." Thus you can use the phrase … **hō ga** … to make a comparison.

Chikatetsu no hō ga hayai.	The city railroad is faster.

To have experienced something already

Formation: **–ta-Form + koto ga arimasu**

literally:	"the thing exists"
Kyōto ni itta koto ga arimasu.	I've already been to Kyoto.

To be able (can)

Formation:
verb stem (Group 1) + –eru
verb stem (Group 2) + –rareru

kiku	to hear	kikeru	to be able to hear
yomu	to read	yomeru	to be able to read
hanasu	to speak	hanaseru	to be able to speak
taberu	to eat	taberareru	to be able to eat

Another way of expressing **to be able (can)**:

Infinitive + koto ga dekiru

Dekiru to be able (can)	koto thing
Nihongo o hanasu koto ga dekimasu.	I can speak Japanese.

Passive Voice

The passive voice is rarely used in Japanese.

Formation:

verb stem (Group 1)   + -areru
verb stem (Group 2)   + -rareru

kiku	to hear	kikareru	is heard
yobu	to call	yobareru	is called
homeru	to praise	homerareru	is praised
miru	to see	mirareru	is seen
taberu	to eat	taberareru	is eaten
Seito wa sensei ni homerareru.		The pupil is praised by the teacher.	

• Once a verb is made passive, it automatically belongs to Verb
Group 2, since all passive forms end in **-eru**.
All the forms that exist in the active voice can also be expressed in
the passive voice.
The forms of **to be able (can)** frequently are identical to the passive
forms.

Kore wa taberaremasu ka?	Can one eat that?
	Is that eaten?

Conditional Form

"if," "in case"

Formation:

–ta-Form   +   –ra

literally:	"direction good is"
ame ga furu to rain	futta + -ra
Moshi ame ga futtara ikimasen.	If it rains, I won't go.
Moshi ojisan ga sore o kiitara bikkuri suru deshō.	If Uncle hears that, he probably will be surprised.

Adjectives

Adjectives are words that more precisely determine a noun. As in English, Japanese adjectives precede the noun they modify. But they also have the properties of verbs, and thus they are known as verbal adjectives.

There are two groups of adjectives, and each group is treated differently.

1. i-adjectives (true adjectives)

i adjectives always end in –**i**, preceded by **a**, **i**, **o**, or **u**.

yasui	cheap	omoshiroi	interesting
furui	old	tōi	far
atarashii	new	chiisai	small
ōkii	bit	takai	expensive

2. na adjectives (quasi-adjectives)

na adjectives are nouns that become adjectives only when **na** is added. Usually they do not end in –**i**. If they do, then the –**i** is preceded by an **e** or a consonant.

kirei	pretty	iya	bad
suki	to like	benri	practical
shizuka	quiet		

Attributive use: the pretty …, the big …
i-adjectives

furui otera	an old temple
atarashii kuruma	a new car
tōi machi	distant city

na adjectives become adjectives by the addition of **na**.

kirei na hana	a pretty flower
suki na hito	a person whom I love/like
yūmei na otera	a famous temple

Predicative use: … is pretty, … is big

Formation: **wa + adjective + desu**

Tatemono wa takai desu.	The building is tall.
Kono hon wa omoshiroi desu.	This book is interesting.

wa + na adjective (without **na**) + **desu**

Kono kissaten wa shizuka desu ne?	This cafe is quiet, isn't it?
Kenchō-ji wa yu¯mei desu ka?	Is the Kencho Shrine famous?

Both groups of adjectives have their own forms for present (affirmative, negative) and past (affirmative, negative).

As with the verbs, there exist different forms for the various social levels of language (colloquial language and polite manner of speech).

i-adjectives

Colloquial language

Present		Past	
affirmative	negative	affirmative	negative
i adjective without -i	**+ –ku nai**	**+ –katta**	**+ –ku nakatta**
atarashi-i new	atarashiku nai not new	atarashikatta was new	atarashiku nakatta was not new
chiisa-i small	chiisaku nai not small	chiisakatta was small	chiisaku nakatta was not small
furu-i old	furuku nai not old	furukatta was old	furuku nakatta was not old
ii / yo-i good	yoku nai not good	yokatta was good	yoku nakatta was not good

• **ii** and **yoi** both mean good. However, only **yoi** is used in connection with –ku or –katta.

Polite speech

Present		Past	
affirmative	negative	affirmative	negative
i adjective without -i	**+ –ku arimasen**	**+ –katta**	**+ –ku arimasen deshita**
omoshiro-i ...teresting	omoshiroku arimasen not interesting	omoshirokatta was interesting	omoshiroku arimasen deshita was not interesting
...zukashi-i	muzukashiku arimasen not difficult	muzukashikatta was difficult	muzukashiku arimasen deshita was not difficult

...ʳ the **i** adjectives is dropped in these forms.

...rence between the colloquial forms and the polite forms

...ɔnly in the negative.

na adjectives

Colloquial language

Present		Past	
affirmative	negative	affirmative	negative
na adjective without na	**+ de wa nai**	**+ datta**	**+ de wa nakatta**
kirei na pretty	kirei de wa nai not pretty	kirei datta was pretty	kirei de wa nakatta was not pretty
benri na practical	benri de wa nai not practical	benri datta was practical	benri de wa nakatta was not practical

Polite speech

Present		Past	
affirmative	negative	affirmative	negative
na adjective without na	**+ de wa arimasen**	**+ deshita**	**+ de wa arimasen deshita**
suki na to like	suki de wa arimasen to dislike	suki deshita to have liked	suki de wa arimasen deshita to have disliked

Adverbs

i adjectives are changed into adverbs by replacing the **-i** with **-ku**.

Adjective		Adverb
chiisai	small	chiisaku
atatakai	warm	atataku
yoi	good	yoku
osoi	late	osoku

Kyōto wa yoku shitte imasu.	I know Kyoto well.
Yoru osoku nemashita.	I went to bed late.
Atataku narimasu.	It's getting warm.

A **ni** is added to the **na** adjectives to make them into adverbs.

Nihongo o **jōzu ni** hanashimasu ne.	You speak Japanese well.
Sore wa **hontō ni** yokatta desu ne.	That was really good.
Kinō **genki ni** kaette kimashita.	Yesterday he came back healthy.

Common adverbs

Totemo omoshiroi desu.	Very interesting.
Taihen yorokonde imasu.	I'm very glad.
Amari oishiku arimasen.	It doesn't taste good.
Hontō ni dame desu ka?	Is it really not possible?
Yukkuri itte kudasai.	Please speak slowly.

Degree of Comparison

Degrees of comparison are expressed by using the adverbs **motto** and **ichiban,** which precede the adjectives.

Adjective	Comparative	Superlative
yasui cheap	motto yasui cheaper	ichiban yasui cheapest
furui old	motto furui older	ichiban furui oldest
yūmei famous	motto yūmei more famous	ichiban yūmei most famous

Kore ga ichiban yasui desu.	This is cheapest.
Sore wa ichiban yūmei na matsuri desu.	This is the most famous festival.

Making a Comparison

When making a comparison, you use not the comparative degree, but the phrase **(no) hō (ga)** the direction of.
The object of the comparison is followed by **yori**.

Tōkyō no hō ga ōkii desu.	Tokyo is bigger.
Shikoku wa Kyūshū **yori** chiisai desu.	Shikoku is bigger than Kyushu.
Kyōto no hō ga Tōkyō **yori** furui desu.	
Tōkyō **yori** Kyōto no hō ga furui desu.	Kyoto is older than Tokyo.

Demonstrative Pronouns

This, that, that over there, here, over there, this way, that way
Demonstrative pronouns give the Japanese language many possibilities
for forming simple sentences. They are structured according to a certain
pattern, which also can be applied to the interrogative word "where."

Position of the speaker with respect to the topic:

ko-	near the speaker
so-	near the person spoken to
a-	farther away from both the speaker and the person spoken to

The following are attached to these syllables:

–re	for things, objects (and also people)
–chira	for people
–ko	for indicating place
–chira	for indicating direction/place

Position of speaker	Place		Thing/Person		Direction/ Place	
ko-	koko	here	kore	this	kochira	here (this way)
so-	soko	there	sore	that	sochira	(that way)
a-	asoko	over there	are	that over there	achira	(that way over there)

• Demonstrative pronouns take the place of nouns and are treated
  as nouns.

Koko wa Ginza desu.	Here is the Ginza.
Asoko wa koen desu.	There is a park.
Kore o kudasai.	This one, please!
Kore wa hon desu.	This is a book.
Are wa Tōdai desu ka?	Is that the University of Tokyo?

This, these, the, that, those
By attaching the syllable **–no** to the prefixes **ko-, so-, a-,** you obtain
demonstrative pronouns, which are always used with a noun.

Kono kamera o kudasai.	This camera, please.
Ano shinbun o kudasai.	The newspaper there, please.
Sono terebi wa ikura desu ka?	How much does that television set cost?

Interrogative Words and Particles

Some interrogatives are structured according to the same pattern as the demonstrative pronouns.

doko?	where?
dore?	which?
dochira?	where to?
dono?	which?

Tōkyō eki **wa doko desu ka?**	Where is the Tokyo train station?
Koko wa **doko desu ka?**	Where are we here?
Dore ga kaitai **desu ka?**	Which one do you want to buy?
Dono hon **desu ka?**	Which book?
Dono gurai?	Which extent? (length, width, distance, time . . .)
Dono gurai tōi?	How far?

• **Dono** can be used only in combination with a noun.

doko + particle

By adding the particles already familiar to us to **doko**, we obtain additional interrogatives. This sometimes results in overlapping meanings, as in the case of **dochira** where to and **doko e**, the latter of which is more common.

doko e?	where to?
doko kara?	where from?
doko de?	where?
doko no?	from where (to be)?

Doko e ikimashō ka?	Where do we want to go?
Doko kara kimashita ka?	Where do you come from?
Doko de gohan o tabemashita ka?	Where did they eat?
Doko no hito?	Where is he from?

dare? (polite form: **donata?**) who?

dare?	who?
dare no?	whose?
dare ni?	to/for whom?

Kono hito wa dare desu ka?	Who is that?
Kore wa dare no hon desu ka?	Whose book is that?
Anata wa donata desu ka?	Who are you?

nan, nani? what?
nan before **d, t, n**; otherwise, usually **nani**

Kore wa nan desu ka?	What is that?
Nani o sashiagemashō ka?	What would you like?
Nani ga mitai desu ka?	What would you like to see?
Hoka ni nani ka?	What else would you like?

ka and **mo** after interrogatives:

doko	where	dokoka	somewhere	dokomo	nowhere
dare	who	dareka	someone/somebody	daremo	no one/nobody
nani	what	nanika	something	nanimo	nothing

• For the negative forms with **mo,** the verb is used in the negative:

Daremo imasen.	No one is there.

dō? how?
sō?

Kore wa dō desu ka?	How about it?
Dō shimashō ka?	How shall we do it?
Sō shimashō?	Shall we do it this way?
Dō itashimashite!	You're welcome! Don't mention it! *(response to a preceding Thank you!)*

itsu? when?

Basu wa itsu kimasu ka?	When will the bus come?
Itsu kara itsu made?	From when until when?
itsuka	sometime
itsumo	always

naze?, dōshite? why?

Naze kimasen ka?	Why doesn't he/she/it come?
Dōshite sore o shimasu ka?	Why are we doing that?

How much? + classifiers

Japanese has different measure words based on the kind and shape of the noun being counted.

Asking about the price:

| Ikura desu ka? | How much does ... cost? How expensive? |
| Hon wa ikura desu ka? | How much does the book cost? |

Asking about the time:

| Nanji desu ka? | What time is it? |

In addition to the phrases for price and time, Japanese uses different classifiers depending on the nature of the object or thing of which some part is being discussed, and on whether it is human or animal in nature. These words are also called counters or measure words, and a small selection of them is presented here.

–nin	people (three or more)
–hiki	animals
–mai	thin, flat things (paper, shirts, tickets)
–satsu	books
–hon	long, narrow objects (rod, trees)
–dai	technical devices

Precise distinctions are made not only in the questions; the numbers in the answers, too, use the same endings.

nan-nin?	how many people?	san-nin	3 people
nan-satsu?	how many books?	yon-satsu	4 books
nan-bon?	how many umbrellas?	rop-pon	6 umbrellas
nan-mai?	how many tickets?	nana-mai	7 tickets
Otona ichimai kudasai		A ticket for adults.	

• There are irregularities in the counters for people:

| hitori (1) | san-nin (3) |
| futari (2) | yo-nin (4) and on up are regular. |

| Itō-san ni wa kodomo ga nannin imasu ka? | How many children does Mrs. Ito have? |

• In the case of the counter **-hon**, **h** may change to **b** or **p**:

ip-pon (1)	rop-pon (6)
ni-hon (2)	nana-hon (7)
san-bon (3)	hap-pon (8)
yon-hon (4)	kyū-hon (9)
go-hon (5)	jup-pon (10)

Banana sanbon onegai shimasu.	Three bananas, please.

ikutsu desu ka?

How much of something whose nature the speaker either won't or can't specify with a classifier. The answer to a question using **ikutsu** is expressed with the original Japanese number system.

Tsukue ga ikutsu arimasu ka?	How many tables are there?
Tsukue ga itsutsu arimasu.	There are 5 tables.

Indications of Place and Time

In English, the spatial and temporal relationship between two things is expressed through prepositions. In Japanese, nouns perform this function, and they are used like nouns in a sentence. If you think of the indication of place and time **mae** as a noun and translate it as "front side," it becomes clear why it stands between the postpositions **no** (genitive) and **ni** (dative for place or time).

Tatemono	no	mae	ni	machimasu.
Building	whose	front side; in front of	at	(I) wait

At the front side of the building I wait.
→ **I'm waiting in front of the building.**

in front of	mae	Eki no mae ni. In front of the train station.
behind	ushiro	Sono ushiro desu. It's behind it.
on the other side	mukō	Gakkō wa mukō ni arimasu. The school is over there.
on this side	temae	Yūbinkyoku wa ginkō no temae desu. The post office is here, next to the bank.
nearby	chikaku	Kono chikaku ni. Near here.
next to	tonari	Ano depāto no tonari desu. Next to the department store over there.
right	migi	Migi ni magaru. Turn right.
left	hidari	Hidari ni magaru. Turn left.
inside	naka	Heya no naka ni. In the room.
outside	soto	Kaisha no soto ni. Outside of the company.
on, above	ue	Tsukue no ue ni. On the table.
under	shita	Tsukue no shita ni. Under the table.
across from	mukai	Eki no mukai ni. Across from the train station.

Connective Expressions

Here are a few of the most important connectives:

and	**to**	Hambāga **to** kōhi o kudasai.
		A hamburger and a coffee, please.
with	**to**	Kare **to** ikimasu.
		("he and I go") I'm going with him.
also	**mo**	Kōhi o nomimasu. Kēki **mo** tabemasu.
		I'm drinking coffee. I'm also eating a cake.
both ... and	**mo ... mo**	Doitsujin **mo** furansujin **mo** imasu.
		Both Germans and Frenchmen are there.
neither ... nor	**mo ... mo** + verneinte verb form	Furansu ni **mo** Itaria ni **mo** ikimasen.
		I'm going neither to France nor to Italy.
either ... or	**ka**	Kyōto **ka** Nara ni ikimasu.
		I'm going either to Kyoto or to Nara.

• Connectives always follow the noun.

Compound Sentences

In Japanese, compound sentences are formed by joining two simple clauses with a particle that is placed between the clauses, or at the end of the first clause. Some of these words are already familiar to us as postpositions or as nouns. All of them link the clauses through their lexical meaning.

kara	*(con.)*	from; therefore → **because**
mae	*(con.)*	in front of → **before**
made		until → **until**
ato		after → **after**
toki	*(n.)*	time → **when, as**
aida	*(n.)*	interval, period of time → **while**

because	**kara/ no de**	Hon o kaimasu **kara**, okane o kudasai.
		("Book I buy, therefore money please")
		Because I'm buying a book, I'm asking you for money.
		Kyō wa doyōbi **da kara**, kaisha wa yasumi desu.
		Because today is Saturday, I have the day off (the company has the day off).

		• **da** is a form of **desu**
		Tomodachi ga kuru **no de**, uchi e kaerimasu. **Because** friends are coming, I'm going home now.
before	**mae ni**	Koko ni kuru **mae ni**, Ōsaka ni sunde imashita. **Before** I came here, I lived in Osaka.
		• **mae** always requires the infinitive form of the verb, then in the second clause the conjugated form.
until	**made**	Goshujin ni au **made**, sore o shirimasen deshita. **Until** I met her husband, I didn't know it.
after	**ato de**	Benkyō shita **ato de** terebi o mimasu. **After** I've done my work, I watch television.
		• **ato de** always requires the **-ta/-da-Form** (Past Tense)
when, as	**toki**	Sore o kiita **toki**, bikkuri shimashita. **When** I heard that, I was surprised.
while	**aida**	Gohan o taberu **aida** wa terebi o mimasen. **While** I eat, I don't watch television.
		• In Japanese, two complete clauses appear in succession, linked by the **te form** in the first clause and the normal verb form in the second clause. In English this is accomplished by using **and**.
		Takushi ni **notte**, depāto e **ikimasu**. I get into the taxi and go to the department store. Kaimono o **shite**, uchi ni **kaerimashita**. I did my shopping and went home.
if	**to**	• **to** follows the verb of the first clause and states the condition for the second clause. Takushi de iku **to**, gofun gurai desu. ("Taxi with to go if, five minutes about to be.") If you go by taxi, it takes about five minutes.
and, but	**ga**	Jitaku no denwa bangō wa 457-4531 desu **ga**, jimusho wa 176-5684 desu. My private number is 457-4531, my office number 176-5684. Samui desu **ga**, soto e ikimasu. It's cold, **but** I'm going outside.

Numbers

The number system is derived from Chinese and is quite simple in structure. All numbers up to 100 billion can be made from just 15 words.

0	rei, zero	6	roku	100	hyaku
1	ichi	7	shichi (nana)	1 000	sen
2	ni	8	hachi	10 000	man
3	san	9	kuu (kyuu)	100 billion	oku
4	shi (yon)	10	juu		
5	go				

11	juu-ichi	(ten one)
12	juu-ni	(ten two)
14	juu-yon	
17	juu-nana	
20	ni-juu	(two ten)
23	ni-juu-san	(two ten three)
30	san juu	(three ten)
31	san -juu- ichi	(three ten one)
2 000	ni-sen	(two thousand)

• The following numbers have phonetic irregularities:

300	sam-byaku
600	rop-pyaku
800	hap-pyaku
3 000	san-zen
8 000	has-sen

Kore wa ikura desu ka?	How much does that cost?
Sore wa ni-sen en desu.	It costs 2,000 yen.

Old Japanese Number System

In addition to the number system derived from Chinese, Japanese has a system that predates the coming of the Chinese writing system to Japan. Only fragments of it are still extant, however: Today the numbers from 1-10 still play a role and are used for formless objects (or whenever you don't know the appropriate counters, or classifiers).

1	hitotsu	6	mutsu
2	futatsu	7	nanatsu
3	mitsu	8	yatsu
4	yotsu	9	kokonotsu
5	itsutsu	10	too

Tamanegi o yotsu to tomato o futatsu kudasai.	4 onions and 2 tomatoes, please.

Japanese—English Dictionary

To render longer Japanese words in the Roman alphabet, the *hyphen* and the *apostrophe* must be used as additional articulation marks, though they are not needed in the Japanese writing system. On occasion we have used the *hyphen* here more often than necessary, to make words more readable or to make their meaning clear from their component parts.

Unlike the hyphen, the *apostrophe* is a mark that directly affects pronunciation: Here the voice must be raised if the word in question is to be understood properly. The mark occurs primarily after the syllabic nasal **n** inside a word, when the next syllable is a vowel or starts with **n**. In the latter case, that is, if an **n** is followed by another **n,** the mark is not absolutely necessary for articulation: hence, *kon'nichi wa* or *konnichi wa,* with the former spelling preferred. But the mark is essential with a vowel that follows a closed syllable.

Example: *necessary apostrophe (raising of voice when speaking)*

In hebonshiki:	gōseisen'i	gōseiseni
Divided into syllables:	gō-sei-**sen-i**	gō-sei-**se-ni**
In syllabic system:	ごうせいせんい	ごうせいせに
Normal way of writing:	合成繊維	—
Meaning:	synthetic fiber	— / no meaning

The example also shows why the apostrophe is not needed in the syllabary, and thus it does not exist there in this function.

The foreign — primarily English — loan words and word components that are normally written in *katakana* are marked with a *. This is meant to make words easier to recognize and understand, and to help locate them in Japanese characters. As you will see at once, Japanese spelling is based on the motto "write as you speak."

There are precise rules for indicating the long vowels, which are shown in the table below compared with the way they are written in the syllabic system.

Comparison table. *Long vowels in* hebonshiki *and syllabary:*

ā	ei	ii	ō	ū
	ē (only loan words)	ī (only loan words)		
ああ	えい	いい	おう おお	うう
アー	エー	イー	オー	ウー

(Long vowels in loan words: *katakana* with a macron, or long mark)

*abogado avocado
abura oil
abura no sukunai low-fat
abura-e oil painting
aburakkoi fatty
*āchi arch
*adaputā adaptor
*aerobikku aerobic
ai love
ai suru love (v.)
aida, … no ~ ni during; between
*aidea idea
*airon o kakeru iron (v.)
aisatsu (o) suru greet (v.)
*aisu ice
*aisu-*hokkē ice hockey
aitai suru oppose (v.)
aite open
aite iru open (adj.)
aji taste
aji ga suru good-tasting
aji o tsukeru season (v.)
*ajia Asia
*ajia Asian
*ajia no, *ajia-jinno Asian
aka red
akachan baby
akari lamp
aka-*wain red wine
akeru open (v.)
akete open (adv.)
aki autumn
akiaki shita bored
akiraka ni clearly
*akuseru gas pedal
*akusesarī accessory
*akushiyon-eiga action movie
amai sweet
ame rain
amemoyō rainy
ami net
*āmondo almond
*āmu-*cheā armchair
ana hole
anata you
ana-usagi rabbit
*andāshatsu undershirt
ane elder sister
annai information
annai-nin guide

ano hito / ano koto that person/that thing
*anorakku parka
anshin suru feel easy (v.)
anshō-bangō PIN
anteizai tranquilizer
anzen kakunin security check
anzen na safe
anzen-*beruto safety belt
anzen-*pin safety pin
anzen-ryōkin deposit
anzu apricot
ao blue
*apāto apartment
*aputo-shiki tetsudō mountain railway
arashi storm
arau wash (v.)
*arerugī allergy
arifureta common
arimasu there is/are
aru have (v.)
*arukōru-bun nashi nonalcoholic
*arukōru-nashi no *bīru nonalcoholic beer
*arumi hoiru aluminum foil
asa morning; linen
asa ni in the morning
asa-gohan breakfast
ase o kaku sweat (v.)
ashi leg
ashi no ura sole
ashi no yubi toe
ashibumi *bōto paddle boat
ashihire flipper
ashita tomorrow
ashita no asa hayaku/ashita no ban early tomorrow morning/tomorrow night
asobi play
asobiba playground
asobi-tomodachi playmate
asobu play (v.)
assatte day after tomorrow
*asuparagasu asparagus
*asupirin aspirin
ataeru give (v.)
atama head
atarashii new
atari surrounding
atatakai warm
ato de later

224

atsui hot; thick (book)
atsui hibi heat wave
atsumeru collect *(v.)*
atsusa heat
au meet *(v.)*
awadate nama-*kurīmu whipped cream
ayamari fault; false
azukeru deposit *(v.)*

B

*bā bar
*bābekyū barbecue
*badominton badminton
*baipasu bypass surgery
baka na dumb
bakkin fine
*bakkugiā reverse gear
*bakku-*mirā rearview mirror
*bakku-*raito taillight
*banana banana
banchi house number
*bando band
*bando belt
*bangarō bungalow
bangō number
banji-jampu bungee jumping
*banpā bumper
bansōkō adhesive tape
*barē ballet
*bārēbōru volleyball
*bariafurī barrier-free
*barukonī balcony
basho place
*basu bus
*basugaun bathrobe
*basukettobōru basketball
*basurūmu bathroom
*basu-*tāminaru bus terminal
*batā butter
*batā-*miruku buttermilk
batsu penalty
*batterī battery
*bebī baby
*bebībetto baby bed
*bebīfōn baby monitor
*bebīfūdo baby food
*bebīrifuto babylift
*bebī-shittā babysitter
*bēju beige
*benchi bench

bengoshi lawyer
benkai excuse
benkyō suru study *(v.)*
benpi constipation
benshō suru compensate *(v.)*
bentsū bowel movement
*beru bell
*beruto belt
bessō vacation house
*besuto vest
*betto bed
*bīchi-*barēbōru beach volleyball
*bīchi-*sandaru beach sandal
bideo camcorder
*bideofirumu video film
*bideokamera video camera
*bideokasetto videocassette
*bideorekōdā video recorder
bien rhinitis
bijutsu-shō art dealer
bikini bikini
bin bottle
binbō poor
*bindingu ski binding
binsen letter paper
*bīru beer
*bīrusu virus
biyō-shi beautician
*biza visa
bō stick
bochi cemetery
bō-*choko chocolate bar
*bodībirudingu bodybuilding
bōen-*renzu telephoto lens
*bokkusu box
bōkō bladder
*bonnetto hood
*bōringu bowling
*bōru ball
*bōrupen ballpoint pen
bōshi hat
*bōto-untenmenkyoshō boat operating license
bubun part
bubun-shatai-hoken partial coverage insurance
budō grape
budōtō glucose
bun sentence
bunbōgu stationery
bunbōgu-ya stationery store
bunka culture

bunkazai-hogo protection of cultural assets
bunshō de written
*burajā brassiere
*burashi brush
*burausu blouse
*burēki brake
*burēki *oiru brake fluid
*burezā-*kōto blazer
*burīfu underpants (man's)
*burōchi brooch
*būru-asobi boule (game)
burūsu blues
bushō na lazy
buta-niku pork
*butikku boutique
byō second
byōin hospital
byōki illness
byōtō hospital ward

C

CD-*pureiyā CD player
cha-iro brown
chakuriku landing
chakushoku suru color (v.)
*chāmingu na charming
*chaperu chapel
*chekkuin suru check in (v.)
chi blood
chichi father
*chīfu chef
*chifusu typhoid
chiiki area
chiisa na kodomo yō *sokkusu anklet
chiisai small
chijin acquaintance
chikai near
chikamichi shortcut
chikatetsu subway
chikazukiyasusa friendliness
chikubi pacifier
chikyū earth
*chīmu team
chinretsu-hin exhibit
*chippu tip
*chippukādo IC card
chirigami tissue
chiryō suru treat (v.)
chishiki knowledge

*chīzu cheese
chizu map
chō intestine
chōdo exact, just
chōdo yoi toki ni timely
chōji clove
chōjō summit
chōkin jewelry-making
*chokki vest
chokkō-bin nonstop flight
chōkoku sculpture
chōkoku-ka sculptor
*chokorēto chocolate
chokusetsu direct
chokutsū through
chōkyori-*basu long-distance bus
chōkyori-*kōsu trail
chōkyori-tsūwa long-distance call
chōmiryō seasoning
chōri suru cook (v.)
chōrui-hogo-chiiki bird sanctuary
chōryoku hearing
chōsa investigation
chōsen Korea
chōsho merit
chōshoku breakfast
chōshoku o toru eat breakfast (v.)
chōshoku-*byuffe breakfast buffet
chōshū listener
chōtatsu suru supply (v.)
chōten peak
chōzō statue
*chūbu tube
chūdan suru interrupt (v.)
chūdoku poisoning
chūgoku China
chūgoku-go Chinese (language)
chūgoku-jin Chinese (person)
chūi caution
chūi suru look out (v.)
chūi wo harau pay attention (v.)
chūji-en inflammation of the middle ear
chūkan-chakuriku stopover
chūmon order
chūō center

chūō no central
chūō-dōri main street
chūō-eki central station
chūō-yūbinkyoku main post office
chūsei Middle Ages
chūsha injection
chūsha suru park *(v.)*
chūsha-jō parking garage
chūshinbu central area
chūshoku lunch

D

da kara therefore
daidokoro kitchen
*daietto diet
*daietto-shoku diet food
daigaku university
dairiten agency
daiseidō cathedral
daizu soybean
dake only
damu dam
dan step
dan no nai tsūro/dan no nai iriguchi stepless access
danbō heating
dan-*katto layer
*dansā dancer
dansei man
*dansu no *bando dance band
*dansu o suru dance *(v.)*
*dansu-jōen dance performance
danwa-shitsu telephone room
dareka somebody
daremo ... nai nobody
daremo everybody
dashi procession
de with
de aru am, are, is *(v.)*
deau meet *(v.)*
deguchi exit
*dejitaru-*kamera digital camera
dekimono boil
dekiru can
*dekki deck
demo but
denkai-shitsu no yōkai electrolyte solution

denki jikake no kurumaisu electrical wheelchair
denki no electric
denki-*renji electric range
denki-*sutando desk lamp
denki-ya electrical appliances store
denkyū lightbulb
denpō telegram
denryū electric current
densen infection
densensei no contagious
denshin-gawase wire transfer
dentaku pocket calculator
denwa telephone
denwa o kakeru/suru telephone *(v.)*
denwa-bangō telephone number
denwa-*bokkusu telephone booth
denwachō telephone book
*deodoranto deodorant
*depāto department store
*derakkusu na deluxe
*dezāto dessert
*disuko disco
dō copper
dō itashimashite You're welcome.
*doa door
doa ni kagi o kakeru lock *(v.)*
*doa no angō door code
*doa no haba door width
*doaman doorman
dōbutsu animal
dōbutsuen zoo
dōgi undershirt
dōgu tool
dōhansha companion
*doitsu Germany
*doitsu-go German (language)
*doitsu-jin German (person)
dōji ni simultaneously
doko ni mo ... nai nowhere
dokoka hoka de somewhere else
dōkoku-jin compatriot
doku poison
doku no aru poisonous
dokushin single
dōkutsu cave

*dokyumentari documentary film
*dōmu dome
dono yō ni how
doraggusutoā drugstore
*doraibu driving
*dorai-*kurīningu dry cleaning
*doraiyā hair dryer
doraiyā o ateru blow-dry (v.)
*dorama drama
*doresshingu dressing
dorobō thief
dōro-chizu road map
dōryō colleague
doryoku suru make an effort (v.)
dōyō ni similar
doyōbi Saturday

E

e picture
e o kaku paint (v.)
... e to
ebi shrimp
egaku draw (v.)
ehagaki picture postcard
eiga film
eigakan movie theater
eigo English
eigyō-jikan opening hours
eihei-kōtai changing of the guard
eisei setsubi sanitary facility
ekaki painter
eki station
*ekisutora extra
ekitai no liquid
en yen
enchō sareta shūmatsu extended weekend
engan coast
engekijō vaudeville
*enjin engine
enki suru postpone (v.)
enshō inflammation
enshutsu direction
ensō musical performance
ensoku excursion
entchō-*kōdo extension cord
erabi dasu select (v.)
erabu choose (v.)

*erebētā elevator
*etchingu etching
EU-kamēkoku no kokumin EU citizen

F

*faindā finder
*fakkusu fax
*fakkusu no kikai fax machine
*fassādo façade
*fasshon-*akusesari costume jewelry
*fāsuto fast
*feā fair
*fēn wind (hot)
*ferī ferry
*fesutibaru festival
*firumu film
*fittonesu-*sentā fitness center
*fōku fork
*fōku to *supūn ... fork and spoon
fuhai shita rotten
fuiuchi attack
fukai deep
fukai na unpleasant
fukaikan nausea
fukanō na impossible
fuke dandruff
fūkei scenery
fukin dish towel
fukkatsusai Easter
fukō bad luck
fukō ni au misfortune, have a (v.)
fuku o kiru dress (v.)
fukumarete iru included
fukumete including
fukushi-jigyō welfare work
fukusō clothes
fuminshō insomnia
fun minute
funayoi suru seasick get (v.)
funsui fountain
*furaipan-ryōri meal cooked on frying pan
furansushiki *toire French-style toilet
*furasshu-souchi flash
furikomi remittance

furoba bathroom
*furonto-*garasu windshield
furui old
furusato hometown
fūshin German measles
futatsume ni second
futekitō na unsuitable
fūtō envelope
futō pier
futō-eki antifreeze
futon futon
futotta fat
futsū de nai unusual
futsū no regular
fuyu winter
fuyu yō *taiya winter tire
fuzui-hiyō extra cost

G

*gādo shita no michi
  underpass
*gaido guide
*gaido-*bukku guidebook
gaikoku foreign country
gaikoku no foreign
gaikoku-jin foreigner
gaikoku-kawase foreign
  exchange
gaishutsu suru go out (v.)
gaiyō no external
gaka painter
gakki o hiku play a musical
  instrument (v.)
gakkō school
gakusetsu movement (music)
gaman patience
gaman dekinai impatient
*gamu chewing gum
gan cancer
ganpeki rock cliff
*garasu glass
*garasu-sei mizusashi carafe
garō art gallery
gasorin o ireru fill with gas (v.)
*gasorin yō *ponpu gas pump
*gasorinkan gas canister
gasshō-dan chorus
*gasu-*kātūshe gas cartridge
*gasukonro portable gas
  cooking stove
*gasurenji gas range

*gāze no hōtai gauze bandage
geijutsu art
geka'i surgeon
geki play
geki-dan theatrical company
gekido shite iru furious
gekijō theater
gekkei menstrual period
gekkeiju laurel tree
gekkeitai sanitary napkin
gen'in ni naru cause (v.)
*genkan-*hōru entrance hall
genkin cash
genkin de harau pay in cash
  (v.)
genkin-jidō-hikidashi-ki ATM
genkō-*raito low beam
genryō material
gensaku original
genya wilderness
geri diarrhea
gesha suru get off (v.)
getsuyōbi Monday
gezai laxative
gikkuri-goshi lumbago
gimu no nai not binding
gin silver
gin no silver (adj.)
ginkō bank
giri no ane sister-in-law (older)
giri no ani brother-in-law
  (older)
giri no imōto sister-in-law
  (younger)
giri no otōto brother-in-law
  (younger)
*girisha no Greek
gogaku-*kōsu language course
gogatsu May
gogo afternoon
gogo ni in the afternoon
gōka na luxurious
gokai misunderstanding
gōkan rape
gōkei total
gomi trash
gomi-bukuro trash bag
*gomu-*bōto rubber dinghy
*gomu-nagagutsu rubber
  boots
gomu-wa rubber band
gomu-*zōri rubber sandals
goro about

*gōru goal
*gorufu golf
*gorufukurabu golf club
*gōru-*kīpā goalkeeper
gosan suru miscalculate (v.)
gozen A.M.
gozen ni in the morning
gozenchū ni during the morning
*gurafu-zasshi illustrated magazine
*guraidingu fly a glider (v.)
*guramu gram
*gurando-*piano grand piano
*gurasu glass
*gurēpufurūtsu grapefruit
*guriru de grilled
*guriru yō sumi charcoal (barbecue)
*gurūpu group
gūzen ni coincidentally
*gyararī gallery
gyōretsu procession
gyōsei administration
gyoson fishing village
gyūniku beef
gyūnyū milk

H

ha tooth
ha ga itamu toothache
haba width
*hābu herb
ha-*burashi toothbrush
hachi bee
hachigatsu August
hachimitsu honey
hada skin
hadaka no naked
hae fly
haguki gum
haha mother
hai lung
*haibīmu high beam
haien pneumonia
hai-iro gray
haiketsu-shō blood poisoning
haikikō exhaust pipe
*haikingu o suru hike (v.)

*haikingu yō chizu hiking map
*haikingu-dō hiking trail
haikyo ruins
hairiyasusa accessibility
*haishīzun high season
ha-ita toothache
haitte kuru come in (v.)
haiyū actor
haizara ashtray
hajime beginning
hajime ni at the beginning
hajimeru begin (v.)
haka grave
haka-ishi tombstone
hakike nausea
hakken discovery
hakken suru discover (v.)
hakkiri shita clear
hakkutsu excavation
hako box
hakobu carry (v.)
hakubutsukan museum
hakushu applause
hama beach
hamaguri clam
hamaki cigar
hamigaki toothpaste
*hamu ham
hana nose
hanabi fireworks
hanaji nosebleed
hanakaze head cold
hanareru away
hanashiai conversation
hanashiau converse (v.)
hanasu speak (v.)
hanataba bouquet
hanaya flower shop
hanbun half
*handobaiku hand-driven bicycle
*handobakku handbag
*handobōru handball
*handobureki hand brake
*handokrīmu hand cream
*handomeido handmade
*hangā hanger
*hangu-*guraidā hang glider
*hangu-*guraidingu hang-gliding
haniwa terra-cotta image
hankagai downtown

230

*hanmā hammer
hanshinfuzui paraplegic
hantai contrary
hantai no opposite
hanzai crime
happa leaf
hara o tateru get angry *(v.)*
hare swelling
hareta swollen
hari needle
harigane wire
haru spring
hasami scissors
hashi bridge
hashika measles
hashira pillar
hashiru run
hashōfū tetanus
hason suru break down *(v.)*
hatake field
hataraku work *(v.)*
hatsudenki generator
hatsuon suru pronounce *(v.)*
hatten suru develop *(v.)*
hayai fast
hayaku quickly
hayari mode
hazukashigariya no shy
*heāgeru hair gel
hebi snake
*heddohōn headphone
*heddo-*raito headlight
*heihō-*mētoru square meter
heijitsu weekday
heikin no average
heisateki na closed
heiya plains
henji o suru answer *(v.)*
henkō suru change *(v.)*
hentōsen tonsils
hentōsen'en tonsillitis
henzutsū migraine
*herumetto helmet
heya room
heya no denwa room
  telephone
*heyāsutairu hairstyle
hi fire; day
hi o tsukeru set fire *(v.)*
hibiku sound *(v.)*
hidari left
hidari no left *(adj.)*
hidoi terrible

hieru freeze *(v.)*
hifu skin
higaeri-ryokō day trip
higaeri-*tsuā day tour
higashi east
higawari-*menyu daily special
hige beard
higeki tragedy
higesori yō awajō no sekken
  shaving foam
higesori yō hake shaving
  brush
higesori yō keshōsui shaving
  lotion
hijō-*burēki emergency brake
hijō-guchi emergency exit
hikari light
hikikae-ken voucher
hikikaesu go back *(v.)*
hikiniku ground meat
hikishio ebb tide
hikitori-*sābisu claim service
hikitsuen-sha nonsmoker
hikiwake draw
hikizuna tow rope
hikō flight
hiku pull *(v.)*
hikui low
hima na unhurried
hinan-goya shelter
hiningu contraceptive device
hinin-yaku contraceptive pill;
  contraceptive material
hinshitsu quality
hinshu variety
*hinto hint
hi-okoshi charcoal starter
hiroi spacious
hiru goro around noon
hiru ni at noon
hiru-gohan lunch
hiruma ni during the day
hissha-geijutsu graphic art
*hitchihaiku suru hitchhike
  (v.)
hiteiteki na negative
hito man
hitobito people
hitokire goto ni kirareta
  *chīzu sliced cheese
hitokumi pair
hitori de alone
hitotsu no one

hitsuji no niku mutton
hitsuyō to suru need *(v.)*
hitsuyō, sewa no ~ na/kaigo ga ~ na in need of care
hitsuzenteki na necessary
hiyake suntan
hiyakedome-*kurīmu suntan cream
hiyō cost
hiyoke sunshade
hiyoke-bōshi sun hat
hiza knee
hizuke date
*hobākurafuto hovercraft
hobo about
hōhō method
hoiku child care
hoji suru hold *(v.)*
hoka no other
hoken insurance
hōkō direction
hokori dust
hokōsha pedestrian
hokōsha-tengoku car-free zone
hōmon visit
hōmon suru visit *(v.)*
*hōmumeido no homemade
hon book
hone bone
honmono genuine article
honmono no genuine
hontō true
hontō ni truly
honya bookstore
honyaku suru translate *(v.)*
honyū-bin baby bottle
honyūbin no ho'onki baby bottle warmer
hōrensō spinach
horo-yane sunroof
*hōru hall
hōseki jewel
hōseki-shō jeweler
hoshi star
hoshō guarantee
hoshō-kin security deposit
hōshū reward
hōsō packing
hosoi thin
hossa spasm
hossori to shita skinny
*hōsu hose

*hosuto host
hōtai bandage
hōtai suru bandage *(v.)*
hotondo almost
hotondo nai hardly
hozon preservation
hozon suru preserve *(v.)*
hozon-kikan preservation period
hūryoku wind velocity
hyakkaten department store
hyaku-nichi-zeki whooping cough
hyōgen expression
hyōgenshugi expressionism
hyōmenteki na superficial
hyōsatsu front door nameplate
hyōshiki sign
*hyūzu fuse

I

i stomach
*iaringu earring
ibiki o kaku snore *(v.)*
ichiba market
ichiban yoi best
ichido once
ichigatsu January
ichigo strawberry
ichijikan-goto ni hourly
ichijiku no mi fig
ichinichi-jōshaken day-long ticket
ichinin-mae portion
ido well
ie house
*igunisshon-ki ignition key
ii good
ijō na unusual
ika squid
iken opinion
iki o suru breathe *(v.)*
ikiru live *(v.)*
ikkai first floor; once
ikkatsu-ryōkin lump-sum fee
iku go *(v.)*
ikuraka no somewhat
ikutsuka no some
ima now; living room
imasu there is, there are
imi meaning

imōto younger sister
inaka countryside
inazuma lightning
inchiki na kitschy
ingen kidney bean
inoru pray (v.)
*inrainā inline skate
inshō-ha impressionists
*inshurin insulin
inu dog
ippai full
irai since
iremono container
irie inlet
iriguchi entrance
iro-enpitsu colored pencil
iro-toridori diverse
irui clothes
iseki ruins
ishi stone
ishi darake no rocky
ishiki fumei no unconscious
ishiki-fumei unconsciousness
ishitsubutsu-toriatsukaijo
  lost-and-found office
isogi no urgent
isogu hurry (v.)
issho ni together
isshūkan go ni after a week
isshūkan yūkō na jōshaken
  weekly ticket
isu chair
*īsutā Easter
itai painful
itami pain
itamidome painkiller
itamu hurt
itaru tokoro de everywhere
itoko cousin
itsū stomachache
itsumo always
iu say (v.)
iwa rock
iwau celebrate (v.)
izen before
izumi spring

J

jagaimo potato
jaguchi faucet
*jakki jack

jama o suru disturb (v.)
*jamu jam
*jazu jazz
*jazu-taisō jazzercise
jibun self
jibun no own
jidai era, period
jidō automatic transmission
jidō-hanbaiki vending machine
jidōsha-tōrokushō car
  registration
jidōshiki no automatic
jidōteki na *doa no kaikōbu
  remote door opener
*jifuteria diphtheria
jijitsu fact
jikan hour; time
jikandōri on time
jiko accident
jikoku-hyō timetable
jimaku subtitle
jimen ground
jimen to onaji takasa no
  ground level
jimusho office
jinbutsu ni kan suru koto
  personal data
jin'en nephritis
jinsei life
jinseki kidney stone
jintai no hibi chapped
jinzō kidney
*jīnzu jeans
jishin self
jisoku speed per hour
jissai actually
jitensha bicycle
jitensha ni noru ride on a
  bicycle (v.)
jitensha yō *herumetto
  bicycle helmet
jitensha-kyōgi bicycle race
jitensha-ryokō bicycle trip
jitensha-senyō-dōro cycling
  path
jitsuyōteki na practical
jiyū na free
jōba horseback riding
jōba-gakkō riding school
jōdan joke
jōei show (movie)
jōen play (theater)
jōen-yoteihyō play schedule

*joggingu-*pantsu jogging pants

*joggingu-zubon jogging trousers

*jogingu o suru jog (v.)

jōheki castle wall

jōhin na elegant

jokō-eki nail polish remover

jōkyō situation

jōryū no distinguished

josei woman

jōshaji no tetsudai help for boarding

jōshaken token; ticket

jōshaken-hatsubaiguchi ticket counter

jōshaken-jidōhanbaiki ticket machine

jōshaken-kokuinki ticket canceling machine

jotei empress

joyū actress

jōzai tablet

jūbun enough

jūbun ni yaketa well-done

jūdensōchi charger

jūdoshōgaisha severely handicapped

jūgatsu October

jūichigatsu November

jūji cross

jukuren shita skilled

jukushita ripe

junbi suru prepare (v.)

jūnigatsu December

junkanki-zai medicine for circulation

junkan-shōgai circulatory ailment

jun-kōsokudōro freeway

jūsho address

jūtai traffic jam

jūtenzai filling

juwaki receiver

jūyō important

jūyō de wa nai unimportant

K

ka mosquito

ka dō ka whether

kaban briefcase

kabe wall

kabin vase

kabocha squash

*kābu curve

kachi no nai worthless

*kādigan cardigan

kado corner

kadōshogai person with reduced mobility

kaeri no kippu return ticket

kaeri-michi return trip

kaeru return, go back (v.)

kaesu give back (v.)

kaette kuru return (v.)

kafukubu abdomen

kagami mirror

kage shadow

kagi key

kagi o kakeru lock (v.)

kago basket

kagu furniture

kahei money

kai floor; shellfish; time(s)

kaidan step

kaidō main road

kaifuku suru recover (v.)

kaiga painting

kaigai overseas

kaigan seashore

kaigō meeting

kaigo ga hitsuyō na in need of care

kaikan collection (mailbox)

kaikan-jikan opening

kaikei check

kaimono o suru shop (v.)

kairo circuit

kairyō-shokuhin-ten health food store

kaisha firm

kaisoku-densha rapid train

kaisuiyokujō bathing beach

kaisuiyokujō no kanshi-nin lifeguard

kaisūken book of tickets

kaiwa conversation

kaiyō ulcer

kaji rudder

*kajino casino

kakaku hyōji price sign

kakato heel

kakawarazu, ... ni mo ~ although

kakebuton comforter
kake-kugi hook
kakeru hang (v.); run (v.); bet (v.)
kaki oyster
kaki genkin Caution: Flammable
kakitome registered mail
kakitomeru write down (v.)
kako past
kakō estuary
kaku write (v.)
kakujin everyone
kakunin suru confirm (v.)
***kamera** camera
***kamera-ya** camera shop
kami god; paper
kami no ke hair
kami o someru dye hair (v.)
kami o tokasu comb hair (v.)
kami o totonoeru fix hair (v.)
kamibukuro paper bag
kamidome hair clip
kamigata hairstyle
kami-*napukin paper napkin
kamisori razor
kamisori no ha razor blade
kamitsure no hana o senjita yakuyu chamomile tea
kamome seagull
kamu bite (v.)
***kan** can
kan tube
***kanadian *sukī** cross-country skiing
kanamono-ya hardware store
kanari rather
kanashii sad
kanazuchi hammer
kandō, (ni) ~ suru be impressed deeply (v.)
kane money
kanemochi rich
***kānēshon** carnation
kangae idea
kangofu nurse (female)
kango-nin nurse (male)
kani crab
kan'i-shindaisha no seki convertible seat of a sleeping car
kanjiru feel (v.)
kanjō-sho bill
kankaku distance; feeling; sense

kanki cold
***kan-kiri** can opener
kankō-annaisho tourist information
kankōdo film speed
kankoku Korea
kankoku no Korean
kankokugo Korean (language)
kankoku-jin Korean (person)
kankō-kyoku tourist office
kankyaku spectator
kankyō environment
kan'mei o ataete impressive
kanmiryō sweetener
kanmuri crown (tooth)
kanō na possible
kanojo she
kanribu management
kansen infection
kansetsu joint
kansha suru thank (v.)
kansō shita kami dry hair (v.)
kansōki clothes dryer
kantan na simple
***kanū** canoe
***kanū o kogu** paddle a canoe (v.)
kanzei no kakaru duty
kanzō liver
kanzume can
kao face
kaori smell
kappatsu na active
***kappu** cup
kara from
***kārā** curler
kara no empty
kara, ... ~ since
karada body
karai hot (spicy)
***kā-rajio** car radio
karakuchi dry (wine)
karashi mustard
karasu-mugi no *furēku oat flakes
kara-unten idling
kare he
kari trial
***karifurawā** cauliflower
***kāringu** curling
karino provisional
kariru borrow (v.)
***kāru** curl

karui light
kasa umbrella
kasai-hōchiki fire alarm
*kasetto cassette
*kasetto-*rekōdā cassette
  recorder
kashikoi intelligent
kashu singer
kasu lend (v.)
kata shoulder, form
katai hard
katamatta solid
katamuki inclination
katei yō hin household goods
katsu win (v.)
katsudōshogai mobility
  impediment
katsura wig
katsuretsu cutlet
kau buy
kawa river
kawaii pretty
kawa-*jaketto leather jacket
kawakasu dry (v.)
kawaku dry
kawariyasui variable
kawase exchange
kawa-seihin-ten leather goods
  shop
kayōbi Tuesday
kayui itchy
kazan volcano
kazan-funka eruption
kazari ornament
kaze wind; cold (sickness)
kaze-muki wind direction
kazoeru count (v.)
kazoku family
kazu number
*kēburu-*kā cable car
*kechiappu ketchup
kega injury
kega o suru be injured (v.)
kega-nin injured person
kegawa fur
keihō-tenmetsu-sōchi hazard
  warning flasher
keiken suru experience (v.)
keikoku ravine
keikoku-sōchi alarm
keikotsu tibia
keimusho prison
keiren cramp

keirin yō jitensha racing bike
keisan suru calculate (v.)
keisatsu police
keisatsu-kan police officer
keisha-*hōmu ramp
keishiki form
keishoku snack
keitai yō CD-*pureiyā
  portable CD player
keitai-denwa cellular phone
ke-ito woolen yarn
keiyaku contract
keiyaku o musubu contract
  (v.)
*kēki cake
*kēki-ya pastry shop
kekkan defect
kekkon suru marry (v.)
kekkon-shiki wedding
  ceremony
kenchiku architecture
kenchikubutsu building
kenchikuka architect
kengaku field trip
kengaku suru tour (v.)
ken'in suru tow (v.)
ken'in-*rifuto ski tow
kenkō na healthy
kenkō-hoken health insurance
kenkō-hoken-shō health
  insurance certificate
kenmon-jo checkpoint
kenpu-zome silk dyeing
kensa inspection
kensa suru inspect (v.)
kesa this morning
keshiin o osu cancel (ticket)
  (v.)
keshiki scenery
keshite ... nai never
keshōhin-ten perfume store
ketsuatsu (kou/tei ~) blood
  pressure (high/low)
ketsu-atsu blood pressure
ketsuekichū no *arukōru
  nōdo no jōgen upper limit of
  blood alcohol content
ketsueki-gata blood type
ketsugi suru determine (v.)
ketsugō connection
kettei suru decide (v.)
ketteiteki na crucial
ketten fault

kewashii steep
ki tree
ki ni iru like (v.)
ki o haru exert (v.)
ki o tsukeru look out (v.)
ki o tsukete carefully
kibishii hard
kibori woodcarving
kichigai crazy
*kidoni-*beruto seat belt (lap type)
kigu appliance
ki-iro yellow
kiji fabric
kikai machine
kikanshi bronchi
kikanshi-en bronchitis
kiken danger
kiken na dangerous
kiki iru listen (v.)
kikinzoku-shō jeweler
kikō climate
kikōchi no kankō excursion at a port of call
kikon married
kiku hear (v.)
kikyō returning to one's hometown
kimeru decide (v.)
kin gold
kinen no chi memorial
kin'en no shashitsu nonsmoking compartment
kinen-butsu monument
kinen-kitte commemorative stamp
kin'en-sha nonsmoking car
kingaku amount of money
kingyōki off season
kin-iro golden
kin'itsu-ryōkin flat fare
kinjo no hito neighbor
kinko safe
kinkō-ressha suburban train
kinkyū-renraku-sōchi emergency phone
kin'niku muscle
kinō yesterday
kinō o hakki suru function (v.)
kinpatsu no blonde
kinpen nearby
kinshi suru forbid (v.)

kinu silk
kinyōbi Friday
kinyū-yōshi form
kippu ticket
kirei na clean
kirei ni suru clean (v.)
kiri fog
kirikizu cut
*kirisuto-kyō Christianity
*kiro kilogram
*kiro/*kiromētoru kilometer
kiroku-eiga documentary film
*kiromēta-ryōkin charge per kilometer
kisen steamer
kisetsu season
kisetsu mae preseason
kisha train
kishi coast
kishōtsūhō weather information
kisoku regulation
kisokuteki na regular
kissaten coffee shop
*kisu kiss
*kisu o suru kiss (v.)
kita north
kitai suru expect (v.)
kitanai dirty
*kitchin kitchen
kitsuen yō shashitsu smoking compartment
kitsuen-sha smoking car
kitte stamp
kitte o haru affix a stamp (v.)
kitte-jidō-hanbaiki stamp dispenser
kizu wound
kizuato scar
kizukau be concerned (v.)
kizuku realize (v.)
kizutsuku injure (v.)
ko piece
kōbai incline
kobamu refuse (v.)
kobetsu separate
kobutsu-shō secondhand dealer
kodoku na lonely
kodomo child
kodomo no byōki children's disease

kodomo yō *pūru swimming pool for children
kodomo yō *shīto child seat
kodomo-fuku children's clothing
kodomo-jōshaken child's ticket
kodomo-waribiki discount for children
kōen park
kofū na old-fashioned
kōgai suburb
kogata-maru-*pan roll
kogata-maru-*pan no *sandoitchi sandwich roll
kōgei handicraft
kogibune rowboat
kōgō empress
kogu row (v.)
kōhai-chi hinterland
*kōhī coffee
*koin-*randorī laundromat
*koin-*rokkā coin-operated locker
kojiakeru pry open (v.)
kōji-genba construction site
kojinteki na personal
kōjō factory
kōka coin
kōka na mono expensive item
kōkai no public
kōkan exchange
kōkan no moteru likeable
kōkan suru exchange (v.)
kōkiatsu high pressure
kōkishin no aru curious
kokka state
*kokku cook
kokkyō border
koko here
kokochiyoi comfortable
kōkogaku archaeology
kōkoku o dasu advertise (v.)
*kokonattsu coconut
kokoro mind
kokoro kara sincere
kokoromi attempt
kokoromu try (v.)
kōkūbin de via airmail
kōkū-gaisha airline
kokuin o osu cancel (v.)
kokumin people
kokunai-sen domestic flight

kokuritsu-kōen national park
kokusai no international
kokusai-sen international flight
kokusai-tsūwa international call
kokuseki nationality
kokuseki hyōjiban nationality sticker
kokyō hometown
kōkyō no public
kokyū-kon'nan difficulty breathing
kōkyū-shokuryōhin-ten delicatessen
komakai fine
komaku eardrum
kome rice
*komedī comedy
*komedian comedian
komi included
komori babysitter
komugiko wheat flour
*kōn corn
kona-yuki powdery snow
konban tonight
konchū insect
*kondōmu condom
kongō shita mixed
kon-iro/anryokushoku dark blue
kono this
kono koro recently
konomashii desirable
konomi taste
konomu like (v.)
*konpasu compass
*konro stove
*konsāto concert
*konsento wall outlet
*kontakuto contact
konyaku-sha fiancé/fiancee
*kopī copy
*koppu cup
*kōrasu chorus
*korekuto-*kōru collect call
*korera cholera
kōri ice
*koruku-sen'nuki corkscrew
kōryū exchange
kōsaten intersection
kōsei-busshitsu antibiotic
koshi hip
kōshiki no official

238

kōshin reverse gear
koshō breakdown; pepper
koshō shite iru out of order
koshō-*sābisu repair service
kōsoku-dōro highway
kōsoku-jidōshadōro-ryōkin highway toll
kossetsu bone fracture
*kōsu course
*kosuchūmu costume
kōsui perfume
kotaeru answer (v.)
kōtei emperor
koten-sakka classic writer
*kōto overcoat
koto thing
kotoba language
*kotoretto cutlet
kōtsū traffic
kottō-ichi flea market
*kotton cotton
kottō-shō antique dealer
kottō-ya antique shop
kōun luck
ko-ushi-niku veal
kowareta broken
kōya wilderness
kōza account
kozeni change
kōzui flood
kozutsumi package
kubi neck
kuchi mouth
kuchi-beni lipstick
kuchibiru lip
kuchi-hige mustache
kudamono fruit
kugatsu September
kujiki sprain
kujō o iu, kujō o mōshitateru complain (v.)
kūki air
kūki-*matto air mattress
kūki-*ponpu air pump
*kukkī cookie
kūkō airport
kūkō-*basu airport bus
kūkō-shiyōryō airport duty
kumo cloud
kumori cloudy
kuni state; country
kunsei smoked goods

kunsei no smoked
*kūrā air-conditioning; radiator
*kurabu club
*kurabu no ie clubhouse
kurai dark
*kurakushon horn
*kurashikku classic
*kurasu class
*kuratchi clutch
*kurejitto-*kādo credit card
kurikaesu repeat (v.)
*kurīmu cream
*kurīmu-*chīzu cream cheese
*kurīningu suru clean (v.)
*kurīningu-ya dry cleaner
*kurisumasu Christmas
*kurisutaru crystal
kuro black
*kurōku cloakroom
kuropan rye bread
kuru come (v.)
kurubushi ankle
kuruma automobile
kuruma de no sōgei-*sābisu transportation service
kuruma no kagi car key
kuruma-isu wheelchair
kuruma-isu yō for a wheelchair
kuruma-isu-riyōsha wheelchair user
kurumi walnut
*kurūzu cruise
kusai stinky
kusari chain
kushami o suru sneeze (v.)
kushi comb
kusuri medicine
kusuri-ya pharmacy
kutsu shoe
kutsu-*burashi shoe brush
kutsu-himo shoelace
kutsū pain
kutsujoku insult
kutsu-*kurīmu shoe polish
kutsurogeru relaxing
kutsushita sock
kutsu-shokunin shoe repair
kutsu-ya shoe store
*kyabetsu cabbage
*kyabin cabin (aircraft)
kyaku guest
kyaku-hon script

*kyampingu-shō camping
  permit
*kyampu-jō campground
*kyampu-jō *gaidobukku
  camping guidebook
*kyandī candy
*kyanpu camping
*kyaputen captain
kyō today
kyo tsukete! Take care!
kyōdai brother
kyōdō no common
kyōgi-jō stadium
kyohi suru refuse (v.)
kyōiku education
kyoka sarete iru permitted
kyōkai church
kyōkai no tō steeple
kyoku-dome general delivery
kyōmibukai interesting
kyori distance
kyōtei suru agree on (v.)
kyū no sudden
kyūden palace
kyūji service
kyūjo help, aid
kyūjo-*bōto lifeboat
kyūka holiday, vacation
kyūka yō setsubi vacation
  facilities
kyūkei break
kyūkei-basho rest area
kyūkei-jo service area
kyūkyū-sha ambulance
kyūmē-dōgi life jacket
kyūmei-ukiwa life belt
kyūri cucumber
kyūsei maiden name
kyūshigai old town

M

machi town
machi no ikkaku block
machiaishitsu waiting room
machigaeru confuse (v.)
machigai mistake
machigau make a mistake (v.)
mada not yet
made till
mado window

madogawa no zaseki window
  seat
mae front
mae e forward
mae ni before
mae no mae one before last
mae, ... no ~ ni before; ago
mae-uri advance sale
*mafurā muffler
*māgarin margarine
mago grandchild
maguro tuna
mahi paralysis
mahōbin thermal flask
mainasu no negative
mainichi every day
*mairudo na mild
maitoshi every year
majime na earnest
makanai board
maku act (theater)
makura pillow
mame bean, pea
mamonaku soon
manabu learn (v.)
manga-eiga cartoon film
*manikyua manicure
mannaka middle
manpuku shita full
manuke na stupid
manzoku suru be satisfied (v.)
marui round
-masen not
*massāgi massage
massugu straight
masui anesthesia
*masukara mascara
mata again
*matchi match
*maton mutton
matsu wait (v.)
matsubazue crutch
matsuri festival
mattaku really
*mattoresu mattress
*mauntenbaiku mountain bike
mawari michi detour
*mayonēzu mayonnaise
mazeta mixed
mazushii poor
me eye
me ga sameru awaken (v.)
me no mienai hito blind

240

megane-ya optician
megusuri eyedrops
mei inscription
meibutsu special product
*meido maid
meikaku na clear
*mein main dish
*meinsutorīto main street
meisho place of interest
meiwaku o kakeru bother (v.)
mejirushi landmark
memai dizziness
memai ga suru be dizzy (v.)
men cotton; noodles; face
menbō cotton swab
menkai-jikan visiting hours
menshiki acquaintance
*mensu menstruation
*menyū menu
menzei-ten duty-free shop
*meron melon
*mētoru meter
mezamashi dokei alarm clock
mezurashii rare
mibun-shōmei-sho ID
michi street, road
michi de on the street
michi ni mayou get lost (v.)
michishio high tide
midokoro highlight
midori green
midori no hoshō-*kādo green
  international auto insurance card
migi right
migi no right (adj.)
mihon-ichi trade fair
mijikai short
mikan mandarin orange
mimi ear
mimi no kikoenai hito deaf
mimi no kusuri ear medicine
mimi o katamukeru listen
  carefully (v.)
mimi-kazari earring
mimizu earthworm
minami south
minato harbor
*mineraruwōtā mineral water
*minibā minibar
*minigorufu miniature golf
minikui ugly
minshū-ongaku folk song
minzoku people; race

minzoku no yoru evening of
  folk music
minzoku-ishō national costume
*miri, *mirimētoru milimeter
miru see, look (v.)
*miruku milk
miryō suru charm (v.)
miryokuteki na attractive
miseru show (v.)
mishiranu unfamiliar
mitasu fill in (v.)
mitsukeru find (v.)
mitsuyu smuggling
miyagemono-ten souvenir
  shop
miyako capital
mizu water
mizu-asobi yō *pūru wading
  pool
mizubōsō chicken pox
mizugi swimsuit
mizuke no ōi juicy
mizu-umi lake
mizu-*tanku water tank
mo also
mō already
mō ippō no another
mochi no yoi durable
mōchōen appendicitis
*modan na modern
*moderu model
mōdōken seeing-eye dog
modosu return (v.)
mōfu blanket
moguru dive (v.)
moji character
mokei model
mokugeki-sha eyewitness
mokuteki purpose
mokuyōbi Wednesday
mokuzai lumber
momiage sideburn
momo peach
mōmoku blind
mon gate
mono thing
monohoshi-zuna clothesline
morau receive (v.)
mori woods
mōshikomi enrollment
mōshikomu enroll (v.)
moshiku wa ... either ... or
mōshitate statement

241

***mōtābōto** powerboat
motenashi hospitality
***mōteru** motel
motsu have *(v.)*
motte iku take along *(v.)*
motte kuru bring along *(v.)*
motto more
moukeru earn *(v.)*
moyōshi-mono entertainment
***mozaiku** mosaic
muji no plain
mukae ni iku go to meet *(v.)*
mukaeru receive *(v.)*
mukaigawa ni opposite from
mukidashino bare
mune chest
muneyake heartburn
mura village
murasaki purple, violet
murasaki igai mussel
muryō free of charge
muryō de gratis
muryō no free
mushi insect
mushiatsui muggy
mushiba cavity
mushita steamed
musubi tsuki connection
musubi-himo string
musuko son
musume daughter
muzei tax-free
muzukashii difficult
myaku pulse
myōji family name
***myūjikaru** musical

N

nagagutsu boots
nagai long
nagame view
nagameru view *(v.)*
nagare stream
nagashi-dai sink
naguriau beat each other *(v.)*
naguritaosu knock down *(v.)*
-nai not
naibu de inside
***naifu** knife
naishukketsu internal bleeding

***naito-*kurabu** nightclub
***naito-*tēburu** night table
***naito-*tēburu no denki-
sutando** night table lamp
naiyō content
naka de inside
naka-niwa courtyard
naku cry *(v.)*
nakusu lose *(v.)*
nama raw
namae name
nama-ensō live performance
nama-*hamu uncured ham
***nanbā-*purēto** license plate
nanchō deaf
nanimo + *Neg.* nothing
nankō ointment
***napukin** napkin
narau learn *(v.)*
narete iru accustomed
naritatsu, ... kara ~ consist of
(v.)
naru, ... ni ~ become
naru, yoko ni ~ lie down *(v.)*
nashi pear
nashi ni without
nasu eggplant
natsu summer
natsume date
***nattsu** nut
nawa rope
naze nara for, because
nebiki discount
negau hope *(v.)*
negi leek
neji screw
nekki heat
neko cat
***nekutai** necktie
nemuru sleep *(v.)*
nen year
nenkin pension
nenrei age
nenryō yō *arukōru fuel
alcohol
nenza shite iru sprained
***neopren-sensui-fuku**
neoprene wet suit
netsu fever
netsu-kikyū hot-air balloon
ni aru there is/are
ni fureru touch *(v.)*
ni hanshite contrary to

ni hantai de aru against
ni iru there is /are
ni kyōmi ga aru, ni kyōmi o motte iru is/are interested in
ni mo kakarawazu in spite of
ni sansei de aru agree with (v.)
ni shinpai suru is/are worried about
ni tai shite opposite from; toward
ni tsuite kangaeru think about (v.)
ni tsuite nayamu is/are troubled by
ni zoku suru belong to (v.)
niban(me) second
nibanme, saigo kara ~ no second from the last
nichi yō zakka keshōhin drugstore items
nichiyōbi Sunday
nichiyōbi ni on Sunday
nigai bitter
nigatsu February
nihon Japan
nihon no Japanese
nihongo Japanese (language)
nihonjin Japanese (person)
nihonshiki *toire Japanese-style toilet
nijū duplicate
nijū no double
nikkō-yoku yō shibafu lawn for sunbathing
niku meat
nikuya butcher
nimotsu baggage
nimotsu-ichiji-azukari-sho baggage room
ningen man
ninjin carrot
nin'niku garlic
ninshin pregnancy
nintai patience
nioi smell
nioi ga suru stink (v.)
niou smell (v.)
nishin herring
nishoku-tsuki two meals included
nisshabyō sunstroke
nitchū in the daytime

nite iru similar
niwa garden
niwaka ame shower
nō brain
no baai in case of
no hoka besides
no hoka ni in addition to
no kawari ni instead of
no naka ni inside
no naka ni/de within
no shita ni under
no shusshin de aru come from (v.)
no tame ni for
no toki when
no tokoro by
no yoko side of
nobasu extend; stretch; postpone
noboriyasusa accessibility
nodo throat
nodo ga kawaita thirsty
nodo no itami throat pain
nodo no kusuri throat medicine
nohara field
nōka farmhouse
nokotte iru remain (v.)
nomi no ichi flea market
nomimizu drinking water
nomimono drink
nomiya tavern
nomu drink (v.)
norikae-*basu transfer bus
norikomu get in (v.)
nōshintō concussion
nōsotchū stroke
*nōtobukku notebook
nōyō abscess
nū sew (v.)
nuku extract (dentistry) (v.)
numachi marshland
nureta wet
nuri'e-chō coloring book
nusumu steal (v.)
nyō urine
nyūji yō *bebīshīto infant seat (car)
nyūjō entrance
nyūjō-ken admission ticket
nyūjō-ryōkin admission fee
nyūkoku immigration

O

o hikitomeru detain (v.)
o omoidasu remember (v.)
o otozureru visit (v.)
o tanoshimi ni suru look forward to (v.)
o tasukeru help (v.)
o tooshite through
o yurusu allow (v.)
ō/ōhi king/queen
obāsan grandmother
obi belt (KIMONO)
ocha tea
ōchō dynasty
odayaka na mild
odoriko dancer
odoroku be frightened; be surprised; be amazed
odoru dance (v.)
oeru finish (v.)
ōfuku no kippu round-trip ticket
*ofusaido offside
ō-goe no loud
o-hairi! Come in!
oikosu pass (v.)
*oiru oil
*oiru-kōkan oil change
oishii delicious
oiwai no kotoba congratulation
oiwai o noberu congratulate (v.)
ojiisan grandfather
ojōsan young lady
oka hill
okan chill
o-kane money
okāsan mother
okashi sweets
okashi na ridiculous
okashi-ya pastry shop
ōkesutora orchestra
ōkii big
okiniiri favorite
ōkisa size
okite iru awake
okonawareru take place (v.)
okosama yō *menyū children's menu
okosu wake up (v.)

oku put (v.)
okure delay
okurimono gift
okuru send (v.); give (v.)
okuru, ato kara ~ forward (v.)
o-kyaku customer
o-matsuri festival
omiyage souvenir
omocha toy
omocha-ya toy store
omoi heavy
omoichigai misunderstanding
omoidasaseru remind (v.)
omosa weight
omoshiroi interesting
omou think (v.)
omutsu-kōkandai changing table
onaji same
onaka stomach
onaka ga haru koto bloated stomach
onaka ga suite iru hungry
ondo temperature
onegai request
onegai suru request (v.)
ongaku music
ongaku o kiku listen to music (v.)
onna no ko girl
onsenchi hot-springs resort
*opera opera
*operetta operetta
*orenji orange
*orenji-*jūsu orange juice
oreta broken
*orību olive
*orību-*oiru olive oil
*orijinaru original
oriomite at a convenient time
oritatamishiki kuruma-isu collapsible wheelchair
oroka na stupid
ōru oar
oshaburi pacifier
oshi deaf-and-dumb person
oshieru teach (v.)
oshime diaper
osoi late
osoraku perhaps
osoreru fear (v.)
osoroshii terrible, fearful
*ōsutoria Austria

244

*ōsutoria-jin Austrian (person)
otafuku-kaze mumps
otera temple
oto sound
otoko no hito man
*ōtomīru oatmeal
otona adult
otōsan father
ototoi day before yesterday
otto husband
ō-uridashi clearance sale
owari end
oya parent
oyashirazu wisdom tooth
oyogu swim *(v.)*
ōyoso nearly; about
oyu hot water

P

*paderu-*bōto paddleboat
*painappuru pineapple
*pairotto pilot
*pākingu-*raito parking light
*pāma permanent wave
*pan bread
*panfuretto pamphlet
*panku flat tire
*pantī panties
*pantī-*sutokkingu pantyhose
*pan-ya bakery
*paraguraidā paraglider
*pāru pearl
*paruketto parquet
*pāsento percent
*paseri parsley
*pasupōto passport
*pasupōto-kensa passport check
*pātī party
*pātī-*sābisu catering
*patokā police car
*paudā powder
*pēji page
*penaruti-*eria penalty area
*pendanto pendant
*penshon pension
*petto pet
*pīman bell pepper
*pinku-iro no pink
*pinpon ping-pong
*pinsetto tweezers

*poketto-ban no hon paperback
*poketto-*naifu pocket knife
*pondo pound
*ponī pony
*poraroido-*kamera Polaroid camera
*posutā poster
*posuto mailbox
pun minute
*puragu plug
*puraibēto private
*purasuchikku plastic
*purasuchikku no fukuro plastic bag
*purattofōmu platform
*puroguramu program
*purotēze artificial limb
*pūru swimming pool
*pūru no kanshi-nin lifeguard

R

rainen next year
raiu thunderstorm
*rajio radio
*raketto racket
rakka suru fall *(v.)*
rakkasan parachute
*ramu-niku lamb
rankan handrail
*ranpu lamp
*rappu foil
ratai-*dessan nude sketch
*rebā-pate liver pâté
*reberu level
*rēdā-*kontorōru radar-controlled
*reginsu leggings
rei example
reigi-tadashii polite
reikyaku-*bakku cooler bag
reikyakuzai coolant
*reinkōto raincoat
reisei na calm
reisui cold water
reizōko refrigerator
rekishi history
*rekkā-*sābisu towing service
*rekkā-sha tow truck
*remon lemon
*remonēdo lemonade

*renji kitchen range
renmei association
renshū suru practice (v.)
*rentogen X-rays
*rentogen-shashin X-ray
  picture
*renzu lens
*rēru rail
*resepushon reception
*rēsu race
*retasu lettuce
rēto rate
rieki profit, gain
*rifuto lift; chairlift
rikai suru understand (v.)
riku land
rikujō-kyōgi athletics
ringo apple
*ringu ring
*rinneru linen
ririku suru take off (v.)
ritsuzō statue
*rittoru liter
riyū reason; ground
rōa to oshi deaf-mute
rōasha deaf-and-dumb person
*robī lobby
roji alley
rokku rock (music)
rokugatsu June
*rōpu rope
*rōrā-*sukēto roller skating
*rose rosé
roshutsu-kei exposure meter
rōsoku candle
rusuban-denwa answering
  machine
*rūto route
ryōgae money changing
ryōhō no both
ryōji-kan consulate
ryoken passport
ryoken-kensa passport
  inspection
ryōkin price, fee
ryokō trip, tour
ryokō suru travel (v.)
ryokō-dantai tour group
ryokō-kaban traveling bag
ryokō-sha traveler; tourist
ryokō-tōchaku-bi arrival date
ryokushoku-hokensho green
  international auto insurance card

ryokyaku passenger
ryōri no hon cookbook
ryōri o suru cook (v.)
ryōri-nin cook
ryōrizumi no cooked
ryōshin parents
ryōshū-sho receipt
ryū dragon
ryūkan influenza
*ryukku-*sakku backpack
ryūkō fashion
*ryūmachi rheumatism
ryūzan miscarriage

S

saba mackerel
sadamerareta fixed, decided
sāfin surfing
*sāfin-*bōdo surfboard
sagasu look for (v.)
sagi fraud
saiban-kan judge
saiban-sho court
saidan altar
saifu wallet
saigo ni finally
saigo no last
saihō-dōgu sewing kit
saikin recently
saikō at most
*saikuringu bicycling
*sain signature
saisho at first
saisho no first
saishoku-shugi vegetarianism
sakai border
sakamichi slope
sakana fish
sakana no hone fish bone
sakana-ya fish store
*sākasu circus
sakaya liquor store
sakebu shout (v.)
sakidatte in advance
*sakkā soccer
*sakkā-*gēmu soccer game
*sakkā-jō soccer stadium
*sakkā-kyōgi soccer game
sakkyoku-ka composer
sakotsu collarbone
sakuranbo cherry

*salada-*byuffe salad buffet
-sama Mr./Mrs./Miss./Ms.
samatageru prevent (v.)
samui cold
samuke chill
-san Mr./Mrs./Miss./Ms.
sanban(me) third
*sandaru sandal
sangatsu March
sanka suru participate (v.)
sankakkei-keikokuhyōji-ki triangular warning sign
sankyaku tripod
sanmyaku mountain range
*san-*oiru suntan oil
sanpo stroll
sanpo o suru take a walk (v.)
sanshoku-tsuki three meals included
sanso-kyūnyūki oxygen mask
sanson mountain village
sara plate
*sarada salad
*sarami salami
sashidashi-nin sender
sashikomi electrical outlet
sashikomu plug in (v.)
sashiosaeru seize (v.)
satō sugar
satsuire wallet
satte away
*sauna sauna
*sawā-*kurīmu sour cream
sebone spine
seibu-geki Western (film)
seibutsu still-life painting
seidōtō brake light
seifu government
seigaku-ka vocalist
seihin product
seikaku na accurate
seiketsu na clean
seiki century
seikyū-sho bill
seimei life
seinen-gappi date of birth
seisan suru settle (v.)
seishōnen youth
seiteki iyagarase sexual harassment
seiyō-yabuichigo blackberry
sekai world
seki cough; seat

seki o suru cough (v.)
sekidome-gusuri cough medicine
sekinin responsibility
sekinin no aru responsible
sekinin-sha person in charge
sekken soap
semai small, narrow
sen line
senaka back
senaka no itami backache
*senchi(mētoru) centimeter
senjitsu other day
senmendai washstand
senmenjo washroom
senmon'i specialist
sen'nuki bottle opener
senpūki electric fan
sensai na delicate
senshitsu cabin
senshū no getsuyōbi a week ago Monday
sensui-dōgu diving equipment
sensui-megane diving goggles
sentakki washing machine
sentaku washing
sentaku-basami clothespin
sentakumono laundry (clothing)
sentaku-ya laundry (shop)
*sento cent
sentsū colic
senzai detergent
*sēringu sailing
*serori celery
*serufu-*sābisu self-service
*serufu-*taimā self-timer
*sētā sweater
setsuzoku connnection
*setto-*rōshon setting lotion
sewa no hitsuyō na in need of care
shagareta hoarse
shakai-hōshi assistance service
shakkin debt
shako garage
*shanpū shampoo
sharin wheel
*sharyō-bangō car number
shashin photograph
shashin o toru take a picture (v.)
shashitsu compartment

shashō conductor
*shatsu shirt
*shawā shower
*shawā yō ekitai-sekken body shampoo
*shawā yō isu shower stool
shazai apology
shiai game
shiawase na happy
shibafu lawn
shibōbun no sukunai gyūnyū lowfat milk
shichigatsu July
shichōsha town hall
shiden streetcar
*shīdī CD
shidō guidance
shidōsha mastermind; leader
shidō-sōchi starter
shigai kyokuban area code
shigai-chīzu street map
shigaisen yobō ultraviolet protection
shigatsu April
shigoto work
shigoto o suru work (v.)
shiharai payment
shiharau pay (v.)
shihei bill
shiji instruction
shiji suru instruct (v.)
shijō market
shika + Neg. only
shikakushōgai blindness
shikakushōgaisha vision-impaired (person)
shikan crown (tooth)
shikashi but
shikichi ground
shiki'i doorsill
shikirinonai-zaseki-ressha car with benches along windows
shikiri-seki box (seat)
shikisha conductor
shima island
shima-meguri island cruise
shimatte iru closed
shimeru close (v.)
shimetta wet
shimi stain
shimo frost
shinai-*basu city bus
shinai-kankō city sightseeing

shinai-tsūwa local call
shinbō patience
shinbun newspaper
shinbun-hanbaiten-shu newspaper distributor
shindan diagnosis
shindan-jikan examination hours
shindansho diagnosis report
shingō traffic light
shiniku gum
shinjirarenai unbelievable
shinjiru believe (v.)
shinjō-sho resume, personal data
shinju pearl
shinkei nerve
shinkei shitsu na nervous
shinken na serious
shinkin-kōsoku coronary
shinkoku report
shin'nen new year
shin'nyū entry
shin'nyūro approach
shinpaku-chōseiki pacemaker
shinpu priest
shinsatsu-jikan examination hours
shinsei na holy
shinseki no related
shinsen fresh
shinsetsu na kind, friendly
shinshitsu bedroom
shinshukusei no aru hōtai elastic bandage
shintaishōgai physical handicap
shinyō trust
shinzō heart
shinzō-hossa heart attack
shinzō-shōgai heart trouble
shio salt
shio-ire salt shaker
shirase notice
shiro white; castle
shiro-kuro-*firumu black-and-white movie
shiro-*pan white bread
shiro-*wain white wine
shiru learn (v.)
*shirubā silver
*shirubā no silver (adj.)
shirushi mark

shisen glance
shishū embroidery
shishutsu suru spend (v.)
shisshin faint
shita tongue
shita ni under
shitabirame sole
shitagi underwear
shitataru drip (v.)
shitate-ya tailor
shite, ... to kōsai ~ iru keep company with (v.)
shitsū toothache
*shītsu to *kabā bed linen
shitsubō shita disappointed
shitsugyō unemployment
shitsumon question
shitte iru know (v.)
shitsumon o suru question (v.)
shiyakusho city office
shiyō-chū occupied
shizen nature
shizen no natural
shizen-dōbutsuen zoo (safari-type)
shizen-hogo-kuiki nature conservation area
shizen-shokuhin-ten natural food store
shizuka na quiet, calm
shizuke-sa quietness
shizuku drop
*shīzun season
*shīzun mae preseason
*shīzun-*offu off-season
*shō show
shōbō-sho fire station
shōchō symbol
shōdaku suru consent (v.)
shōdoku suru sterilize (v.)
shōdoku-eki disinfectant
shoen premiere
shōgaisha techō ID for the handicapped
shōgaisha yō ... for the handicapped
shōgaisha yō no chūsha-jō parking for the handicapprd
shōgaisha yō *toire toilet for the handicapped
shōgaisha-renmei association of the handicapped

shohō suru prescribe (v.)
shohōsen prescription
shōka digestion
shōka furyō indigestion
shōkai introduction
shōkaki fire extinguisher
shokki tableware
shokubutsu plant
shokubutsu-en botanical garden
shokuchūdoku food poisoning
shokudō esophagus
shokudō-sha dining car
shokugyō occupation
shokugyo-betsu denwa-chō yellow pages
shokuhin-ten grocery store
shokuji meal
shokuji no ato after a/the meal
shokuji no mae ni before a/the meal
shokuji o suru eat a meal (v.)
shokuyoku appetite
shōkyaku burn
shomei signature
shōmei suru certify (v.)
shomei suru sign (v.)
shōmei-sho certificate
shōnen boy
shōnimahi polio
shōnin witness
shōrai future
shōrai no future (adj.)
shōri victory
*shōru shawl
*shorudā-*bakku shoulder bag
shorui papers
shorui-kaban briefcase
shōsetsu novel
shōtai suru invite (v.)
*shōto short circuit
shōtotsu crash
shōtsu shorts
*shō-*uindō shop-window
shōzō portrait
shū week
shū goto ni weekly
shūchaku-eki terminal station
shuchō suru assert (v.)
shudan medium (art)
shūdōin monastery
shuei guard
shūgeki attack

shūi surroundings
shujin husband
shujutsu surgery
shūkai gathering
shukketsu bleeding
shukketsu suru bleed (v.)
shukkoku departure from a
country
shukuga celebration
shukuhaku lodging
shukuji congratulatory address
shūkyō religion
shūmatsu ni during the
weekend
shūmatsu-ikkatsu-ryōkin
weekend package rate
*shunōkeru snorkel
*shunōkeru suru snorkel (v.)
shuppatsu departure
shuppatsu suru leave (v.),
depart (v.)
shuppatsu-jikan departure
time
shuppi expense
shūri suru repair (v.)
shūri-dōgu repair kit
shurui kind
shūryō completion
shussei-chi place of birth
shuto capital
shuwa sign language
shuyaku leading role
shūyū excursion
*shyanpan champagne
*sinfonī(-*konsāto) symphony
sō de aru shall
sōba market price
sobo grandmother
sode sleeve
soegi splint
sofu grandfather
sōji cleaning
sōji suru clean (v.)
sokei-*heruniya inguinal
hernia
*soketto socket
*sokksu socks
soko bottom, there
sōkō drive
sokutatsu special delivery
solo solo
songai damage
songai o ataeru damage (v.)

sonkei respect
sono ato after that
sono hoka ni besides
sono tochi koyū no
indigenous
sō-on noise
sora sky
*sorariumu solarium
soretomo or
sori sleigh
soroban abacus
*sōseji sausage
*sōsharusutēshon social-work
facility
soshite and
*sōsu sauce
sotchū stroke
soto outdoors
soto ni outside
sōzōteki na creative
su vinegar
subarashii wonderful
subeki de aru should
subete all
*suchuwādo/*suchuwādesu
steward/stewardess
sude ni already
sugiru too much
sugite over
sugu ni immediately
sugureta excellent
sui-chū *kamera underwater
camera
suichū-yokusen hydrofoil
suiei swimming
suiei yō kutsu swimming shoes
sui-ei yō *uingu fin
(swimming)
suiei-bō swimming cap
suiei-*kōsu swimming course
suiei-*pantsu swimming trunks
suiei-senshu swimmer
suijō-*sukī water ski
suika watermelon
suiminyaku sleeping pill
suiro canal
suisaiga watercolor
suisaiga o kaku paint
watercolors (v.)
suisen flush
*suisu Switzerland
*suisu-*furan Swiss franc
*suisu-jin Swiss (person)

*suitchi switch
*suitchi o ireru switch on *(v.)*
suitō canteen
suiyōbi Wednesday
suji-chigai strain
*sukāfu scarf
*sukāto skirt
*suketchi sketch
*sukēto skating, skate
*sukētobōdo skateboard
*sukēto-*rinku skating rink
*sukī ski
suki na liking
*sukī no shidō-in ski instructor
*sukī o suru ski *(v.)*
*sukī-gakkō ski school
*sukī-gutsu ski boots
*sukī-*kōsu ski course
*sukī-*sutokku ski poles
*sukī-*zubon ski pants
sukoshi a little, some
sukunaku to mo at least
sukūtā scooter
sumai house
sumomo plum
suna no shiro sand castle
suna-ba sandbox
*sunappu-*shashin snapshot
sunda clear
*sunō-*taiya snow tire
*supāku-*puragu spark plug
*sūpā-*māketto supermarket
*supea spare tire
*supīkā speaker
*supōtsu sport
*supōtsu-*man athlete
*supōtsushūzu sneakers
*supōtsu-yōhin sports goods
suppai sour
*sūpu soup
*supūn spoon
*sūpu-zara soup dish
*suraisu slice
*suranpu slump
suri pickpocket
*surippu slip
*surippu no *patto panty liner
*surira-shōsetsu-eiga thriller
  film
*surōpu ramp
suru do *(v.)*
susumeru recommend *(v.)*
*sutajio studio

*sutanpu stamp
*sutātā starter
*sutāto-hojo-*kōdo jumper
  cable
suteki na pretty
*sutekki cane
*sutendo-*gurasu stained glass
*sutoppuraito stop light
*sutorō straw
*sūtsu suits
suwaru sit *(v.)*
suyaki unglazed pottery
*suzuki sea bass

T

*tabako cigarette, tobacco
*tabako o suu smoke *(v.)*
*tabako-ya cigar store
taberareru edible
taberu eat *(v.)*
tabi ni deru travel *(v.)*
tabidatsu depart *(v.)*
tabun perhaps
tachiagaru stand up *(v.)*
tachisaru leave *(v.)*
tachi-uo swordfish
tada de free
tadashii right
taeru, yoko ~ lay down *(v.)*
taichō ga ii fit
taida na lazy
taiho suru arrest *(v.)*
taionkei thermometer
taira na flat
tairiku continent
taishikan embassy
taishō object
taishū-engeki popular play
taisō gymnastics
*taiya tire
*taiya ga pechanko/panku
  flat tire
taiyō sun
taizai stay
takai high; expensive
takasa height
taki waterfall
takkyū ping-pong
tako kite
takoage kite-flying
*takomētā tachometer

takusan no many
*takushi-*doraibā* cab driver
*takushi-noriba taxi stand
takuwae supply
tamago egg
tamanegi onion
tame, ... no ~ ni because of
tamesu try (v.)
*tāminaru terminal
tango word
tani valley
tanjō-bi birthday
tankikan no short-term
tanku tank
tan'nō gallbladder
tanoshimi fun, pleasure, enjoyment
tanoshimu enjoy (v.); amuse (v.)
tanpen-eiga short feature
*tanpon tampon
tansu chest of drawers
tantō responsible
*taoru towel
tarege straight hair
tarinai missing
tasai na colorful
tashika na certain, sure
tassuru reach (v.)
tasuke help
tatemono building
tate-*saizu vertical format
tatoe example
tatsu stand (v.)
*tawā tower
tawashi pot cleaner
te hand
te no nigiri grip
te-arai-ba lavatory
teate suru treat (v.)
*tēbakku tea bag
tebukuro gloves
*tēburu-*kurosu tablecloth
tegami letter
teian proposal
teibō dike
teikiatsu low atmospheric pressure
teikyō suru offer (v.)
teinei na polite
teiryū-jo bus stop
tenbōdai observation platform
tengoku heaven

tenimotsu-hassō-*kauntā baggage counter
tenimotsu-hikiwatashi-jo baggage claim
tenimotsu-toriatsukai-madoguchi baggage window
*tenisu tennis
tenji braille
tenjihin exhibit
tenjikai exhibition
tenjō ceiling
tenka ignition
tenkan epilepsy
tenka-sōchi ignition system
tenkeiteki na typical
tenkiyohō weather forecast
tennō emperor
tenpi de yaku cook in an oven (v.)
tenraku suru fall (v.)
tensō suru forward (v.)
tenteki intravenous drip
*tento tent
*tento no *pōru tent pole
*tento o haru pitch a tent (v.)
*tento yō *rōpu rope for a tent
tenugui washcloth
terasu balcony
*terasu terrace
*terebi television
*terebi-shitsu television room
*terehon-*kādo telephone card
*terekkusu telex
*tēru-*raito taillight
tesuri handrail
tesūryō handling fee
*tetanusu tetanus
tezukuri no handmade
*tishu tissue paper
*tī-supūn teaspoon
to with
tō tower
to and
to iu call (v.)
to shite as
tobakujō casino
tobidatsu takeoff
tobu fly (v.)
tōchaku arrival
tōchaku suru arrive (v.)
tōchaku-jikan arrival time
tochi ground
tochū de on the way

tōdai lighthouse
todana cupboard
todoke deru report (v.)
todokede report
todoku reach (v.)
todomaru remain (v.)
tōge mountain pass
tōgei pottery
tōgeihin pottery goods
tōi far
*toire toilet
*toiretto-*pēpā toilet paper
tōji at that time
tōjō-guchi boarding gate
tōjō-ken boarding pass
tokei-ya watchmaker's
torobi de yaita simmered
tōketsu suru freeze (v.)
tōketsu shita frozen
tōki china
tokidoki sometimes
tokoya barber
tōku distant
toku ni especially
tokubetsu na special
tokubetsu ni specially
tomare! Halt!
tomaru hold (v.); stay (v.)
*tomato tomato
tomegane clasp
tomegu ski binding
tomeru stop (v.)
tomodachi friend
tōmorokoshi corn
tōnan theft
tonari no hito neighbor
*tonneru tunnel
tōnori long ride
tōnyō-byō diabetes
tōnyōbyō-kanja diabetic
toppatsu-jiken incident
toppū gust
*toraberāzu-*chekku traveler's
  check
*torakku truck
*toranku-*supēsu trunk space
*toreirā trailer
tori bird
toriatsukau handle (v.)
toride fortress
torikaeru exchange (v.);
  replace (v.); change (v.)
torikesu cancel (v.)

tori-niku chicken
torisaru remove (v.)
toriwake above all; in particular
toru take (v.)
*torukoishi-iro turquoise
toshi age; year; city
toshi no ichi year-end fair
*tōsutā toaster
*tōsuto toast
totemo very
totetsumonai stupendous
totsuzen suddenly
totte handle
tōyu kerosene
tozan mountain climbing
*T-*shatsu T-shirt
*tsuā tour
tsubasa wing
tsuchi earth
tsūchi notice
tsūchi suru notify (v.)
tsue, mōjin yō ~ white cane
  (for the blind)
tsugi no next
tsui ni finally
tsuika no additional
tsuite, ... ni ~ about
tsūjō usually
tsūjō no usual
tsūka currency
tsukamaeru catch (v.)
tsūkan-tesūryō customs
  clearance fee
tsukareru get tired (v.)
tsukareta tired
tsukau make use of (v.)
tsukeru, ... ni ~ land (v.)
tsukeru, mi ni ~ put on (v.)
tsuketasu add (v.)
tsuki moon, month
tsukisoinin attendant
tsukisou accompany (v.)
tsukizuki monthly
tsukue desk
tsukuru make (v.)
tsuma wife
tsumaranai dull
tsumari thus
tsumatta stuffed
tsumayōji toothpick
tsumbo to oshi deaf-and-
  dumb
tsume-kiri nail clipper

tsumetai cold
tsumi crime
tsunbo deaf
tsune ni always
tsurete iku take along (v.)
tsurete kuru bring along (v.)
tsuri fishing
tsuri o suru fish (v.)
*tsūrisuto tourist
tsurutsuru no kōri icy ground
tsutsumi packet
tsutsumu pack up (v.)
tsuyoi strong
tsuzuku continue (v.)
tsuzuru spell (v.)
*turekkingu-jitensha
  mountain bike

U

uchi house
uchi ni iru at home
ude arm
ude ni maku ukiwa water
  wing
ude-dokei wristwatch
udewa bracelet
udon noodles
ue above
ue e upward
ue, ... no ~ ni on; thereon
*uēbu o tsukeru get a perm
  (v.)
*uētā waiter
*uētoresu waitress
ugoku move (v.)
*uinkā turn signal
ukairo detour
uketori ni iku fetch (v.)
uketori-nin addressee
uketoru receive (v.)
uketsuke reception
uke-zara saucer
ukiwa life preserver
ukiyoe woodcut print in the Edo
  period
uma horse
uma ni noru ride a horse (v.)
umare no, umareta born
umi sea; pus
umi no yōsu sea motion
unagi eel

unchin fare
undō-jō playground
unga canal
unten suru drive (v.)
unten-menkyo-shō driver's
  license
unten-shu driver
unten-sōchi gears
ura-dōri back street
ureshii glad
ureyuki sale
urikire sold out
uritsukushi clearance sale
uru sell (v.)
*ūru wool
urusai noisy
ushiro e backward
ushiro ni in the back
ushiro, no ~ ni at the back of
usu-aoi/usu-midori light
  blue/light green
usui weak (coffee)
usukukitta niku cold meat
  (sliced)
uta song
utau sing (v.)
utsu beat up (v.)
utsukushii beautiful
utsurikawari passage
utsuru, hito ni ~ contagious
uwagi jacket

W

wa ring
*wāgon baggage cart
*wain wine
*waingurasu wineglass
*wain-ya wine store
*waipā windshield wiper
wakai young
wakamono youth
wakare o tsugeru say good-
  bye (v.)
wakeme part (hair) (v.)
wakimichi bypass
wakimizu spring
wan bay
*wanpīsu one-piece dress
warau laugh (v.)
wareru break (v.)
wareta broken

waribiki discount
warimashi-ryōkin surcharge
warui bad
wasabi horseradish (Japanese)
wasureru forget (v.)
wata cotton
watashi I
watashi no tame ni for me
watashitachi we
watashitachi no our
watasu hand over (v.)

Y

yachin rent
yado accommodation
yagi-nyū-chīzu goat cheese
yaita roasted
yakedo-gusuri burn ointment
yaku about; baked; roasted
yakusho government office
yakusō herb
yakusoku promise; deadline;
  appointment
yama mountain
yama no eki mountain station
yameru stop (v.)
yamome no widowed
yane roof
yanushi landlord
yaoya vegetable store
yappari after all
yasai vegetable
yasashii kind; gentle; simple
yasei wild
yaseta thin
yasui cheap
yasumu rest (v.)
yawarakai soft
yobidashi call
yobi-*taiya spare tire
yobō-sesshu vaccination
yobō-sesshu-techō vaccination
  record
yōchi site
*yōdo iodine
*yoga yoga
*yōguruto yogurt
yoi good
yōki container
yokogiru go across (v.)

yoko-naga(-ban) horizontal
  format
yokotawatte iru lying down
yoku often, frequently
yokusuberu (tsurutsuru no)
  kōri slippery ice
yoku tsukawareru usual,
  customary
yoku yō *surippa bathroom
  slippers
yokushitsu bathroom
yokusō bathtub
yomu read (v.)
yōnyū-*chīzu sheep cheese
yopparatta drunken
yori ijō more
yoriyoi better
yorokobashii delightful
yorokonde with pleasure
*yōroppa Europe
*yōroppa no European
*yōroppa-jin European (person)
yoru night, evening
yoru no ifuku evening clothes
yōsai fortress
yose vaudeville theater, music
  hall
yōshi form; paper
yōshiki style
yoso de elsewhere
yōtsū backache
*yotto yacht, sailboat
*yotto-asobi sailing
yowai weak
yoyaku reservation, booking;
  person-to- person call
yoyaku suru reserve (v.), book
  (v.)
yubi finger
yūbin-bangō zip code
yūbin-hagaki postcard
yūbinkyoku post office
yūbin-ryōkin postage
yūbin-yokin-tsūchō postal
  savings book
yudeta *hamu boiled ham
yūdō-*rūpu guide loop
yue ni therefore
yūenchi amusement park
yui-itsu only
yuka floor
yukai na cheerful
yuki snow

yuki-megane ski goggles
yukkuri slow
yūkō na valid
yume dream
yūmei na famous
yumigata bow shaped
yūri advantage
*Yūrō euro
yūshoku dinner

Z

zairyō material
zakotsu-shinkētsū sciatica
zan'nen regrettable
zan'nen ni omou regret *(v.)*
zan'nen-nagara unfortunately
zappi incidental expenses
zaseki-shiteiken reserved-seat
  ticket
zasshi magazine

zatsuon noise
zayaku suppository
zeikan customs
zeikan-shinsei customs
  declaration
zenbu all
zenbu no entire
zensai appetizer
zenshatai-hoken
  comprehensive auto insurance
zensoku asthma
zentō-dōen sinusitis
zenzen Not at all.
zettai ni absolutely
zōkin cleaning rag
zokuaku na kitschy
*zubon trousers
zunō brain
zutsū headache
zutsū-yaku headache medicine
zūzūshii impudent

A

a little sukoshi
A.M. gozen
abacus soroban
abdomen kafukubu
about tsuite, ... ni ~; hobo, goro, ōyoso
above ue
above all toriwake
abscess nōyō
absolutely zettai ni
accessibility hairiyasusa, noboriyasusa
accessory akusesarī
accident jiko
accommodation yado
accompany (v.) tsukisou
account kōza
accurate seikaku na
accustomed narete iru
acquaintance chijin, menshiki
act (theater) maku
action movie akushiyon-eiga
active kappatsu na
actor haiyū
actress joyū
actually jissai
adaptor adaputā
add (v.) tsuketasu
additional tsuika no
address jūsho
addressee uketori-nin
adhesive tape bansōkō
administration gyōsei
admission fee nyūjō-ryōkin
admission ticket nyūjō-ken
adult otona
advance sale mae-uri
advantage yūri
advertise (v.) kōkoku o dasu
aerobics aerobikku
affix a stamp (v.) kitte o haru
after all yappari
after a/the meal shokuji no ato

after that sono ato
after a week isshūkan go ni
afternoon gogo
again mata
against ni hantai de aru
age nenrei, toshi
agency dairiten
ago ... mae ni
agree on (v.) kyōtei suru
agree with (v.) ni sansei de aru
aid kyūjo
air kūki
air mattress kūki-matto
air pump kūki-ponpu
air-conditioning kūrā
airline kōkū-gaisha
airport kūkō
airport bus kūkō-basu
airport duty kūkō-shiyōryō
alarm keikoku-sōchi
alarm clock mezamashi dokei
all zenbu, subete
allergy arerugī
alley roji
allow (v.) o yurusu
almond āmondo
almost hotondo
alone hitori de
already mō, sude ni
also mo
altar saidan
although kakawarazu, ... ni mo ~
aluminum foil arumi-hoiru
always itsumo, tsune ni
am (v.) de aru
amazed, be (v.) odoroku
ambulance kyūkyū-sha
amount (of money) kingaku
amuse (v.) tanoshimu
amusement park yūenchi
and soshite, to
anesthesia masui
animal dōbutsu
ankle kurubushi

anklet chiisa na kodomo yō sokkusu
another mō ippō no
answer (v.) henji o suru, kotaeru
answering machine rusuban-denwa
antibiotic kōsei-busshitsu
antifreeze futō-eki
antique dealer kottō-shō
antique shop kottō-ya
apartment apāto
apology shazai
appendicitis mōchōen
appetite shokuyoku
appetizer zensai
applause hakushu
apple ringo
appliance kigu
appointment yakusoku
approach shin'nyūro
apricot anzu
April shigatsu
arch āchi
archaeology kōkogaku
architect kenchikuka
architecture kenchiku
are (v.) de aru
area chiiki
area code shigai kyokuban
arm ude
armchair āmu-cheā
around noon hiru goro
arrest (v.) taiho suru
arrival tōchaku
arrival date ryokō-tōchaku-bi
arrival time tōchaku-jikan
arrive (v.) tōchaku suru
art geijutsu
art dealer bijutsu-shō
art gallery garō
artificial limb purotēze
as to shite
ashtray haizara
Asia ajia
Asian ajia-jin, ajia no, ajia-jin no
asparagus asuparagasu
aspirin asupirin
assert (v.) shuchō suru
assistance service shakai-hōshi

association renmei
association of the handicapped shōgaisha-renmei
asthma zensoku
at a convenient time oriomite
at first saisho
at home uchi ni iru
at least sukunaku to mo
at most saikō
at noon hiru ni
at that time tōji
at the back of ushiro, no ~ ni
at the beginning hajime ni
athlete supōtsu-man
athletics rikujō-kyōgi
ATM genkin-jidō-hikidashi-ki
attack fuiuchi, shūgeki
attempt kokoromi
attendant tsukisoinin
attractive miryokuteki na
August hachigatsu
Austria ōsutoria
Austrian (person) ōsutoria-jin
automatic jidōshiki no; jidō
automobile kuruma
autumn aki
average heikin no
avocado abogado
awake okite iru
awaken me ga sameru
away hanareru, satte

B

baby bebī; akachan
baby bottle honyū-bin
baby bottle warmer honyūbin no ho'onki
baby crib bebībeddo
baby food bebīfūdo
baby monitor bebīfōn
babylift bebīrifuto
babysitter komori, bebī sittā
back senaka
back street ura-dōri
backache yōtsū, senaka no itami

backpack ryukku-sakku
backward ushiro e
bad warui
bad luck fukō
badminton badominton
baggage nimotsu
baggage cart wagon
baggage claim tenimotsu-hikiwatashi-jo
baggage counter tenimotsu-hassō-kauntā
baggage room nimotsu-ichiji-azukari-sho
baggage window tenimotsu-toriatsukai-madoguchi
bake (v.) yaku
bakery pan-ya
balcony barukonī
ball bōru
ballet barē
ballpoint pen bōrupen
banana banana
band bando
bandage hōtai
bandage (v.) hōtai suru
bank ginkō
bar bā
barbecue bābekyū
barber tokoya
bare mukidashi no
barrier-free bariafurī
basket kago
basketball basukettobōru
bathing beach kaisuiyokujō
bathrobe basugaun
bathroom yokushitsu; furoba; basurūmu
bathroom slippers yoku yō surippa
bathtub yokusō
battery batterī
bay wan
be frightened (v.) odoroku
be from (v.) no shusshin de aru
be impressed deeply (v.) kandō suru
be injured (v.) kega suru
be interested in (v.) ni kyōmi ga aru; ni kyōmi o motte iru
be troubled by (v.) ni tsuite nayamu

be worried about (v.) ni shinpai suru
beach hama
beach sandal bīchi-sandaru
beach volleyball bīchi-barēbōru
bean mame
beard hige
beat each other (v.) naguriau
beat up (v.) utsu
beautician biyō-shi
beautiful utsukushii
because nazenara
because of tame, --- no ~ ni
become naru, ... ni ~
bed linen shītsu to kabā
bed beddo
bedroom shinshitsu
bee hachi
beef gyūniku
beer bīru
before ... no mae ni, mae ni
before a/the meal shokuji no mae ni
begin (v.) hajimeru
beginning hajime
beige bēju
believe (v.) shinjiru
bell beru
bell pepper pīman
belong to (v.) ni zoku suru
belt (KIMONO) obi
belt bando, beruto
bench benchi
besides sono hoka ni, no hoka
best ichiban yoi
bet (v.) kakeru
better yoriyoi
be worried about (v.) ni shinpai suru
bicycle jitensha
bicycle race jitensha-kyōgi
bicycle trip jitensha-ryokō
bicycling saikuringu
bike helmet jitensha yō herumetto
big ōkii
bikini bikini
bill shihei, kanjō-sho, seikyū-sho
bird tori

259

bird sanctuary chōrui-hogo-chiiki
birthday tanjōbi
bite (v.) kamu
bitter nigai
black kuro
black-and-white movie shiro-kuro-firumu
blackberry seiyō-yabuichigo
bladder bōkō
blanket mōfu
blazer burezā-kōto
bleed (v.) shukketsu suru
bleeding shukketsu
blind me no mienai hito; mōmoku
blindness shikakushōgai
bloated stomach onaka ga haru koto
block machi no ikkaku
blonde kinpatsu no
blood chi
blood poisoning haiketsu-shō
blood pressure (high/low) ketsuatsu (kou/tei~)
blood type ketsueki-gata
blouse burausu
blow-dry (v.) doraiyā o ateru
blue ao
blues burūsu
board makanai
boarding gate tōjō-guchi
boarding pass tōjō-ken
boat operating license bōto-untenmenkyoshō
body karada
body shampoo shawā yō ekitai-sekken
bodybuilding bodībirudingu
boil dekimono
boiled ham yudeta hamu
bone fracture kossetsu
bone hone
book (v.) yoyaku suru
book hon
book of tickets kaisūken
booking yoyaku
bookstore honya
boots būtsu
border sakai, kokkyō
bored akiaki shita
born umare no; umareta

borrow (v.) kariru
botanical garden shokubutsu-en
both ryōhō no
bother (v.) meiwaku o kakeru
bottle bin
bottle opener sen'nuki
bottom soko
boule (game) būru-asobi
bouquet hanataba
boutique butikku
bow-shaped yumigata
bowel movement bentsū
bowling bōringu
box bokkusu, hako
box (seat) shikiri-seki
boy shōnen
bracelet udewa
braille tenji
brain zunō, nō
brake burēki
brake fluid burēki oiru
brake light seidōtō
brassiere burajā
bread pan
break (v.) wareru
break kyūkei
break down (v.) hason suru
breakdown koshō
breakfast asa-gohan, chōshoku
breakfast buffet chōshoku-byuffe
breathe (v.) iki o suru
bridge hashi
briefcase kaban; shorui-kaban
bring along (v.) tsurete kuru; motte kuru
broken kowareta, wareta, oreta
bronchi kikanshi
bronchitis kikanshi-en
brooch burōchi
brother kyōdai
brother-in-law (younger) giri no otōto
brother-in-law (older) giri no ani
brown cha-iro
brush burashi
building tatemono, kenchikubutsu

bumper banpā
bungalow bangarō
bungee jumping banjī-jampu
burn shōkyaku
burn ointment yakedo-gusuri
bus basu
bus stop teiryū-jo
bus terminal basu-tāminaru
but demo, shikashi
butcher nikuya
butter batā
buttermilk batā-miruku
buy kau
by no tokoro
bypass wakimichi
bypass surgery baipasu

C

cab driver takushī-doraibā
cabbage kyabetsu
cabin senshitsu
cabin (aircraft) kyabin
cable car kēburu-kā
cake kēki
calculate (v.) keisan suru
call yobidashi
call (v.) to iu
calm reisei na; shizukesa
camcorder bideo
camera kamera
camera shop kamera-ya
chamomile tea kamitsure no
  hana no senjita yakuyu
campground kyanpu-jō
camping kyanpu
camping guidebook kyanpu-
  jō gaidobukku
camping permit kyanpingu-
  shō
can kanzume, kan; dekiru
can opener kan-kiri
canal unga, suiro
cancel (v.) kyanseru
cancel (ticket) (v.) keshiin o
  osu
cancer gan
candle rōsoku
candy kyandī
cane sutekki
canoe kanū

canteen suitō
capital shuto, miyako
captain kyaputen
car-free zone hokōsha-
  tengoku
car key kuruma no kagi
car number sharyō-bangō
car radio kā-rajio
car registration jidōsha-
  tōrokushō
carafe garasu-sei-mizusashi
cardigan kādigan
care, in need of sewa no
  hitsuyō na, kaigo ga hitsuyō
  na
carefully ki o tsukete
carnation kānēshon
carrot ninjin
carry (v.) hakobu
cartoon film manga-eiga
cash genkin
casino kajino; tobakujō
cassette kasetto
cassette recorder kasetto-
  rekōdā
castle shiro
castle wall jōheki
cat neko
catch (v.) tsukamaeru
catering pātī-sābisu
cathedral daiseidō
cauliflower karifurawā
cause (v.) gen'in ni naru
caution chūi
Caution: Flammable Kaki
  genkin!
cave dōkutsu
cavity mushiba
CD shīdī
CD player CD-pureiyā
ceiling tenjō
celebrate (v.) iwau
celebration shukuga
celery serori
cellular phone keitai-denwa
cemetery bochi
cent sento
center chūō
centimeter senchi(mētoru)
central chūō no
central area chūshinbu
central station chūō-eki

century seiki
certain tashika na
certificate shōmei-sho
certify (v.) shōmei suru
chain kusari
chair isu
chairlift rifuto
champagne shanpan
change kozeni
change (v.) torikaeru; henkō suru
changing of the guard eihei-kōtai
changing table omutsu-kōkandai
chapel chaperu
chapped akagireshita
character moji
charcoal (barbecue) guriru yō sumi
charcoal starter hi-okoshi
charge per kilometer kiromēta-ryōkin
charger jūdensōchi
charm (v.) miryō suru
charming chāmingu na
cheap yasui
check kaikei
check in (v.) chekkuin suru
checkpoint kenmon-jo
cheerful yukai na
cheese chīzu
chef chīfu
cherry sakuranbo
chest mune
chest of drawers tansu
chewing gum gamu
chicken tori-niku
chicken pox mizubōsō
child kodomo
child care hoiku
child seat kodomo yō shīto
child's ticket kodomo-jōshaken
children's clothing kodomo-fuku
children's disease kodomo no byōki
children's menu okosama yō menyū
chill okan, samuke
China chūgoku

Chinese (person) chūgoku-jin
Chinese (language) chūgoku-go
chocolate bar bō-choko
chocolate chokorēto
cholera korera
choose (v.) erabu
chorus kōrasu; gasshō-dan
Christianity kirisuto-kyō
Christmas kurisumasu
church kyōkai
cigar hamaki
cigar store tabako-ya
cigarette tabako
circuit kairo
circulatory ailment junkan-shōgai
circus sākasu
city toshi
city bus shinai-basu
city office shiyakusho
claim service hikitori-sābisu
clam hamaguri
clasp tomegane
class kurasu
classic kurashikku
clean (v.) kurīningu suru, sōji suru, kirei ni suru
clean kirei na, seiketsu na
cleaning rag zōkin
cleaning sōji
clear meikaku na, sunda, hakkiri shita
clearance sale ō-uridashi; uritsukushi
clearly akiraka ni
climate kikō
cloakroom kurōku
close (v.) shimeru
closed heisateki na, shimatte iru
clothes dryer kansōki
clothes irui, fukusō
clothesline monohoshi-zuna
clothespin sentaku-basami
cloud kumo
cloudy kumori
clove chōji
club kurabu
club house kurabu no ie
clutch kuratchi
coast kishi, engan

coconut kokonattsu
coffee kōhī
coffee shop kissaten
coin kōka
coin-operated locker koin-rokkā
coincidentally gūzen ni
cold kanki, tsumetai, kaze, samui
cold meat (sliced) usuku kitta niku
cold water reisui
colic sentsū
collapsible wheelchair oritatamishiki kuruma-isu
collarbone sakotsu
colleague dōryō
collect (v.) atsumeru
collect call korekuto-kōru
collection (mailbox) kaikan
color (v.) chakushoku suru
colored pencil iro-enpitsu
colorful tasai na
coloring book nuri'e-chō
comb kushi
comb hair (v.) kami o tokasu
come (v.) kuru
come in (v.) haitte kuru
Come in! Ohairi!
comedian komedian
comedy komedī
comfortable kokochiyoi
comforter kakebuton
commemorative stamp kinen-kitte
common kyōdō no, arifureta
companion dōhansha
compartment shashitsu
compass konpasu
compatriot dōkoku-jin
compensate (v.) benshō suru
complain (v.) kujō o iu/kujō o mōshitateru
completion shūryō
composer sakkyoku-ka
comprehensive auto insurance zenshatai-hoken
concerned (to be) kizukau
concert konsāto
concussion nōshintō
condom kondōmu
conductor shashō, shikisha

confirm (v.) kakunin suru
confuse (v.) machigaeru
congratulate (v.) oiwai o noberu
congratulation oiwai no kotoba
congratulatory address shukuji
connection ketsugō, musubi tsuki, setsuzoku
consent (v.) shōdaku suru
consist of (v.) naritatsu, ... kara ~
constipation benpi
construction site kōji-genba
consulate ryōji-kan
contact kontakuto
contagious hito ni utsuru, densensei no
container iremono; yōki
content naiyō
continent tairiku
continue (v.) tsuzuku
contraceptive device hiningu
contraceptive material hininyaku
contraceptive pill hinin-yaku
contract keiyaku
contract (v.) keiyaku o musubu
contrary hantai
contrary to ni hanshite
conversation hanashiai; kaiwa
converse (v.) hanashiau
convertible seat (sleeping car) kan'i-shindaisha no seki
cook kokku, ryōri-nin
cook (v.) chōri suru, ryōri
cook in an oven (v.) tenpi de yaku
cookbook ryōri no hon
cooked ryōrizumi no
cookie kukkī
coolant reikyakuzai
cooler bag reikyaku-bakku
copper dō
copy kopī
corkscrew koruku-sen'nuki
corn kōn, tōmorokoshi
corner kado
coronary shinkin-kōsoku
cost hiyō

costume kosuchūmu
costume jewelry fasshon-akusesari
cotton kotton, men, wata
cotton swab menbō
cough seki
cough (v.) seki o suru
cough medicine sekidome-gusuri
count (v.) kazoeru
country kuni
countryside inaka
course kōsu
court saiban-sho
courtyard naka-niwa
cousin itoko
crab kani
cramp keiren
crash shōtotsu
crazy kichigai
cream kurīmu
cream cheese kurīmu-chīzu
creative sōzōteki na
credit card kurejitto-kādo
crime hanzai, tsumi
cross jūji
cross-country skiing kanadian sukī
crown kanmuri
crown (tooth) shikan
crucial ketteiteki na
cruise kurūzu
crutch matsubazue
cry (v.) naku
crystal kurisutaru
cucumber kyūri
culture bunka
cup kappu, koppu
cupboard todana
curious kōkishin no aru
curl kāru
curler kārā
curling kāringu
currency tsūka
curve kābu
customary yoku tsukawareru
customer o-kyaku
customs zeikan
customs clearance fee tsūkan-tesūryō
customs declaration zeikan-shinsei

cut kirikizu
cutlet katsuretsu
cycling path jitensha-senyō-dōro

D

daily special higawari-menyū
daily ticket ichinichi-jōshaken
dam damu
damage (v.) songai o ataeru
damage songai
dance (v.) odoru; dansu o suru
dance band dansu no bando
dance performance dansu-jōen
dancer odoriko
dandruff fuke
danger kiken
dangerous kiken na
dark kurai
dark blue kon-iro
dark green anryokushoku
date natsume; hizuke
date of birth seinen-gappi
daughter musume
day hi
day after tomorrow asatte
day before yesterday ototoi
day tour higaeri-tsuā
day trip higaeri-ryokō
deadline yakusoku
deaf tsunbo; mimi no kikoenai hito
deaf-and-dumb tsunbo to oshi
deaf-and-dumb person oshi; rōasha
deaf-mute rōa to oshi
debt shakkin
December jūnigatsu
decide (v.) kettei suru, kimeru
decided sadamerareta
deck dekki
deep fukai
defect kekkan
delay okure
delicate sensai na
delicious oishii
delightful yorokobashii
deluxe derakkusu na

deodorant deodoranto
depart (v.) shuppatsu suru, tabidatsu
department store hyakkaten, depāto
departure shuppatsu
departure from a country shukkoku
departure time shuppatsu-jikan
deposit (v.) azukeru
deposit anzen-ryōkin
desirable konomashii
desk tsukue
desk lamp dennki-sutando
dessert dezāto
detain (v.) o hikitomeru
detergent senzai
determine (v.) ketsugi suru
detour ukairo, mawari michi
develop (v.) hatten suru
diabetes tōnyō-byō
diabetic tōnyōbyō-kanja
diagnosis shindan
diagnosis report shindansho
diaper oshime
diarrhea geri
diet daietto
diet food daietto-shoku
difficult muzukashii
difficulty breathing kokyū-kon'nan
digestion shōka
digital camera dejitaru-kamera
dike teibō
dining car shokudō-sha
dinner yūshoku
diphtheria jifuteria
direct chokusetsu
direction enshutsu, hōkō
dirty kitanai
disappointed shitsubō shita
disco disuko
discount waribiki; nebiki
discount for children kodomo-waribiki
discover (v.) hakken suru
discovery hakken
dish towel fukin
disinfectant shōdoku-eki
distance kyori, kankaku

distant tōku
distinguished jōryū no
disturb (v.) jama o suru
dive (v.) moguru
diverse iro-toridori
diving equipment sensui-dōgu
diving goggles sensui-megane
dizziness memai
dizzy (be) memai ga suru
do (v.) suru
documentary film kiroku-eiga, dokyumentarī
dog inu
dome dōmu
domestic flight kokunai-sen
doorman doaman
door doa
door code doa no angō
door width doa no haba
doorsill shiki'i
double nijū no
downtown hankagai
dragon ryū
drama dorama
draw (v.) egaku
draw hikiwake
dream yume
dress (v.) fuku o kiru
dressing doresshingu
drink nomimono
drink (v.) nomu
drinking water nomimizu
drip (v.) shitataru
drive (v.) unten suru
drive sōkō
driver unten-shu
driver's license unten-menkyo-shō
driving doraibu
drop shizuku
drugstore nichi yō zakka keshōhin ten, doraggusutoā
drunken yopparatta
dry kawaku
dry (v.) kawakasu
dry cleaner kurīningu-ya
dry cleaning dorai-kurīningu
dry hair kansō shita kami
dry (wine) karakuchi
dull tsumaranai

dumb baka na
duplicate nijū
durable mochi no yoi
during; between aida, ... no
  ~ ni
during the day hiruma ni
during the morning
  gozenchū ni
during the weekend
  shūmatsu ni
dust hokori
duty kanzei no kakaku
duty-free shop menzei-ten
dye hair (v.) kami o someru
dynasty ōchō

E

ear medicine mimi no kusuri
ear mimi
eardrum komaku
early tomorrow morning
  ashita no asa hayaku
earn (v.) mōkeru
earnest majime na
earring mimi-kazari, iaringu
earth tsuchi, chikyū
earthworm mimizu
east higashi
Easter īsutā, fukkatsusai
eat (v.) taberu
eat a meal (v.) shokuji o suru
eat breakfast (v.) chōshoku o
  toru
ebb tide hikishio
edible taberareru
education kyōiku
eel unagi
egg tamago
eggplant nasu
either ... or moshiku wa
elastic bandage shinshukusei
  no aru hōtai
elder sister ane
electric denki no
electric current denryū
electric fan senpūki
electric range denki-renji
electric wheelchair denki-
  kurumaisu

electrical appliances store
  denki-ya
electrical outlet sashikomi
electrolyte solution denkai-
  shitsu no yōkai
elegant jōhin na
elevator erebētā
elsewhere yoso de
embassy taishikan
embroidery shishū
emergency brake hijō-burēki
emergency exit hijō-guchi
emergency phone kinkyū-
  renraku-sōchi
emperor tennō, kōtei
empress kōgō, jotei
empty kara no
end owari
engine enjin
English eigo
enjoy (v.) tanoshimu
enjoyment tanoshimi
enough jūbun
enroll (v.) mōshikomu
enrollment mōshikomi
entertainment moyōshi-
  mono
entire zenbu no
entrance iriguchi, nyūjō
entrance hall genkan-hōru
entry shin'nyū
envelope fūtō
environment kankyō
epilepsy tenkan
era jidai
eruption kazan-funka
esophagus shokudō
especially toku ni
estuary kakō
etching etchingu
EU citizen EU-kameikoku no
  kokumin
euro yūro
Europe yōroppa
European yōroppa no
European (person) yōroppa-
  jin
evening yoru
evening clothes yoru no ifuku
evening of folk music
  minzoku no yoru
every day mainichi

every year maitoshi
everybody daremo
everyone kakujin
everywhere itaru tokoro de
exact chōdo
examination hours shinsatsu-jikan, shindan-jikan
example rei, tatoe
excavation hakkutsu
excellent sugureta
exchange kōkan, kawase, kōryū
exchange (v.) torikaeru, kōkan suru
excursion shūyū, ensoku
excursion at a port of call kikōchi no kankō
excuse benkai
exert (v.) ki o haru
exhaust pipe haikikō
exhibit tenjihin, chinretsu-hin
exhibition tenjikai
exit deguchi
expect (v.) kitai suru
expense shuppi
expensive takai
expensive item kōka na mono
experience (v.) keiken suru
exposure meter roshutsu-kei
expression hyōgen
expressionism hyōgenshugi
extend (v.) nobasu
extended weekend enchō sareta shūmatsu
extension cord enchō-kōdo
external gaiyō no
extra ekisutora
extra cost fuzui hiyō
extract (dentistry) (v.) nuku
eye me
eyedrops megusuri
eyewitness mokugeki-sha

F

fabric kiji
façade fassādo
face kao
fact jijitsu
factory kōjō
faint shisshin

fair feā
fall (v.) rakka suru, tenraku suru
false ayamari
family kazoku
family name myōji
famous yūmei na
far tōi
fare unchin
farmhouse nōka
fashion ryūkō
fast fāsuto, hayai
fat futotta
father chichi, otōsan
fatty aburakkoi
faucet jaguchi
fault ketten, ayamari
favorite okiniiri
fax machine fakkusu no kikai
fax fakkusu
fear (v.) osoreru
fearful osoroshii
February nigatsu
fee ryōkin
feel (v.) kanjiru
feel easy (v.) anshin suru
feeling kankaku
ferry ferī
festival o-matsuri, fesutibaru, matsuri
fetch (v.) uketori ni iku
fever netsu
fiancé/fiancee konyaku-sha
field hatake, nohara
field trip kengaku
fig ichijiku no mi
fill in (v.) mitasu
fill with gas (v.) gasorin o ireru
filling jūtenzai
film eiga, firumu
film speed kankōdo
fin (swimming) ashihire, suiei yō uingu
finally tsui ni, saigo ni
find (v.) mitsukeru
finder faindā
fine komakai, bakkin
finger yubi
finish (v.) oeru
fire hi
fire alarm kasai-hōchiki

fire extinguisher shōkaki
fire station shōbō-sho
fireworks hanabi
firm kaisha
first saisho no
first floor ikkai
fish (v.) tsuri o suru
fish sakana
fish bone sakana no hone
fish store sakana-ya
fishing tsuri
fishing village gyoson
fit taichō ga ii
fitness center fittonesu-sentā
fixed sadamerareta
flash furasshu-sōchi
flat taira na
flat fare kin'itsu-ryōkin
flat tire taiya ga pechanko;
  panku
flea market kottō-ichi, nomi
  no ichi
flight hikō
flood kōzui
floor yuka, kai
flower shop hanaya
flush suisen
fly hae
fly (v.) tobu
fly a glider (v.) guraidingu
  suru
fog kiri
foil rappu
folk song minshū-ongaku
food poisoning
  shokuchūdoku
for no tame ni, naze nara
for a wheelchair kuruma-isu
  yō
for me watashi no tame ni
for the handicapped
  shōgaisha yō ...
forbid (v.) kinshi suru
foreign gaikoku no
foreign country gaikoku
foreign exchange gaikoku-
  kawase
foreigner gaikoku-jin
forget (v.) wasureru
fork fōku
fork and spoon fōku to supūn

form keishiki, yōshi, kata,
  kinyū-yōshi
fortress toride, yōsai
forward (v.) tensō suru, okuru,
  mae e, ato kara ~
fountain funsui
fraud sagi
free tada de, muryō no, jiyū na
free of charge muryō
freeway jun-kōsokudōro
freeze (v.) tōketsu suru, hieru
French-style toilet
  furansushiki toire
frequently yoku
fresh shinsen
Friday kinyōbi
friend tomodachi
friendliness chikazukiyasusa
friendly shinsetsu na
from kara
front mae
front door nameplate
  hyōsatsu
frost shimo
frozen tōketsu shita
fruit kudamono
fuel alcohol nenryō yō
  arukōru
full manpuku shita, ippai
fun tanoshimi
function (v.) kinō o hakki suru
fur kegawa
furious gekido shite iru
furniture kagu
fuse hyūzu
futon futon
future shōrai
future (adj.) shōrai no

G

gain rieki
gallbladder tan'no
gallery gyararī
game shiai
garage shako
garden niwa
garlic nin'niku
gas canister gasorinkan;
  gasubonbe
gas cartridge gasu-kātūshe

268

gas pedal akuseru
gas pump gasorin yō ponpu
gas range gasurenji
gate mon
gathering shūkai
gauze bandage gāze no hōtai
gears unten-sōchi
general delivery kyoku-dome
generator hatsudenki
gentle yasashii
genuine honmono no
genuine article honmono
German (person) doitsu-jin
German (language) doitsu-
  go
German measles fūshin
Germany doitsu
get a perm (v.) uēbu o
  tsukeru
get angry (v.) hara o tateru
get in (v.) norikomu
get lost (v.) michi ni mayou
get off (v.) gesha suru
get seasick (v.) funayoi suru
get tired (v.) tsukareru
gift okurimono
girl onna no ko
give (v.) ataeru, okuru
give back (v.) kaesu
glad ureshii
glance shisen
glass gurasu, garasu
gloves tebukuro
glucose budōtō
go (v.) iku
go across (v.) yokogiru
go back (v.) kaeru
go out (v.) gaishutsu suru
go to meet (v.) mukae ni iku
goal gōru
goalkeeper gōru-kīpā
goat cheese yagi-nyū-chīzu
god kami
gold kin
golden kin-iro
golf gorufu
golf club gorufukurabu
good yoi, ii
good-tasting aji ga suru
government seifu
government office yakusho
gram guramu

grand piano gurando-piano
grandchild mago
grandfather ojiisan, sofu
grandmother sobo, obāsan
grape budō
grapefruit gurēpu-furūtsu
graphic art hissha-geijutsu
gratis muryō de
grave haka
gray hai-iro
Greek girisha no
green international auto
  insurance card midori no
  kokusai jidōsha hoken kādo,
  ryokushoku-kokusai-jidōsha-
  hokensho
greenpea gurinpīsu
greet (v.) aisatsu (o) suru
grilled guriru de
grip te no nigiri
grocery store shokuhin-ten
ground shikichi, tochi, jimen
ground level jimen to onaji
  takasa no
ground meat hikiniku
group gurūpu
guarantee hoshō
guard shuei
guest kyaku
guidance shidō
guide gaido, annai-nin
guide loop yūdō-rūpu
guidebook gaido-bukku
gum haguki, shiniku
gust toppū
gymnastics taisō

H

hair kami no ke
hair clip kamidome
hair dryer doraiyā
hair gel heāgeru
hairstyle kamigata;
  heyāsutairu
half hanbun, hanbun no
hall hōru
Halt! Tomare!
ham hamu
hammer kanazuchi, hanmā
hand te

hand brake handoburēki
hand cream handokurīmu
hand over *(v.)* watasu
hand-driven bicycle
  handobaiku
handbag handobakku
handball handobōru
handicraft kōgei
handle *(v.)* toriatsukau
handle totte
handling fee tesūryō
handmade handomeido,
  tezukuri no
handrail tesuri, rankan
hang *(v.)* kakeru
hang glider hangu-guraidā
hang-gliding hangu-
  guraidingu
hanger hangā
happy shiawase na
harbor minato
hard kibishii, katai
hard of hearing nanchō
hardly hotondo nai
hardware store kanamono-ya
hat bōshi
have *(v.)* aru, motsu
hazard warning flasher
  keihō-tenmetsu-sōchi
he kare
head atama
head cold hanakaze
headache zutsū
headache medicine zutsū-
  yaku
headlight heddo-raito
headphone heddohōn
health food store kenkō-
  shokuhin-ten
health insurance kenkō-
  hoken
health insurance certificate
  kenkō-hoken-shō
healthy kenkō na
hear *(v.)* kiku
hearing chōryoku
heart shinzō
heart attack shinzō-hossa
heart trouble shinzō-shōgai
heartburn muneyake
heat nekki, atsusa

heat wave atsui hibi
heating danbō
heaven tengoku
heavy omoi
heel kakato
height takasa
helmet herumetto
help *(v.)* o tasukeru
help kyūjo, tasuke
help for boarding jōshaji no
  tetsudai
herb hābu, yakusō
here koko
herring nishin
high takai
high beam haibīmu
high pressure kōkiatsu
high season haishīzun
high tide michishio
high-class grocery store
  kōkyū-shokuryōhin-ten
highlight midokoro
highway kōsoku-dōro
highway toll kōsoku-
  jidōshadōro-ryōkion
hike *(v.)* haikingu o suru
hiking map haikingu yō chizu
hiking trail haikingu-dō
hill oka
hint hinto
hinterland kōhai-chi
hip koshi
history rekishi
hitchhike *(v.)* hitchihaiku suru
hoarse shagareta
hold *(v.)* hoji suru, tomaru
hole ana
holiday kyūka
holy shinsei na
homemade hōmumeido no
hometown kokyō, furusato
honey hachimitsu
hood bonnetto
hook kake-kugi
hope *(v.)* negau
horizontal format yoko-
  naga(-ban)
horn kurakushon
horse uma
horseback riding jōba
horseradish (Japanese)
  wasabi

270

hose hōsu
hospital byōin
hospital ward byōtō
hospitality motenashi
host hosuto
hot atsui
hot pepper tōgarashi
hot (spicy) karai
hot water oyu
hot-air balloon netsu-kikyū
hot-springs resort onsenchi
hour jikan
hourly ichijikan-goto ni
house ie, sumai, uchi
house number banchi
household goods katei yō hin
hovercraft hobākurafuto
how dono yō ni
hungry onaka ga suite iru
hurry (v.) isogu
hurt itamu
husband otto, shujin
hydrofoil suichū-yokusen

I

I watashi
IC card chippukādo
ice aisu, kōri
ice hockey aisu-hokkē
icy ground tsurutsuru no kōri
ID mibun-shōmei-sho
ID for the handicapped
  shōgaisha techō
idea aidea, kangae
idling kara-unten
ignition tenka
ignition key igunisshon-kī
ignition system tenka-sōchi
illness byōki
illustrated magazine gurafu-
  zasshi
immediately sugu ni
immigration nyūkoku
impatient gaman dekinai
important jūyō
impossible fukanō na
impressionists inshō-ha
impressive kan'mei o ataete
impudent zūzūshii
in addition to no hoka ni

in advance sakidatte
in case of no baai
in particular toriwake
in spite of ni mo kakawarazu
in the afternoon gogo ni
in the back ushiro ni
in the daytime nitchū
in the morning asa ni
in the morning gozen ni
incident toppatsu-jiken
incidental expenses zappi
inclination katamuki
incline kōbai
included komi, fukumarete iru
including fukumete
indigenous sono tochi koyū
  no
indigestion shōka furyō
infant seat (car) nyūji yō bebī
  shīto
infection densen, kansen
inflammation enshō
inflammation of the middle
  ear chūji-en
influenza ryūkan
information annai
inguinal hernia sokei-herunia
injure (v.) kizutsuku
injured person kega-nin
injury kega
inlet irie
inline skate inrainā
inscription mei
insect mushi, konchū
inside naibu de, no naka ni,
  naka de
insomnia fuminshō
inspect (v.) kensa suru
inspection kensa
instead of no kawari ni
instruct (v.) shiji suru
instruction shiji
insulin inshurin
insult kutsujoku
insurance hoken
intelligent kashikoi
interesting omoshiroi,
  kyōmibukai
internal bleeding
  naishukketsu
international kokusai no

271

international call kokusai-tsūwa

international flight kokusai-sen

interrupt (v.) chūdan suru

intersection kōsaten

intestine chō

intravenous drip tenteki

introduction shōkai

investigation chōsa

invite (v.) shōtai suru

iodine yōdo

iron (v.) airon o kakeru

is (v.) de aru

island shima

island cruise shima-meguri

itchy kayui

J

jack jakki

jacket uwagi

jam jamu

January ichigatsu

Japan nihon

Japanese nihon no

Japanese (language) nihongo

Japanese (person) nihonjin

Japanese-style toilet nihonshiki toire

jazz jazu

jazzercise jazu-taisō

jeans jīnzu

jewel hōseki

jeweler kikinzoku-shō, hōseki-shō

jewelry making chōkin

jog (v.) jogingu o suru

jogging pants jogingu-pantsu

jogging trousers jogingu-zubon

joint kansetsu

joke jōdan

judge saiban-kan

juicy mizuke no ōi

July shichigatsu

jumper cable sutāto-hojo-kōdo

June rokugatsu

just chōdo

K

keep company with (v.) shite, ... to kōsai ~ iru

kerosene tōyu

ketchup ketchappu

key kagi

kidney jinzō

kidney bean ingen

kidney stone jinseki

kilogram kiro

kilometer kiro, kiromētoru

kind yasashii, shinsetsu na; shurui

king ō

kiss (v.) kisu o suru

kiss kisu

kitchen daidokoro, kitchin

kitchen range renji

kite tako

kite-flying takoage

kitschy zokuaku na, inchiki na

knee hiza

knife naifu

knock down (v.) naguritaosu

know (v.) sitte iru

knowledge chishiki

Korea kankoku, chōsen

Korean kankoku no

Korean (language) kankokugo

Korean (person) kankoku-jin

L

lake mizu-umi

lamb ramu-niku

lamp ranpu, akari

land (v.) tsukeru, ... ni ~

land riku

landing chakuriku

landlord yanushi

landmark mejirushi

language kotoba

language course gogaku-kōsu

last saigo no

late osoi

later ato de

laugh (v.) warau

laundromat koin-randorī

laundry (clothing)
   sentakumono
laundry (shop) sentaku-ya
laurel tree gekkeiju
lavatory te-arai-ba
lawn shibafu
lawn for sunbathing nikkō-
   yoku yō no shibafu
lawyer bengoshi
laxative gezai
lay down (v.) taeru, yoko ~
layer dan-katto
lazy bushō na, taida na
leader shidōsha
leading role shuyaku
leaf happa
learn (v.) manabu, narau; shiru
leather goods shop kawa-
   seihin-ten
leather jacket kawa-jaketto
leave (v.) shuppatsu suru,
   tachisaru
leek negi
left (adj.) hidari no
left hidari
leg ashi
leggings reginsu
lemon remon
lemonade remonēdo
lend (v.) kasu
lens renzu
letter tegami
letter paper binsen
lettuce retasu
level reberu
license plate nanbā-purēto
lie down (v.) naru, yoko ni ~
life seimei; jinsei
life belt kyūmei-ukiwa
life jacket kyūmei-dōgi
life preserver ukiwa
lifeboat kyūjo-bōto
lifeguard pūru no kanshi-nin,
   kaisuiyokujō no kanshi-in
lift rifuto
light hikari, karui
light blue usu-aoi
light green usu-midori
lightbulb denkyū
lighthouse tōdai
lightning inazuma
like (v.) konomu, ki ni iru

likeable kōkan no moteru
liking suki na
line sen
linen asa, rinneru
lip kuchibiru
lipstick kuchi-beni
liquid ekitai no
liquor store sakaya
listen (v.) kiki iru
listen carefully (v.) mimi o
   katamukeru
listen to music (v.) ongaku o
   kiku
listener chōshū
liter rittoru
live (v.) ikiru
live performance nama-ensō
liver kanzō
liver pâté rebā-pate
living room ima
lobby robī
local call shinai-tsūwa
lock (v.) doa ni kagi o kakeru,
   kagi o kakeru
lodging shukuhaku
lonely kodoku na
long nagai
long ride tōnori
long-distance bus chōkyori-
   basu
long-distance call chōkyori-
   tsūwa
look (v.) miru
look for (v.) sagasu
look forward to (v.) o
   tanoshimi ni suru
look out (v.) ki o tsukeru; chūi
   suru
lose (v.) nakusu
lost-and-found office
   ishitsubutsu-toriatsukaijo
loud ō-goe no
love ai
love (v.) ai suru
low hikui
low atmospheric pressure
   teikiatsu
low beam genkō-raito
low-fat abura no sukunai
lowfat milk shibōbun no
   sukunai gyūnyū
luck kōun

273

lumbago gikkuri-goshi
lumber mokuzai
lump-sum fee ikkatsu-ryōkin
lunch chūshoku, hiru-gohan
lung hai
luxurious gōka na
lying down yokotawatte iru

M

machine kikai
mackerel saba
magazine zasshi
maid meido
mailbox posuto
main dish mein
main post office cūō-
  yūbinkyoku
main road kaidō
main street chūō-dōri,
  meinsutorīto
make (v.) tsukuru
make a mistake (v.)
  machigau
make an effort (v.) doryoku
  suru
make use of (v.) tsukau
man otoko no hito, hito,
  dansei, ningen
management kanribu
mandarin orange mikan
manicure manikyua
many takusan no
map chizu
March sangatsu
margarine māgarin
mark shirushi
market shijō; ichiba
market price sōba
married kikon
marry (v.) kekkon suru
marshland numachi
mascara masukara
massage massāji
mastermind shidōsha
match matchi
material genryō, zairyō
mattress mattoresu
May gogatsu
mayonnaise mayonēzu
meal shokuji

meal cooked on frying pan
  furaipan-ryōri
meaning imi
measles hashika
meat niku
medicine kusuri
medicine for circulation
  junkanki-zai
medium (art) shudan
meet (v.) deau, au
meeting kaigō
melon meron
memorial kinen no chi
menstrual period gekkei
menstruation mensu
menu menyū
merit chōsho
meter mētoru
method hōhō
middle mannaka
Middle Ages chūsei
migraine henzutsū
mild odayaka na, mairudo na
milimeter miri
milk gyūnyū, miruku
mind kokoro
mineral water mineraruwōtā
miniature golf minigorufu
minibar minibā
minute pun, fun
mirror kagami
miscalculate (v.) gosan suru
miscarriage ryūzan
misfortune, have a (v.) fukō
  ni au
Miss - san, - sama
missing tarinai
mistake machigai
misunderstanding gokai,
  omoichigai
mixed mazeta, kongō shita
mode hayari
model moderu, mokei
modern modan na
monastery shūdōin
Monday getsuyōbi
money kahei, o-kane
money changing ryōgae
month tsuki
monthly tsukizuki
monument kinen-butsu
moon tsuki

274

more yori ijō, motto
morning asa
mosaic mozaiku
mosquito ka
motel mōteru
mother okāsan, haha
mountain yama
mountain bike mauntenbaiku, turekkingu-jitensha
mountain climbing tozan
mountain pass tōge
mountain railway aputo-shiki tetsudō
mountain range sanmyaku
mountain station yama no eki
mountain village sanson
mouth kuchi
move (v.) ugoku
movement (music) gakusetsu
movie theater eigakan
Mr. - san, - sama
Mrs. - san, - sama
Ms. - san, - sama
muffler mafurā
muggy mushiatsui
mumps otafuku-kaze
muscle kin'niku
museum hakubutsukan
music ongaku
music hall yose
musical myūjikaru
musical performance ensō
mussel murasaki igai
mustache kuchi-hige
mustard karashi
mutton maton, hitsuji no niku

N

nail clipper tsume-kiri
nail polish remover jokō-eki
naked hadaka no
name namae
napkin napukin
narrow semai
national costume minzoku-ishō
national park kokuritsu-kōen
nationality kokuseki

nationality sticker kokuseki hyōjiban
natural shizen no
natural food store shizen-shokuhin-ten
nature shizen
nature conservation area shizen-hogo-kuiki
nausea fukaikan, hakike
near chikai
nearby kinpen
nearly ōyoso
necessary hitsuzenteki na
neck kubi
necktie nekutai
need (v.) hitsuyō to suru
needle hari
negative hiteiteki na, mainasu no
neighbor kinjo no hito, tonari no hito
neoprene wet suit neopren-sensui-fuku
nephritis jin'en
nerve shinkei
nervous shinkei shitsu na
net ami
never kesshite ... nai
new atarashii
new year shin'nen
newspaper shinbun
newspaper distributor shinbun -hanbaiten-shu
next tsugi no
next year rainen
night yoru
night table naito-tēburu
night table lamp naito-tēburu no denki-sutando
nightclub naito-kurabu
nobody daremo ... nai
noise sōon, zatsuon
noisy urusai
nonalcoholic arukōru-bun nashi
nonalcoholic beer arukōru-nashi no bīru
nonsmoker hikitsuen-sha
nonsmoking car kin'en-sha
nonsmoking compartment kin'en no shashitsu
nonstop flight chokkō-bin

noodles udon, men
north kita
nose hana
nosebleed hanaji
not -masen, -nai
Not at all. zenzen
not binding gimu no nai
not yet mada
notebook nōtobukku
nothing nanimo
notice tsūchi, shirase
notify (v.) tsūchi suru
novel shōsetsu
November jūichigatsu
now ima
nowhere doko ni mo ... nai
nude sketch ratai-dessan
number kazu, bango
nurse (female) kangofu
nurse (male) kango-nin
nut nattsu

O

oar ōru
oat flakes karasu-mugi no furēku
oatmeal ōtomīru
object taishō
observation platform tenbōdai
occupation shokugyō
occupied shiyō-chū
October jūgatsu
offer (v.) teikyō suru
office jimusho
official kōshiki na
off-season kingyōki; shīzun-ofu
offside ofusaido
often yoku
oil abura, oiru
oil change oiru-kōkan
oil painting abura-e
ointment nankō
old furui
old town kyūshigai
old-fashioned kofū na
olive orību
olive oil orību-oiru
on ue, ... no ~ ni

on Sunday nichiyōbi ni
on time jikandōri
on the street michi de
on the way tochū de
once ichido, ikkai
one hitotsu no
one before last mae no mae
one-piece dress wanpīsu
onion tamanegi
only yui-itsu, shika, dake
open (v.) akeru
open (adv.) akete
open aite
open (adj.) aite iru
opening kaikan-jikan
opening hours eigyō-jikan
opera opera
operetta operetta
opinion iken
oppose (v.) aitai suru
opposite hantai no
opposite from ni tai shite, mukaigawa ni
optician megane-ya
or soretomo
orange orenji
orange juice orenji-jūsu
orchestra ōkesutora
order chūmon
original orijinaru, gensaku
ornament kazari
other hoka no
other day senjitsu
our watashitachi no
out of order koshō shite iru
outdoors soto
outside soto ni
over sugite
overcoat kōto
overseas kaigai
own jibun no
oxygen mask sanso-kyūnyūki
oyster kaki

P

pacemaker shinpaku-chōseiki
pacifier oshaburi, chikubi
package kozutsumi
packet tsutsumi
packing hōsō

paddle a canoe *(v.)* kanū o kogu
paddleboat padoru-bōto
page pēji
pain kutsū, itami
painful itai
painkiller itamidome
paint *(v.)* e o kaku
paint watercolors *(v.)* suisaiga o kaku
painter ekaki, gaka
painting kaiga
pair hitokumi
palace kyūden
pamphlet panfuretto
panties pantī
panty liner surippu no patto
pantyhose pantī-sutokkingu
paper kami, yōshi
paper bag kamibukuro
paper napkin kami-napukin
paperback poketto-ban no hon
papers shorui
parachute rakkasan
paraglider paraguraidā
paralysis mahi
paraplegic hanshinfuzui
parent oya
parents ryōshin
park kōen
park *(v.)* chūsha suru
parka anorakku
parking chūsha
parking garage chūsha-jō
parking for the handicapprd shōgaisha yō no chūsha-jō
parking light pākingu-raito
parquet paruketto
parsley paseri
part bubun
part (hair) wakeme
partial coverage insurance bubun-shatai-hoken
participate *(v.)* sanka suru
party pātī
pass *(v.)* oikosu
passage utsurikawari
passenger ryokyaku
passenger car shikirinonai-zaseki-ressha

passport pasupōto, ryoken
passport check pasupōto-kensa
passport inspection ryoken-kensa
past kako
pastry shop okashi-ya, kēki-ya
patience nintai, gaman; shinbō
pay *(v.)* shiharau
pay attention *(v.)* chūi o harau
pay in cash *(v.)* genkin de harau
payment shiharai
pea mame
peach momo
peak chōten
pear nashi
pearl shinju, pāru
pedestrian hokōsha
penalty area penarutī-eria
penalty batsu
pendant pendanto
pension nenkin, penshon
people hitobito, kokumin, minzoku
pepper koshō
percent pāsento
perfume kōsui
perfume store keshōhin-ten
perhaps tabun, osoraku
period jidai
permanent wave pāma
permitted kyoka sarete iru
person in charge sekinin-sha
person with reduced mobility kadōshōgai, katsudōshōgai
personal kojinteki na
personal data shinjō-sho, jinbutsu ni kansuru koto
pet petto
pharmacy kusuri-ya
photograph shashin
physical handicap shintai shōgai
pickpocket suri
picture e
picture postcard ehagaki
piece ko
pillar hashira

pillow makura
pilot pairotto
PIN anshō-bangō
pineapple painappuru
ping-pong pinpon, takkyū
pink pinku-iro no
pitch a tent (v.) tento o haru
place basho
place of birth shussei-chi
place of interest meisho
plain muji no
plains heiya
plant shokubutsu
plastic purasuchikku
plastic bag purasuchikku no
  fukuro
plate sara
platform purattofōmu
play (v.) asobu
play geki, asobi
play a musical instrument
  (v.) gakki o hiku
play schedule jōen-yoteihyō
play (theater) jōen
playground asobiba, undō-jō
playmate asobi-tomodachi
pleasure tanoshimi
plug puragu
plug in (v.) sashikomu
plum sumomo
pneumonia haien
pocket calculator dentaku
pocket knife poketto-naifu
poison doku
poisoning chūdoku
poisonous doku no aru
Polaroid camera poraroido-
  kamera
police keisatsu
police car patokā
police officer keisatsu-kan
polio shōnimahi
polite teinei na, reigi-tadashii
pony ponī
poor mazushii, binbō
popular play taishū-engeki
pork buta-niku
portable CD player keitai yō
  CD-pureiyā
portable gas cooking stove
  gasukonro
portion ichinin-mae

portrait shōzō
possible kanō na
post office yūbin-kyoku
postage yūbin-ryōkin
postal savings book yūbin-
  yokin-tsūchō
postcard yūbin-hagaki
poster posutā
postpone (v.) enki suru;
  nobasu
pot cleaner tawashi
potato jagaimo
pottery tōgei
pottery goods tōki; tōgeihin
pound pondo
powder paudā
powdery snow kona-yuki
powerboat mōtābōto
practical jitsuyōteki na
practice (v.) renshū suru
pray (v.) inoru
pregnancy ninshin
premiere shoen
prepare (v.) junbi suru
prescribe (v.) shohō suru
prescription shohōsen
preseason shīzun mae, kisetsu
  mae
preservation hozon
preservation period hozon-
  kikan
preserve (v.) hozon suru
pretty suteki na, kawaii
prevent (v.) samatageru
price ryōkin
price sign kakaku hyōji
priest shinpu
prison keimusho
private puraibēto
procession dashi, gyōretsu
product seihin
profit rieki
program puroguramu
promise yakusoku
pronounce (v.) hatsuon suru
proposal teian
protection of cultural assets
  bunkazai-hogo
provisional karino
pry open (v.) kojiakeru
public kōkyō no, kōkai no
pull (v.) hiku

pulse myaku
purple murasaki
purpose mokuteki
pus umi
put (v.) oku
put on (v.) tsukeru, mi ni ~

Q

quality hinshitsu
queen ōhi
question shitsumon
question (v.) shitsumon o suru
quickly hayaku
quiet shizuka na

R

rabbit ana-usagi
race rēsu, minzoku
racing bike keirin yō jitensha
racket raketto
radar-controlled rēdā-kontorōru
radiator kūrā
radio rajio
rail rēru
rain ame
raincoat reinkōto
rainy amemoyō
ramp surōpu, keisha-hōmu
rape gōkan
rapid train kaisoku-densha
rare mezurashii
rate rēto
rather kanari
ravine keikoku
raw nama
razor kamisori
razor blade kamisori no ha
reach (v.) todoku, tassuru
read (v.) yomu
realize (v.) kizuku
really mattaku
rearview mirror bakku-mirā
reason riyū
receipt ryōshū-sho
receive (v.) uketoru, mukaeru, morau
receiver juwaki

recently saikin, kono goro
reception resepushon, uketsuke
recommend (v.) susumeru
recover (v.) kaifuku suru
red aka
red wine aka-wain
refrigerator reizōko
refuse (v.) kobamu, kyohi suru
registered mail kakitome
regret (v.) zan'nen ni omou
regrettable zan'nen
regular futsū no, kisokuteki na
regulation kisoku
related shinseki no
relaxing kutsurogeru
religion shūkyō
remain (v.) nokotte iru, todomaru
remember (v.) o omoidasu
remind (v.) omoidasaseru
remittance furikomi
remote door opener jidōteki na doa no kaikōbu
remove (v.) torisaru
rent yachin
repair (v.) shūri suru
repair service koshō sābisu
repair tools shūri-dōgu
repeat (v.) kurikaesu
replace (v.) torikaeru
report todokede, shinkoku
report (v.) todoke deru
request onegai
request (v.) onegai suru
reservation yoyaku
reserve (v.) yoyaku suru
reserved-seat ticket zaseki-shiteiken
respect sonkei
responsibility sekinin
responsible tantō, sekinin no aru
rest (v.) yasumu
rest area kyūkei-basho
resume shinjō-sho
return kaeru
return (v.) modosu; kaette kuru; hikikaesu
return ticket kaeri no kippu
return trip kaeri-michi

returning to one's hometown kikyō
reverse gear bakkugiā, kōshin
reward hōshū
rheumatism ryūmachi
rhinitis bien
rice kome
rich kanemochi
ride a bicycle *(v.)* jitensha ni noru
ride a horse *(v.)* uma ni noru
ridiculous okashi na
riding school jōba-gakkō
right migi, tadashii
right *(adj.)* migi no
ring ringu, wa
ripe jukushita
river kawa
road michi
road map dōro-chizu
roast *(v.)* yaku
roasted yaita
rock iwa
rock cliff ganpeki
rock (music) rokku
rocky ishi darake no
roll kogata-maru-pan
roller skating rōrā-sukēto
roof yane
room heya
room telephone heya no denwa
rope rōpu, nawa
rope for a tent tento yō rōpu
rosé roze
rotten fuhai shita
round marui
round-trip ticket ōfuku no kippu
route rūto
row *(v.)* kogu
rowboat kogibune
rubber band gomu-wa
rubber boots gomu-nagagutsu
rubber dinghy gomu-bōto
rubber sandals gomu-zōri
rudder kaji
ruins iseki, haikyo
run *(v.)* hashiru, kakeru
rye bread kuropan

sad kanashii
safe kinko, anzen na
safety belt anzen-beruto
safety pin anzen-pin
sailboat yotto
sailing yotto-asobi, sēringu
salad sarada
salad buffet sarada-byuffe
salami sarami
sale ureyuki
salt shio
salt shaker shio-ire
same onaji
sand castle suna no shiro
sandal sandaru
sandbox suna-ba
sandwich roll kogata-maru-pan no sandoitchi
sanitary facility eisei-setsubi
sanitary napkin gekkeitai
satisfied (be) manzoku suru
Saturday doyōbi
sauce sōsu
saucer uke-zara
sauna sauna
sausage sōsēji
say *(v.)* iu
say good-bye *(v.)* wakare o tsugeru
scar kizuato
scarf sukāfu
scenery keshiki, fūkei
school gakkō
sciatica zakotsu-shinkeitsū
scissors hasami
scooter sukūtā
screw neji
script kyaku-hon
sculptor chōkoku-ka
sculpture chōkoku
sea umi
sea bass suzuki
sea motion umi no yōsu
seagull kamome
seashore kaigan
season shīzun, kisetsu
season *(v.)* aji o tsukeru
seasoning chōmiryō
seat seki

seat belt (lap type) kidonī-
beruto
second byō, niban(me),
futatsume ni
second from the last
nibanme, saigo kara ~ no
secondhand dealer kobutsu-
shō
security check anzen kakunin
security deposit hoshō-kin
see (v.) miru
seeing-eye dog mōdōken
seize (v.) sashiosaeru
select (v.) erabi dasu
self jibun; jishin
self-service serufu-sābisu
self-timer serufu-taimā
sell (v.) uru
send (v.) okuru
sender sashidashi-nin
sense kankaku
sentence bun
separate kobetsu
September kugatsu
serious shinken na
service kyūji
service area kyūkei-jo
set fire (v.) hi o tsukeru
set hair (v.) kami o totonoeru
setting lotion setto-rōshon
settle (v.) seisan suru
severely handicapped
jūdoshōgaisha
sew (v.) nuu
sewing kit saihō-dōgu
sexual harassment seiteki
iyagarase
shadow kage
shall sō de aru
shampoo shanpū
shaving brush higesori yō
hake
shaving foam higesori yō
awajō no sekken
shaving lotion higesori yō
keshōsui
shawl shōru
she kanojo
sheep cheese yōnyū-chīzu
shellfish kai
shelter hinan-goya
shirt shatsu

shoe kutsu
shoe brush kutsu-burashi
shoe polish kutsu-kurīmu
shoe repair kutsu-shūri
shoe store kutsu-ya
shoelace kutsu-himo
shop (v.) kaimono o suru
shop-window shō-uindō
short mijikai
short circuit shōto
short feature tanpen-eiga
short-term tankikan no
shortcut chikamichi
shorts shōtsu
should subeki de aru
shoulder kata
shoulder bag shorudā-bakku
shout (v.) sakebu
show shō
show (v.) miseru
show (movie) jōei
shower shawā, niwaka ame
shower stool shawā yō isu
shrimp ebi
shuttle bus norikae-basu
shy hazukashigariya no
side of no yoko
sideburn momiage
sightseeing (city) shinai-
kankō
sign (v.) shomei suru
sign hyōshiki
sign language shuwa
signature shomei, sain
silk kinu
silk dyeing kenpu-zome
silver shirubā; gin
silver (adj.) shirubā no, gin no
similar nite iru, dōyō ni
simmered torobi de nita
simple kantan na, yasashii
simultaneously dōji ni
since irai, kara
sincere kokoro kara
sing (v.) utau
singer kashu
single dokushin
sink nagashi-dai
sinusitis zentō-dōen
sister-in-law (older) giri no
ane

sister-in-law (younger) giri
  no imōto
sit (v.) suwaru
site yōchi
situation jōkyō
size ōkisa
skate sukēto
skateboard sukētobōdo
skating sukēto
skating rink sukēto-rinku
sketch suketchi
ski (v.) sukī o suru
ski sukī
ski binding bindingu, tomegu
ski boots sukī-gutsu
ski course sukī-kōsu
ski goggles yuki-megane
ski instructor sukī no shidōin
ski pants sukī-zubon
ski poles sukī-sutokku
ski school sukī-gakkō
ski tow ken'in-rifuto
skilled jukuren shita
skin hifu, hada
skinny hossori to shita
skirt sukāto
sky sora
sleep (v.) nemuru
sleeping pill suiminyaku
sleeve sode
sleigh sori
slice suraisu
sliced cheese hitokire goto ni
  kirareta chīzu
slip surippu
slippery ice yokusuberu
  (tsurutsuru no) kōri
slope sakamichi
slow yukkuri
slump suranpu
small semai, chiisai
smell kaori, nioi
smell (v.) nioi ga suru, niou
smoke (v.) tabako o suu
smoked kunsei no
smoked goods kunsei
smoking car kitsuen-sha
smoking compartment
  kitsuen yō shashitsu
smuggling mitsuyu
snack keishoku
snake hebi

snapshot sunappu-shasin
sneakers supōtsushūzu
sneeze (v.) kushami o suru
snore (v.) ibiki o kaku
snorkel (v.) shunōkeru suru
snorkel shunōkeru
snow yuki
snow tire sunō-taiya
soap sekken
soccer game sakkā-gēmu;
  sakkā-kyōgi; sakkā
soccer stadium sakkā-jō
social-work facility
  sōsharusutēshon
socket soketto
socks sokkusu, kutsushita
soft yawarakai
solarium sorariamu
sold out urikire
sole ashi no ura, shitabirame
solid katamatta
solo soro
some sukoshi, ikutsuka no
somebody dareka
sometimes tokidoki
somewhat ikuraka no
somewhere else dokoka hoka
  de
son musuko
song uta
soon mamonaku
sound oto
sound (v.) hibiku
soup sūpu
soup dish sūpu-zara
sour suppai
sour cream sawā-kurīmu
south minami
souvenir o-miyage
souvenir shop miyagemono-
  ten
soybean daizu
spacious hiroi
spare tire supea, yobi-taiya
spark plug supāku-puragu
spasm hossa
speak (v.) hanasu
speaker supīkā
special tokubetsu na
special delivery sokutatsu
special product meibutsu
specialist senmon'i

specially tokubetsu ni
spectator kankyaku
speed per hour jisoku
spell (v.) tsuzuru
spend (v.) shishutsu suru
spinach hōrensō
spine sebone
splint soegi
spoon supūn
sport supōtsu
sports goods supōtsu-yōhin
sprain kujiki
sprained nenza shite iru
spring wakimizu; izumi, haru
square meter heihō-mētoru
squash kabocha
squid ika
stadium kyōgi-jō
stain shimi
stained glass sutendo-gurasu
stamp sutanpu, kitte
stamp dispenser kitte-jidō-
  hanbaiki
stand (v.) tatsu
stand up (v.) tachiagaru
star hoshi
starter shidō-sōchi, sutātā
state kuni, kokka
statement mōshitate
station eki
stationery bunbōgu
stationery store bunbōgu-ya
statue chōzō, ritsuzō
stay taizai
stay (v.) tomaru
steal (v.) nusumu
steamed mushita
steamer kisen
steep kewashii
steeple kyōkai no tō
step dan; kaidan
stepless access dan no nai
  tsūro
stepless entrance dan no nai
  iriguchi
sterilize (v.) shōdoku suru
steward suchuwādo
stewardess suchuwādesu
stick bō
still-life painting seibutsu
stinky kusai
stomach i, onaka

stomachache itsū
stone ishi
stop (v.) tomaru, yameru
stoplight sutoppuraito
stopover chūkan-chakuriku
storm arashi
stove konro
straight massugu
straight hair tarege
strain suji-chigai
straw sutorō
strawberry ichigo
stream nagare
street michi
street map shigai-chizu
streetcar shiden
stretch (v.) nobasu
string musubi-himo
stroke nōsotchū, sotchū
stroll sanpo
strong tsuyoi
studio sutajio
study (v.) benkyō suru
stuffed tsumatta
stupendous totetsumonai
stupid manuke na, oroka na
style yōshiki
subtitle jimaku
suburb kōgai
suburban train kinkō-ressha
subway chikatetsu
sudden kyū no
suddenly totsuzen
sugar satō
suits sūtsu
summer natsu
summit chōjō
sun taiyō
sun hat hiyoke-bōshi
Sunday nichiyōbi
sunroof horo-yane
sunshade hiyoke
sunstroke nisshabyō
suntan hiyake
suntan cream hiyakedome-
  kurīmu
suntan oil san-oiru
superficial hyōmenteki na
supermarket sūpā-māketto
supply (v.) chōtatsu suru
supply takuwae
suppository zayaku

surcharge warimashi-ryōkin
sure tashika na
surfboard sāfin-bōdo
surfing sāfin
surgeon geka'i
surgery shujutsu
surprised (to be) odoroku
surroundings atari, shūi
sweat (v.) ase o kaku
sweater sētā
sweet amai
sweetener kanmiryō
sweets okashi
swelling hare
swim (v.) oyogu
swimmer suiei-senshu
swimming suiei
swimming cap suiei-bo
swimming course suiei-kōsu
swimming pool pūru
swimming pool for children
kodomo yō pūru
swimming shoes suiei yō
kutsu
swimming trunks suiei-pantsu
swimsuit mizugi
Swiss (person) suisu-jin
Swiss franc suisu-furan
switch suitchi
switch on (v.) suitchi o ireru
Switzerland suisu
swollen hareta
swordfish tachi-uo
symbol shōchō
symphony shinfonī(konsāto)

T

T-shirt T-shatsu
tablecloth tēburu-kurosu
tablet jōzai
tableware shokki
tachometer takomētā
taillight tēru-raito; bakku-raito
tailor shitate-ya
take (v.) toru
take along (v.) motte iku;
tsurete iku
take off (v.) ririku suru
take place (v.) okonawareru

take a picture (v.) shashin o
toru
take a walk (v.) sanpo suru
Take care! Ki o tsukete!
takeoff ririku
tampon tanpon
tank tanku
taste aji, konomi
tavern nomiya
tax-free muzei
taxi stand takushī-noriba
tea ocha
tea bag tībakku
teach (v.) oshieru
team chīmu
teaspoon tī-supūn
telegram denpō
telephone denwa
telephone (v.) denwa o
kakeru/suru
telephone book denwachō
telephone booth denwa-
bokkusu
telephone card terefon-kādo
telephone number denwa-
bangō
telephone room denwa-shitsu
telephoto lens bōen-renzu
television terebi
television room terebi-shitsu
telex terekkusu
temperature ondo
temple otera
tennis tenisu
tent tento
tent pole tento no pōru
terminal tāminaru
terminal station shūchaku-eki
terra-cotta image haniwa
terrace terasu
terrible osoroshii, hidoi
tetanus hashōfū
thank (v.) kansha suru
that person/that thing ano
hito/ano koto
theater gekijō
theatrical company geki-dan
theft tōnan
there soko
there is/are imasu, ni iru, ni
aru, arimasu
therefore yue ni, da kara

thermal flask mahōbin
thermometer taionkei
thick (book) atsui
thief dorobō
thin hosoi, yaseta
thing mono, koto
think (v.) omou
think about (v.) ni tsuite
  kangaeru
third sanban(me)
thirsty nodo ga kawaita
this kono
this morning kesa
three meals included
  sanshoku-tsuki
thriller film surira-shōsetsu-
  eiga
throat nodo
throat medicine nodo no
  kusuri
throat pain nodo no itami
through o tōshite
thunderstorm raiu
thus tsumari
tibia keikotsu
ticket jōsha-ken, kippu
ticket canceling machine
  jōshaken-kokuinki
ticket counter jōshaken-
  hatsubaiguchi
ticket machine jōshaken-
  jidōhanbaiki
till made
time jikan
time(s) kai
timely chōdo yoi toki ni
timetable jikokuhyō
tip chippu
tire taiya
tired tsukareta
tissue chirigami
tissue paper tishū
to ... e
toast tōsuto
toaster tōsutā
today kyō
toe ashi no yubi
together issho ni
toilet toire
toilet for the handicapped
  shōgaisha yō toire
toilet paper toiretto-pēpā

tomato tomato
tombstone haka-ishi
tomorrow ashita
tomorrow night ashita no
  ban
tongue shita
tonight konban
tonsillitis hentōsen'en
tonsils hentōsen
too much sugiru
tool dōgu
tooth ha
toothache ha-ita, shitsū, ha ga
  itamu
toothbrush ha-burashi
toothpaste hamigaki
toothpick tsumayōji
total gōkei
touch (v.) ni fureru
tour tsuā, ryokō
tour (v.) kengaku suru
tour group ryokō-dantai
tourist ryokōsha, tsūtisuto
tourist information kankō-
  annaisho
tourist office kankō-kyoku
tow (v.) ken'in suru
tow rope hikizuna
tow truck rekkā-sha
toward ni taishite
towel taoru
tower tō, tawā
towing service rekkā-sābisu
town machi
town hall shichōsha
toy omocha
toy store omocha-ya
trade fair mihon-ichi
traffic kōtsū
traffic jam jūtai
traffic light shingō
tragedy higeki
trail chōkyori-kōsu
trailer toreirā
train kisha
tranquilizer anteizai
translate (v.) honyaku suru
transportation service
  kuruma de no sōgei sābisu
trash gomi
trash bag gomi-bukuro

travel *(v.)* ryokō suru, tabi ni deru
traveler ryokō-sha
traveler's check toraberāzu-chekku
traveling bag ryokō-kaban
treat *(v.)* teate suru, chiryō suru
tree ki
trial kari
triangular warning sign sankakkei-keikokuhyōji-ki
trip ryokō
tripod sankyaku
trousers zubon
truck torakku
true hontō
truly hontō ni
trunk space toranku-supēsu
trust shinyō
try *(v.)* tamesu, kokoromu
tube kan, chūbu
Tuesday kayōbi
tuna maguro
tunnel tonneru
turn signal uinkā
turquoise torukoishi-iro
tweezers pinsetto
two meals included nishoku-tsuki
typhoid chifusu
typical tenkeiteki na

U

ugly minikui
ulcer kaiyō
ultraviolet protection shigaisen-yobō
umbrella kasa
unbelievable shinjirarenai
unconscious ishiki fumei no
unconsciousness ishiki-fumei
uncured ham nama-hamu
under shita ni, no shita ni
underpants (man's) burīfu
underpass gādo shita no michi
undershirt andāshatsu, dōgi
understand *(v.)* rikaisuru

underwater camera suichū-kamera
underwear shitagi
unemployment shitsugyō
unfamiliar mishiranu
unfortunately zan'nen-nagara
unglazed pottery suyaki
unhurried hima na
unimportant jūyō de wa nai
university daigaku
unpleasant fukai na
unsuitable futekitō na
unusual ijō na, futsū de nai
upper limit of blood alcohol content ketsuatsuchū no arukōru nōdo no jōgen
upward ue e
urgent isogi no
urine nyō
usual yoku tsukawareru, tsūjō no
usually tsūjō

V

vacation kyūka
vacation facilities kyūka yō setsubi
vacation house bessō
vaccination yobō-sesshu
vaccination record yobō-sesshu-techō
valid yūkō na
valley tani
variable kawariyasui
variety hinshu
vase kabin
vaudeville engekijō
vaudeville theater yose
veal ko-ushi-niku
vegetable yasai
vegetable store yaoya
vegetarianism saishoku-shugi
vending machine jidō-hanbaiki
vertical format tate-saizu
very totemo
vest chokki, besuto
via airmail kōkūbin de
victory shōri
video camera bideokamera

video film bideofirumu
video recorder bideorekōdā
videocassette bideokasetto
view nagame
view (v.) nagameru
village mura
vinegar su
violet murasaki
virus bīrusu
visa biza
vision-impaired (person) shikakushōgaisha
visit (v.) hōmon suru, otozureru
visit hōmon
visiting hours menkai-jikan
vocalist seigaku-ka
volcano kazan
volleyball barēbōru
voucher hikikae-ken

W

wading pool mizu-asobi yō pūru
wait (v.) matsu
waiter uētā
waiting room machiaishitsu
waitress uētoresu
wake up (v.) okosu
wall kabe
wall outlet konsento
wallet satsuire, saifu
walnut kurumi
warm atatakai
wash (v.) arau
washcloth tenugui
washing sentaku
washing machine sentakki
washroom senmenjo
washstand senmendai
watchmaker's tokei-ya
water mizu
water ski suijō-sukī
water tank mizu-tanku
water wings ude ni maku ukiwa
watercolor suisaiga
waterfall taki
watermelon suika
we watashitachi

weak yowai
weak (coffee) usui
weather forecast tenkiyohō
weather information kishōtsūhō
wedding ceremony kekkon-shiki
Wednesday suiyōbi
week shū
weekday heijitsu
weekend package rate shūmatsu-ikkatsu-ryōkin
weekly shū goto ni
weekly ticket isshūkan yūkō na jōshaken
weight omosa
welfare work fukushi-jigyō
well ido
well-done jūbun ni yaketa
Western (film) seibu-geki
wet nureta, shimetta
wheat flour komugiko
wheel sharin
wheelchair kuruma-isu
wheelchair user kuruma-isu-riyōsha
when no toki
whether ka dō ka
whipped cream awadate nama-kurīmu
white shiro
white bread shiro-pan
white cane (for the blind) tsue, mōjin yō ~
white wine shiro-wain
whooping cough hyaku-nichi-zeki
widowed yamome no
width haba
wife tsuma
wig katsura
wild yasei, yasei no
wilderness kōya, genya
win (v.) katsu
wind kaze
wind (hot) fēn
wind direction kaze-muki
wind velocity hūryoku
window mado
window seat madogawa no zaseki
windshield furonto-garasu

windshield wiper waipā
wine wain
wine store wain-ya
wineglass wain gurasu
wing tsubasa
winter fuyu
winter tire fuyu yō taiya
wire harigane
wire transfer denshin-gawase
wisdom tooth oyashirazu
with to, de
with pleasure yorokonde
within no naka ni/de
without nashi ni
witness shōnin
woman josei
wonderful subarashii
woodcarving kibori
woodcut print in the Edo
  period ukiyoe
woods mori
wool ūru
woolen yarn keito
word tango
work (v.) hataraku; shigoto o
  suru
work shigoto
world sekai
worthless kachi no nai
wound kizu
wrap (v.) tsutsumu
wristwatch ude-dokei
write (v.) kaku
write down (v.) kakitomeru
written bunshō de

X

X-ray (v.) rentogen-shashin
X-ray rentogen

Y

yacht yotto
year nen, toshi
year-end fair toshi no ichi
yellow ki-iro
yellow pages shokugyō-betsu
  denwa-chō
yen en
yesterday kinō
yoga yoga
yogurt yōguruto
young wakai
young lady ojōsan
younger sister imōto
youth wakamono, seishōnen
You're welcome. dō
  itashimashite

Z

zip code yūbin-bangō
zoo dōbutsuen
zoo (safari-type) shizen-
  dōbutsuen